Texts and Traditions of Medieval Pastoral Care

ESSAYS IN HONOUR OF BELLA MILLETT

Pastoral and devotional literature flourished throughout the Middle Ages, and its growth and transmutations form the focus of this collection. Ranging historically from the difficulties of localizing Anglo-Saxon pastoral texts to the reading of women in late medieval England, the individual essays survey its development and its transformation into the literature of vernacular spirituality. They offer close examinations of both particular manuscripts, and of individual texts, including an anonymous *Speculum iuniorum*, the *Speculum religiosorum* of Edmund of Abingdon and later vernacular compositions and translations, such as *Handlyng Synne* and Bonaventure's *Lignum Vitae*. The reading and devotional use of texts by women and solitaries are also considered. They therefore form an appropriate tribute to the work of Bella Millett, whose research has done so much to advance our knowledge of the field.

YORK MEDIEVAL PRESS

York Medieval Press is published by the University of York's Centre for Medieval Studies in association with Boydell & Brewer Limited. Our objective is the promotion of innovative scholarship and fresh criticism on medieval culture. We have a special commitment to interdisciplinary study, in line with the Centre's belief that the future of Medieval Studies lies in those areas in which its major constituent disciplines at once inform and challenge each other.

All enquiries of an editorial kind, including suggestions for monographs and essay collections, should be addressed to: The Academic Editor, York Medieval Press, University of York, Centre for Medieval Studies, The King's Manor, York, YO1 7EP (E-mail: gmg501@york.ac.uk).

Publications of York Medieval Press are listed at the back of this volume.

Texts and Traditions of Medieval Pastoral Care

ESSAYS IN HONOUR OF BELLA MILLETT

Edited by

Cate Gunn and Catherine Innes-Parker

THE UNIVERSITY *of York*

YORK MEDIEVAL PRESS

First published 2009

A York Medieval Press publication
in association with The Boydell Press
an imprint of Boydell & Brewer Ltd
PO Box 9   Woodbridge   Suffolk IP12 3DF   UK
and of Boydell & Brewer Inc.
668 Mt Hope Avenue   Rochester   NY 14620   USA
website: www.boydellandbrewer.com
and with the
Centre for Medieval Studies, University of York

ISBN   978 1 903153 29 1

The publisher has no responsibility for the continued existence or accuracy
of URLs for external or third-party internet websites referred to in this book,
and does not guarantee that any content on such websites is, or will remain,
accurate or appropriate.

A CIP catalogue record for this book is available
from the British Library

Printed in Great Britain by
CPI Antony Rowe, Chippenham and Eastbourne

CONTENTS

ACKNOWLEDGEMENTS

The editors would like to acknowledge the contributions of those whose work has made this volume possible. My research assistant Jennifer Tasker helped with proof-reading and details of format and style. We wish to thank the Social Sciences and Humanities Research Council of Canada for funding that made the research and production of this book possible. We also thank the University of Prince Edward Island for its support. English at the University of Southampton was pleased to be able to assist with publication of this volume.

Our work on this book has been a great joy, but it has also required long hours and the encouragement of our families. Catherine's husband, Kim, and her three children, Ian, Averil and David, were unflaggingly understanding and resourceful. The continuing support of Cate's husband, Tim Everitt, financial as well as emotional, made it possible for her to work on this book. We are grateful for the love and support of our families.

NOTES ON CONTRIBUTORS

Alexandra Barratt was educated at New Hall, University of Cambridge, and the Centre for Medieval Studies, University of Toronto, and has taught at the University of Waikato, New Zealand, where she is Professor of English, for more than thirty years. She has edited a number of Middle English prose texts, including Dame Eleanor Hull's translation of a French commentary on the Penitential Psalms, and an anthology of women's writing in Middle English (recently revised and reprinted). She has also published several articles on *Ancrene Wisse* and other medieval texts of religious instruction.

Mishtooni Bose was Lecturer in Medieval Literature and Culture in the Department of English at the University of Southampton from 1998 to 2004. In 2004 she became Christopher Tower Official Student and Tutor in Medieval Poetry in English at Christ Church, Oxford, and CUF Lecturer in the Faculty of English at Oxford. The author of several recent and forthcoming articles on intellectual life in late medieval England, focusing on Reginald Pecock, Thomas Gascoigne and Wyclif's opponents, she is currently completing a study of the way in which Church reform was explored in late medieval English poetry and prose.

Joseph Goering is Professor of History at the University of Toronto; his primary research and teaching interests are in medieval church history and institutions, intellectual history (especially the schools of law and theology) and popular religion. He has published work on twelfth- and thirteenth-century topics, including papal and episcopal politics, parish priests, pastoral care, penance and transubstantation. He is currently preparing a critical edition of the anonymous mid-thirteenth century *Speculum iuniorum*.

Brian Golding was a close colleague of Bella's for over thirty years. He has written widely on the medieval English church, particularly monasticism, Gerald of Wales, and the Norman Conquest.

Catherine Annette Grisé is Associate Professor in the Department of English and Cultural Studies at McMaster University. Her research interests include Middle English devotional manuscripts and early printed books, late medieval women's devotional culture, and monastic literary production and reception. Forthcoming book projects include a co-edited collection of essays on devotional reading and practices in late medieval England, and a monograph on the insular reception of continental holy women and their texts.

Cate Gunn wrote her PhD thesis on *Ancrene Wisse* under the supervision of Bella Millett while teaching for the Continuing Education department of the University of Essex; a revised version of her thesis has been published as *Ancrene Wisse: From Pastoral Theology to Vernacular Spirituality*. She now researches and writes on pastoral theology and literature as an independent scholar.

Ralph Hanna is Professor of Palaeography in the University of Oxford and tutorial fellow in English at Keble College. He has written on a variety of facets of later medieval literary culture, particularly the transmission of texts. His major interests remain language contact in England, regionalism in the Middle Ages, alliterative poetry, and above all, *Piers Plowman*. He has recently published a book of literary history, *London Literature, 1300–1380*.

Robert Hasenfratz, Professor of English and Medieval Studies at the University of Connecticut, completed his PhD at the Pennsylvania State University. His publications include an edition of *Reading Old English* (co-authored with Thomas Jambeck), *Ancrene Wisse* (TEAMS), and *Beowulf Scholarship: An Annotated Bibliography, 1979–1990*.

Catherine Innes-Parker is Professor of English at the University of Prince Edward Island. She has published widely on *Ancrene Wisse* and its associated texts, and is currently completing an edition of the Wooing Group. Her most recent research involves vernacular passion meditation, focusing particularly on vernacular versions of Bonaventure's *Lignum Vitae*.

E. A. Jones is Senior Lecturer in English Medieval Literature and Culture at the University of Exeter. He works on late medieval religious literature and culture, with a particular interest in hermits, anchorites and other 'semi-religious' vocations. He is the organizer and editor of the Exeter Symposia on the Medieval Mystical Tradition.

Elaine Treharne is Professor of Early English at Florida State University and Visiting Professor of Medieval Literature at the University of Leicester. She has edited numerous Old and Middle English texts, and published extensively in the fields of early medieval manuscript and literary studies. She is the Co-Director of the AHRC-funded project, 'The Production and Use of English Manuscripts, 1060 to 1220' (www.le.ac.uk/ee/em1060to1220/index.htm); founding convenor of the English Association Special Interest Group in the History of Manuscripts and Texts; General Editor of Essays and Studies; a former Chair and President of the English Association; and Medieval Editor for *Review of English Studies*, *Literature Compass*, and *Speculum*. Her current research project focuses on Arts and Crafts to Modernism and the emergence of the modern field of Manuscript Studies.

Nicholas Watson is Professor of English at Harvard University. He is author of *Richard Rolle and the Invention of Authority* (1991); co-translator (with Anne Savage) of *Anchoritic Spirituality: Ancrene Wisse and Associated Works* (1991); editor of Richard Rolle's *Emendatio vitae* (1994); co-editor (with Jocelyn Wogan-Browne, Andrew Taylor, and Ruth Evans) of *The Idea of the Vernacular: An Anthology of Middle English Literary Theory, 1280–1520* (1999); co-editor (with Fiona Somerset) of a volume of essays, *The Vulgar Tongue: Medieval and Post-Medieval Vernacularity* (2003); and co-editor (with Jacqueline Jenkins) of *The Writings of Julian of Norwich: 'A Vision Showed to a Devout Woman' and 'A Revelation of Love'* (2006). He has also written many articles on the religious writing of the English late Middle Ages. At present, he is finishing an edition, translation and study (with Claire Fanger) of John of Morigny's *Liber florum doctrine celestis* and writing a monograph, *Balaam's Ass: Vernacular Theology and Religious Secularization in Later Medieval England*.

Jocelyn Wogan-Browne is Professor of Medieval Literature at the University of York. She has taught in Australia, Europe, America and the UK and has written, edited and translated works concerned with medieval women, virginity, saints' lives and vernacularity in medieval England. She co-edits the French of England Translation Series with Thelma Fenster in which they have published *Matthew Paris: The History of St Edward the King* (FRETS 1, Tempe AZ, 2008); *Matthew Paris: The Life of St Alban*, together with further volumes by other scholars, is forthcoming. She recently edited a collection of thirty-three essays, *Language and Culture in Medieval Britain: The French of England c.1100–c.1500* (York Medieval Press, forthcoming), and currently teaches several courses in the language and literary culture of the French of England to History and English postgraduates at the Centre for Medieval Studies in York.

PREFACE
BELLA MILLETT

Derek Pearsall

I first met Bella in the 1970s when I was external examiner at Southampton. She was young and mini-skirted, and, though Bella could never be called flighty, she was something of a distraction for the older and more susceptible members of faculty. Her career prospered as she concentrated her research with unusually precise determination upon the early Middle English period and in particular upon the *Ancrene Wisse* group of texts, and upon the spiritual reading and guidance that might be specifically associated with female readers. These research interests, first demonstrated as early as 1983 in an impeccable edition of *Hali Meithhad*, a treatise of advice for women contemplating a life of devout virginity, have been steadily followed up in a series of important and influential essays demonstrating and developing Bella's skill and erudition in bringing new life to a significant and treasured corner of English devotion, and female reading and prayer.

Most of the earlier work, from the 1980s, is on the 'Katherine Group', a collection of devotional writings written mostly for (and possibly even by?) devout women in the South-West Midlands in the first half of the thirteenth century. She gives a general account of their affiliations with the alliterative tradition in prose and verse, some judicious speculations about their audience, and a shrewd analysis of their textual history and the problems of editing them (which she had already largely solved for one of them). In about 1990, Bella began to write more particularly about *Ancrene Wisse*, a 'Guide for Anchoresses' written by their spiritual (male) counsellor in the 1220s. Bella writes authoritatively about the prose style and rhetoric of the work, about its literary affiliations, and about its approach to confession and the life of spiritual perfection. She also demonstrated a keen interest in the special textual problems presented by *Ancrene Wisse*, which survives in different forms in a number of closely related early manuscripts, and in the usefulness of current theories of *mouvance* among French scholars to the prospective editor of the work.

The crown of her achievement (so far!) is the edition of the *Ancrene Wisse* now published by the Early English Text Society. The project has a long prehistory. The EETS decided as long ago as the 1930s that *Ancrene Wisse* (then generally called *Ancrene Riwle*), because of the complexities of its textual generation, with multiply layered revision by an author or authors, could not be edited except in diplomatic transcripts of individual manuscripts. These came out in eleven volumes (including two Latin manuscripts and one French) at irregular intervals through the next fifty-five years, the first in 1944, the most important, the text contained in Cambridge, Corpus Christi College Library MS 402, edited by J. R.R Tolkien in 1962, and the last in 1999. This series of separate editions of individual manuscripts, though understandable as a solution to an intractable problem, has not been much of a help to readers in enabling them to grasp the relationships of the English texts as a whole and in their full manuscript context.

Bella has not accepted this state of affairs. She determined that the apparent restlessness of textual affiliation among the manuscripts of *Ancrene Wisse* was capable of being understood as a whole, if not reduced to a pattern, and, what is more, that it could be represented more or less as a single text on the page, not a 'critical edition' but a single text with variants incorporated or recorded on the page in a typologically transparent manner. I have been closely involved in this project over the past few years, not as an advisor, I think (Bella needs little of the advice that I could give), but as a sympathetic reader and mediator of the collective opinion of the Council of the EETS. The project has mutated in various ways in the processes of growth and revision. For instance, the original plan to include a translation of the whole text was not accepted: the translation itself is superb, and I am pleased to see that it is to be published elsewhere, but it would not be usual for an EETS edition to include a translation.

Throughout, I have been impressed and inspired by Bella's dedication and determination, her brilliance as a scholar and textual critic, and her certainty of touch in an often baffling field of enquiry. The edition, in two volumes, will already have appeared before the present volume is published. It is not often that a Festschrift appears more or less simultaneously with the dedicatee's *magnum opus*, but I have no doubt that the publication of the latter will show my praise to have fallen short. At last the greatest work of medieval English prose, one of the great achievements, I would say, of all English prose writing, will come forth in full dress.

The collection of essays that follows celebrates different aspects of Bella's work – her impact generally on the regeneration of interest in early Middle English religious writing, her expertise as a manuscript and textual scholar, her pioneering work on female reading practice in the period and her great contribution to the understanding of medieval spirituality and particularly of female devotion. It is a worthy tribute to a wonderful scholar.

BIBLIOGRAPHY OF BELLA MILLETT'S WRITINGS

Books

(trans.), *Ancrene Wisse/ Guide for Anchoresses: A Translation based on Cambridge, Corpus Christi College, MS 402* (Exeter, 2009)

(ed.), *Ancrene Wisse: A Corrected Edition of the Text in Cambridge, Corpus Christi College, MS 402, with Variants from Other Manuscripts: Drawing on the Uncompleted Edition by E. J. Dobson, with a Glossary and Additional Notes by Richard Dance*, vol. 2, EETS OS 326 (Oxford, 2006)

(ed.), *Ancrene Wisse: A Corrected Edition of the Text in Cambridge, Corpus Christi College, MS 402, with Variants from Other Manuscripts: Drawing on the Uncompleted Edition by E. J. Dobson, with a Glossary and Additional Notes by Richard Dance*, vol. 1, EETS OS 325 (Oxford, 2005)

(with the assistance of G. B. Jack and Y. Wada), *Ancrene Wisse, The Katherine Group, and the Wooing Group*, Annotated Bibliographies of Old and Middle English Literature (Cambridge, 1996)

(ed., with Jocelyn Wogan-Browne), *Medieval English Prose for Women: Selections from the Katherine Group and Ancrene Wisse* (London, 1990; rev. edn. Oxford, 1992)

(ed.), *Hali Meithhad*, EETS OS 284 (London, 1982)

Articles

'The "Conditions of Eligibility" in *The Wohunge of ure Lauerd*', in *The Milieu and Context of The Wooing Group*, ed. Susannah M. Chewning (Cardiff, forthcoming 2009)

'"He speaks to Me as if I was a public meeting": Rhetoric and Audience in the Works of the *Ancrene Wisse* Group', in *Rhetoric of the Anchorhold: Place, Space and Body within the Discourses of Enclosure*, ed. L. Herbert McAvoy (Cardiff, 2008) pp. 50–65

'The Pastoral Context of the Lambeth and Trinity Homilies', in *Essays in Manuscript Geography: Vernacular Manuscripts of the English West Midlands from the Conquest to the Sixteenth Century*, ed. W. Scase (Turnhout, 2007), pp. 43–64

'The Discontinuity of English Prose: Structural Innovation in the Lambeth and Trinity Homilies', in *Text and Language in Medieval English Prose: A Festschrift for Tadao Kubouchi*, ed. J. Fisiak, J. Scahill, and A. Oizumi (Frankfurt, 2005), pp. 129–50

'The *Ancrene Wisse* Group', in *A Companion to Middle English Prose*, ed. A. S. G. Edwards (Cambridge, 2004), pp. 1–17

'Wessex Parallel WebTexts: developing an online tutorial', *English Subject Centre Bulletin* 6 (2003), 5–6

'The Genre of *Ancrene Wisse*' in *A Companion to Ancrene Wisse*, ed. Y. Wada (Cambridge, 2003), pp. 29–44

'*Ancrene Wisse* and the Life of Perfection', *Leeds Studies in English* 33 (2002), 53–76

'*Ancrene Wisse* and the Book of Hours', in *Writing Religious Women: Female Spiritual and Textual Practices in Late Medieval England*, ed. D. Renevey and C. Whitehead (Cardiff, 2000), pp. 21–40

'*Ancrene Wisse* and the Conditions of Confession', *English Studies* 80 (1999), 193–215

'Peintunge and Schadewe in *Ancrene Wisse* Part 4', *Notes and Queries* n.s. 43 (1996), 399–403

'The Songs of Entertainers and the Songs of the Angels: Vernacular Lyric Fragments in Odo of Cheriton's *Sermones de Festis*', *Medium Aevum* 64 (1995), 17–36

'Mouvance and the Medieval Author: Re-editing *Ancrene Wisse*', in *Late-Medieval Religious Texts and their Transmission*, ed. A. J. Minnis (Cambridge, 1994), pp. 9–20

'How Green is the Green Knight?', *Nottingham Medieval Studies* 38 (1994), 138–51

'Women in No Man's Land: English Recluses and the Development of Vernacular Literature in the Twelfth and Thirteenth Centuries', in *Women and Literature in Britain, 1150–1500*, ed. C. M. Meale (Cambridge, 1994), pp. 86–103

'The Origins of *Ancrene Wisse*: New Answers, New Questions', *Medium Aevum* 61 (1992), 206–28

'The Textual Transmission of *Seinte Iuliene*', *Medium Aevum* 59 (1990), 41–54

'Some Editorial Problems in the Katherine Group', *English Studies* 71 (1990), 386–94

'The Audience of the Saints' Lives of the Katherine Group', *Reading Medieval Studies* 16 (1990), 127–56

'The Saints' Lives of the Katherine Group and the Alliterative Tradition', *Journal of English and Germanic Philology* 87 (1988), 16–34

'Chaucer, Lollius, and the Medieval Theory of Authorship', in *Reconstructing Chaucer: Selected Essays from the 1984 New Chaucer Society Congress*, ed. Paul Strohm and T. J. Heffernan (Knoxville TN, 1985)

'*Hali Meithhad, Sawles Warde*, and the Continuity of English Prose', in *Five Hundred Years of Words and Sounds: A Festschrift for Eric Dobson*, ed. E. G. Stanley and D. Gray (Cambridge, 1983)

Electronic publications

2003 *Ancrene Wisse* Preface: a trial electronic edition for EETS, produced with the support of an AHRB Resource Enhancement Scheme grant. http://tei. oucs.ox.ac/EETS

2002 'What is mouvance?', an on-line tutorial produced with the support of the English Subject Centre as part of the Wessex Parallel WebTexts project. http://soton.ac.uk/~wpwt/mouvance/mouvance.htm

Forthcoming

'Change and Continuity: The English sermon before 1250' in *The Oxford Handbook of Medieval Literature in English*, ed. Elaine Treharne and Greg Walker (Oxford, forthcoming 2010)

ABBREVIATIONS

Aelred, *De institutione*	Aelred of Rievaulx, *De Institutione Inclusarum* in *Opera Omnia* ed. A. Hoste and C. H. Talbot, CCCM I (Turnholt, 1971), pp. 637–82.
AHRC	Arts and Humanities Research Council
Ancrene Wisse, ed. Millett	*Ancrene Wisse: A Corrected Edition of the Text in Cambridge, Corpus Christi College, MS 402, with variants from other manuscripts* by Bella Millett with R. Dance, EETS no. 325, vol. 1 (Oxford, 2005); vol. 2 (Oxford, 2006)
ANTS	Anglo-Norman Text Society
Baldwin, *Masters, Princes and Merchants*	J. W. Baldwin, *Masters, Princes and Merchants: the Social Views of Peter the Chanter and his Circle*, 2 vols. (Princeton, 1970)
Bell, *What Nuns Read*	D. N. Bell, *What Nuns Read: Books and Libraries in Medieval English Nunneries* (Kalamazoo 1995)
CCCM	Corpus Christianorum, Continuatio Medievalis (Turnhout, 1966–)
CCSL	Corpus Christianorum, Series Latina (Turnhout, 1953–)
Chobham, *Summa Confessorum*	Thomae de Chobham, *Summa Confessorum*, ed. F. Broomfield (Louvain, 1968)
Chobham, *Summa de Arte Praedicandi*	Thomas de Chobham, *Summa de Arte Praedicandi*, ed. F. Morenzoni, CCCM 82 (Turnhold, 1988)
Dean and Boulton, *Anglo-Norman Literature*	R. Dean, with the collaboration of M. B. M. Boulton, *Anglo-Norman Literature: A Guide to Texts and Manuscripts*, ANTS Occasional Publications 3 (London, 1999)
Edmund, *Mirour*	*Mirour de Seinte Eglyse (St Edmund of Abingdon's Speculum Ecclesiae)*, ed. A. D. Wilshere (London, 1982)
Edmund, *Speculum*	Edmund of Abingdon, *Speculum Religiosorum and Speculum Ecclesie* ed. H. P. Forshaw, Auctores Britannici Medii Aevi, 3 (London, 1973)
EETS	Early English Text Society (London, 1864 -)
FMLS	Forum for Modern Language Studies
Franzen, *Tremulous Hand*	C. Franzen, *The Tremulous Hand of Worcester: A Study of Old English in the Thirteenth Century* (Oxford, 1991)
Gerald of Wales, *Gemma*	*Giraldi Cambrensis: Gemma Ecclesiastica*, ed. J. S. Brewer (Rolls Series, London, 1862)
Goering, *William de Montibus*	J. Goering, *William de Montibus: The Schools and the Literature of Pastoral Care* (Toronto, 1992)

Grosseteste, *Templum Dei*	Robert Grosseteste, *Templum Dei ed. from MS 27 Emmanuel College Cambridge* by J. Goering and F. A. C. Mantello (Toronto, 1984)
Gunn, *AW From Pastoral Literature*	C. Gunn, *Ancrene Wisse: From Pastoral Literature to Vernacular Spirituality* (Cardiff, 2008)
Hanna, *Pursuing History*	R. Hanna, *Pursuing History: Middle English Manuscripts and Their Texts* (Stanford, 1996),
Hartung, *Manual*	*A Manual of the Writings in Middle English 1050–1500*, Volume 9, ed. A. E. Hartung (New Haven, 1993)
Horstmann, *Yorkshire Writers*	*Yorkshire Writers: Richard Rolle and His Followers*, ed. C. Horstmann, 2 vols (London, 1895–96; reprinted Cambridge, 1999)
Hull, *Seven Psalms*	*The Seven Psalms: A Commentary on the Penitential Psalms translated from French into English by Dame Eleanor Hull*, ed. A. Barratt, EETS os 307 (Oxford, 1995), p. 204.
Jolliffe, *Check-list*	P. S. Jolliffe, *A Check-list of Middle English Prose Writings of Spiritual Guidance*, Subsidia Mediaevalia II (Toronto, 1974)
Ker, *Catalogue Containing Anglo-Saxon*	N. R. Ker, *Catalogue of Manuscripts Containing Anglo-Saxon* (Oxford, 1990 [1957])
Love, *Mirror* (2005)	Nicholas Love, *The Mirror of the Blessed Life of Jesus Christ: A Full Critical Edition based on Cambridge University Library Additional MSS 6578 and 6686 with Introduction, Notes and Glossary* ed. M. G. Sargent (Exeter, 2005)
Macpherson, 'Rule of Life'	'A Rule of Life for a Recluse', trans. M. P. Macpherson in *Aelred of Rievaulx: Treatises and Pastoral Prayer*, Cistercian Fathers Series 2 (Kalamazoo, 1971), 41–102
MLR	*Modern Language Review*
Myrour of Recluses ed. Harley	*The Myrour of Recluses: A Middle English Translation of* Speculum Inclusorum, ed. M. P. Harley (Madison, 1995)
MRTS	Medieval and Renaissance Text Series
ODNB	*Oxford Dictionary of National Biography* (Oxford, 2004) www.oxforddnb.com
Old English Homilies, I	*Old English Homilies and Homiletic Treatises … of the Twelfth and Thirteenth Centuries, ed. from MSS in the British Museum, Lambeth and Bodleian Libraries … by* R. Morris, 1st series in 2 parts, EETS nos. 29 and 34 (London, 1867–8)
Old English Homilies, II	*Old English Homilies of the Twelfth Century ed. … by* R. Morris, EETS 53 (London, 1873)
Parkes, '*Ormmulum*'	M. B. Parkes, 'On the Presumed Date and Possible Origin of the Manuscript of the "*Ormmulum*"', Oxford,

	Bodleian Library, MS Junius 1', in *Scribes, Scripts and Readers: Studies in the Communication, Presentation and Dissemination of Medieval Texts* (London, 1991), pp. 187–200; (rep. from *Five Hundred Years of Words and Sounds: A Festschrift for Eric Dobson*, ed. E. G. Stanley and D. Grey (Cambridge, 1983), pp. 115–27)
PL	*Patrologia Latina*, ed. J. P. Migne (Paris, 1841–61)
Raymond of Penyafort, *Summa*	S. Raimundus de Pennaforte, *Summa de paenitentia*, ed. X. Ochoa and A. Diez (Rome, 1976)
RES	*Review of English Studies*
Rhetoric of the Anchorhold	*Rhetoric of the Anchorhold: Space, Place and Body within the Discourses of Enclosure* ed. L. McAvoy (Cardiff, 2008)
Savage and Watson, *Anchoritic Spirituality*	*Anchoritic Spirituality: Ancrene Wisse and Associated Works*, trans. and ed. A. Savage and N. Watson (New York: 1991)
Scase, *Manuscript Geography*	*Essays in Manuscript Geography: Vernacular Manuscripts of the English West Midlands from the Conquest to the Sixteenth Century*, ed. W. Scase (Turnhout, 2007)
Sharpe, *Handlist*	R. Sharpe, *A Handlist of the Latin Writers of Great Britain and Ireland Before 1540* (Brussels, 1997)
STC	*A Short-title Catalogue of Books Printed in England, Scotland, and Ireland, and of English Books Printed Abroad, 1475–1640*, first compiled by A. W. Pollard and G. R. Redgrave; 2nd rev. ed, begun by W. A. Jackson and F. S. Ferguson, completed by K. F. Pantzer (London, 1976–1986)
VCH	The Victoria History of the Counties of England
Wallace, *Cambridge History*	*The Cambridge History of Medieval English Literature*, ed. D. Wallace (Cambridge, 1999)
Women and Literature	*Women and Literature in Britain: 1150–1500*, ed. C. M Meale (Cambridge, 1993)
Writing Religious Women	*Writing Religious Women: Female Spiritual and Textual Practices in Late Medieval England*, ed. D. Renevey and C. Whitehead (Cardiff, 2000)

Introduction

Catherine Innes-Parker and Cate Gunn

Bella Millett is best known for her work on the early thirteenth-century English guide for anchoresses, *Ancrene Wisse*, culminating in her recently published *Corrected Edition of the Text in Cambridge, Corpus Christi College, MS 402 with Variants from Other Manuscripts*. The very title suggests Millett's approach: magisterial, thorough and correct, yet acknowledging variations; never boastful but always respectful of her material; never assuming knowledge in her readers, but never patronizing. The precision and clarity Millett brings to her editing are also the hallmarks of her writing – which has a wider range than the early thirteenth century English works she is normally associated with. Her essay on the Green Man, for example, is a fine example of her analytic thinking and lucid writing. She has written about the practice of editing and on the use of computers and the internet for teaching and presenting: her home page includes a list of electronic publications.

In her writing on *Ancrene Wisse* and other associated works Millett has suggested new ways of reading *Ancrene Wisse*, including as a work of vernacular literature aimed primarily at women and as a precursor to the Books of Hours popular in the later Middle Ages. Importantly, she challenged the received wisdom of her quondam supervisor, Eric Dobson, asking new questions about the origins of *Ancrene Wisse*. The questioning of received authority is a recurring theme in this volume: Joseph Goering questions an attribution suggested by Leonard Doyle, and Elaine Traherne's paper traces the mechanism by which an originally tentative attribution can, by gradual accretion, gain unquestioned authority. It is by going back to original sources – often the manuscripts themselves – that our contributors are able to address new questions, and occasionally come up with new answers. By returning to the manuscripts of the Lambeth Homilies, Ralph Hanna suggests new answers to the questions about the production of pastoral manuscripts – including those of *Ancrene Wisse* – in the thirteenth century.

The title of this collection of essays – *Texts and Traditions of Medieval Pastoral Care* – gives a broad scope while retaining a definite focus. The pastoral and devotional literature considered in this collection was all written in, or in some way associated with, England in the Middle Ages. This is a category into which *Ancrene Wisse* itself would fit.[1] While a number of the contributors to this collection pay tribute to Millett's work on *Ancrene Wisse*, the essays reflect the broader scope of her research, most notably in the area of pastoral literature. Millett has recently published two important articles on early English homily collections, 'The Pastoral Context of the Lambeth and Trinity Homilies', and 'The Discontinuity of English Prose: Structural Innovation in the Lambeth and Trinity Homilies',[2] both dealing with pastoral context. A number of the contributors make use of these papers; Jocelyn Wogan-Browne, for example, points out that Bella Millett has recently shown that

> a group of late twelfth- and early thirteenth-century English homilies, far from being a dying flicker of Anglo-Saxon tradition, is much more likely to have its true context in response to concern at diocesan level with meeting the need for vernacular pastoralia. These homilies, she argues, use older as well as newer material, but are fundamentally a fresh response and redeployment of existing homiletic tradition.

The development of new thinking on pastoral care, which was to be formulated in the decrees of the Fourth Lateran Council of 1215, had an influence on the literature of pastoral care, both the Latin *pastoralia* emanating from France in the twelfth century, and vernacular literature which developed in response to the requirements of parish priests faced with newly formulated duties towards the laity, in particular the requirement to hear confessions, impose penance and teach their parishioners the basics of the faith. The influence of the Parisian theology school was evident in England from early on – one of the best known of the English writers influenced by Paris is Thomas of Chobham, to whose writings a number of our contributors refer. Bella Millett once suggested that Odo of Cheriton is equally important but since he is not so accessible less work has been done on him; some of the papers in this collection strive to raise awareness of other neglected writers of pastoral literature. Authors of thirteenth-century Latin *pastoralia* discussed here include Gerald of Wales, Edmund of Abingdon and the anonymous author of *Speculum iuniorum*.

With the rise of lay literacy and the demand for guidance literature in the vernacular, the literature of pastoral care continued to expand and diversify in the fourteenth and fifteenth centuries. Not all vernacular texts of guidance were directed specifically at lay readers – Mannyng's *Handlyng Synne* and Gascoigne's *Liber Veritatum* were, in the first place, directed at an audience of priests who, in the authors' view, were neglecting their pastoral duties. Other

---

1   Cate Gunn's PhD thesis, written under the supervision of Bella Millett examined *Ancrene Wisse* as a work of pastoral literature. Bella was a model supervisor, providing full support and always generous with the fruit of her own research, such as that on *Ancrene Wisse* and the conditions of confession.
2   A complete bibliography of Bella Millett's work appears in this volume.

texts were, like *Ancrene Wisse*, written in the first instance for audiences of devout women, yet their authors were clearly aware of a wider lay audience. But more and more, devotional literature in the vernacular was commissioned by and written or, more often, translated for a specifically lay audience. Lay readers enthusiastically embraced the emotional and very personal devotion expressed in new translations of continental mystical and devotional literature. Yet, at the same time, the clerical desire to make devotional texts accessible to the laity through translation created a potential for the laity to bypass the instruction urged by the carefully crafted guidance literature for parish priests. Instead of relying on the parish priest for teaching the basic tenets of belief, readers of vernacular guidance texts could become, in effect, independent of the very authors so concerned with their instruction. This created a sense of unease amongst clerical authors, which, as Jocelyn Wogan-Brown points out, had also existed at the time of the Fourth Lateran Council. In the late fourteenth and early fifteenth centuries, pastoral concerns often turned to the problem of avoiding error as much as offering basic instruction. The most well-known (and widely read) text which reflects such concerns is Nicholas Love's *Mirror of the Blessed Life of Jesus Christ*, the translation of the Pseudo-Bonaventuran *Meditationes Vitae Christi*, one of the few texts actually authorized by Archbishop Thomas Arundel under the rubric of the *Constitutiones* of 1409. Yet, despite its overt concern with the correction of Lollardy, Love's *Mirror* also reflects the same concerns with guiding the laity through meditation on Christ's life and passion as does Hilton's letter *Of Mixed Life*.[3] Indeed, in some ways, Arundel's *Constitutiones* can be seen, like the edicts of the Fourth Lateran Council, as much a response to the need for a new kind of pastoral literature as a reaction to the rising threat of Lollardy. Like the author of *Ancrene Wisse*, fifteenth-century authors combine devotional guidance with instruction on the correct understanding of religious concepts and practices, whether as a response to error, or out of concern that their readers 'get it right'. Such texts are designed for a wide audience, whose access to guidance might range from having a learned personal mentor to relying solely on the book itself.

All the texts discussed in this collection are associated with England (or Wales) but are not necessarily in English: in Goering's assessment of the *Speculum iuniorum* he argues that it 'deserves pride of place among the masterpieces of Latin pastoral literature written for the education of priests and pastors of souls in England during the thirteenth and fourteenth centuries'. The Latin versions of Edmund's *Speculum religiosorum* are discussed by Cate Gunn and the vernacular translations by Nicholas Watson. Wogan-

---

[3] See Love, *Mirror* (2005), intro., p. 33. For the problematic issues surrounding Arundel's *Constitutiones* and censorship, see K. Kerby-Fulton, *Books under Suspicion: Censorship and Tolerance of Revelatory Writing in Late Medieval England* (Notre Dame IN, 2006).

Browne looks at francophone pastoral writings produced in the multilingual culture of thirteenth-century England; in particular she examines the French verse translation by the Augustinian canon Angier of Gregory the Great's *Dialogues*. Catherine Innes-Parker shows that a late medieval English text, *Þe passion of oure Lord* is an unrecognized translation and adaptation of Bonaventure's *Lignum Vitae*, while the subject of Robert Hasenfratz's paper is the translation of William of Waddington's French *Manuel des Péchés* into English as the well-known late medieval text, *Handlyng Synne*.

As well as a variety of languages, there are many genres which can be included under the heading of 'pastoral literature': handbooks of preaching, guides to confession, guides to the anchoritic life, sermons, and meditative and devotional guides. E. A. Jones considers both works designed to guide anchorites and works of pastoral care written by anchorites. Brian Golding raises the question of how *pastoralia* is to be defined. Elsewhere, Joseph Goering draws on the definition of *pastoralia* provided by his mentor, Leonard Boyle, as a genre encompassing, 'the many and diverse works produced in the thirteenth and subsequent centuries to educate clerics (and, gradually, the laity) in those things pertaining to the care of souls'.[4] Goering has asserted that all pastoral texts have in common 'a desire to convey in writing ... the basic knowledge and skills necessary for exercising the pastoral care of souls in the parishes of Latin Christendom';[5] and Richard Newhauser has also pointed out that the definition of *pastoralia* is more to do with content than form.[6] Golding, however, suggests that the formal deficiencies of the text he is examining, the *Gemma Ecclesiastica* of Gerald of Wales, raise questions about the definition of pastoral literature.

Golding argues that the *Gemma* 'is not a coherent work of moral and spiritual reform' and 'does not appear "fit for purpose"'. The classic definition, in the sense of a complete taxonomy of all branches of *pastoralia*, is provided by Leonard Boyle in his paper on 'The Fourth Lateran Council and Manuals of Popular Theology', and takes the form of a schematic diagram. It is this structured, scholastic definition that Golding is calling into question since Gerald's 'hodge podge' cannot be located within it. The *Gemma* was written as a didactic work, informed by Gerald's practical experience as an archdeacon and influenced by Parisian theological theory but much of it was irrelevant to the stated audience of parish priests and lesser clerics. Golding points out that previous writers on Gerald of Wales's *Gemma* have presumed that it was written 'to instruct the clergy of St Davids in the rudiments of theology';

---

4   Goering, *William de Montibus*, p. 59.
5   J. Goering, 'Pastoralia: The Popular Literature of the Care of Souls', in *Medieval Latin: An Introduction and Bibliographical Guide*, ed. F. A. C. Mantello and A. G. Rigg (Washington DC, 1996), pp. 670–6 (p. 670).
6   R. Newhauser, *The Treatise on Vices and Virtues in Latin and the Vernacular*, Typologie des Sources du Moyen Âge Occidental, Fasc. 68 (Turnhout, 1993), pp. 59, 60.

he concludes that it is only when this presumption is questioned that 'the importance of the *Gemma* in the development of pastoral literature appears'.

The work Goering analyses here provides an excellent example of a text that was designed for the education of clerics, though whether lowly parish priests would have had access to such work remains unknown. Written in the mid-thirteenth century, the anonymous *Speculum iuniorum* harvested material from the Parisian theological masters and organized it according to classic scholastic methods of division and subdivision. The author seems to have been English, since all the extant manuscripts are apparently of English provenance, and was probably a Dominican. Through close attention to the text, Goering is able to show that he was probably writing at the same time as Simon of Hinton was writing his *Summa ad instructionem iuniorum*. Although part of the larger movement of the development of pastoral literature in England, this anonymous *Speculum* deals with material 'in an original and unusual fashion'. The work quotes from a great number of contemporary and near-contemporary authors to construct what is indeed a mirror of the pastoral literature of the mid-thirteenth century. Goering is preparing a critical edition of this text which will allow it to 'take its rightful place among the major achievements of the pastoral writings of thirteenth- and fourteenth-century England'.

Both Golding and Goering provide careful analysis of the texts under their consideration. Other contributors turn to the physical manifestation of the texts as manuscripts to shed light on the place of pastoral literature in England in the Middle Ages. Both Elaine Treharne and Ralph Hanna use a fresh look at known manuscripts to provide new answers to old questions. Treharne takes Bella Millett's reappraisal of our understanding of the location of origin of *Ancrene Wisse* and associated texts as an inspiration for her own questioning about the localization of manuscripts. Treharne is particularly concerned with the writing, copying and disseminating of pastoral literature in English in the two centuries immediately following the Norman conquest. Worcester was an important scriptorium at this period, but Treharne suggests that its high profile can deter scholars from reassessing the evidence. She argues that Worcester should not be seen in isolation but as the 'core of an important regional network of affiliated monasteries' and that we should perhaps think of it as 'a conglomeration of associated scriptoria and writing environments' rather than an individual centre.

Ralph Hanna is also concerned with manuscripts containing vernacular pastoral literature; his essay uses palaeographical and codicological evidence – especially that of quiring – to provide a new assessment of the production of the early thirteenth century manuscript, Lambeth Palace, MS 487, containing a collection of homilies in the vernacular, known as the 'Lambeth Homilies'. It also examines two manuscripts containing works of the *Ancrene Wisse* group: MS Royal 17 A.xxvii and MS Cotton Titus D.xviii. The essay argues that the compilation of Lambeth 487 and Titus D.xviii was a process over time, the scribe using source material that was probably not continuously available. One can construct a narrative of a book's production by coordinating codicological information; Hanna provides such a narrative for Lambeth 487, and using this as an exemplar concludes that such book histories might lead one to query Dobson's view of 'Wigmore texts' as a concerted local canon, the designed product of an 'AB community'. Codicological evidence, like that provided by Lambeth 487, might well imply a much less centralized and organized group of texts, available only fitfully and sporadically to book producers and the readers they served.

The question of the manuscript context of vernacular guidance texts designed specifically for a lay audience is taken up by Jocelyn Wogan-Browne, who argues that 'clerical writers ... tend to articulate explicitly and copiously the rationale and aims of their work and the common interests, as they see them, of themselves and their audiences'. Wogan-Browne examines Angier of St Frideswide's creation of a vernacular *accessus* in his translation of Gregory the Great's *Dialogues* into Anglo-Norman verse. Through the careful articulation of structure and the inclusion of finding aids in the manuscript itself, Angier makes not only the content but the text itself accessible to 'an inclusive and varied group of readers or hearers'. Like the author of *Ancrene Wisse*, Angier expects his readers to organize their own reading time, choosing for themselves what they will read and when. For such independent reading, Angier provides every means possible to ensure that 'questions, objections and *correct* answers are clearly and unambiguously *readable* as well as audible'. Wogan-Browne shows the willingness of clerical writers to adapt not only their material, but also their authorial stance to the needs of emerging lay audiences.

The concept of readers as consumers is addressed by Alexandra Barratt in the context of guidance literature for women. Barratt argues that advice to women blurs the monastic boundaries between *lectio*, *oratio* and *meditatio*, and that reading is conflated not only with prayer and meditation, but also with work. Yet, in spite of a repeated advocacy of reading as 'good prayer' (found in texts from *Ancrene Wisse* to the *Chastising of God's Children*), Barratt argues that there is a vagueness about what, specifically, women religious should read. While most texts assume some sort of *lectio divina*, access to the Bible was problematic. Nevertheless, two texts stand out in being specifically recommended for reading: the Pseudo-Bonaventuran *Meditationes Vitae Christi* and *Stimulus Amoris*, both of which were available in vernacular translations by the late fourteenth century.

C. Annette Grisé also addresses the development of vernacular devotional texts for women, but takes it one step further, arguing that 'pious women participated in an intermediate system of peer-to-peer care, sharing and teaching ... through vernacular books'. Through an examination of a group of texts associated with Syon Abbey, Grisé shows how women readers became writers who recorded their own devotional practices to share these experiences with their peers or translated the works of others both as a form of spiritual exercise and as a means of widening the audience for such texts.

The adaptation and translation of pastoral texts is addressed by a number of essays in this collection. Vernacular translations of texts designed for the education of the clergy often reflect the emergence of a new audience. Cate Gunn explores adaptation and translation of Edmund of Abingdon's *Speculum religiosorum*, a guide to the 'perfect life'. Once again, the definition of *pastoralia* is raised: Gunn states, 'the *Speculum* is concerned with the ascent to contemplation but its interest is not limited to those in a dedicated religious life; the catechetical material was useful for those in charge of lay people and the work as a whole can be considered a work of *pastoralia*'. Gunn shows that through being translated from Latin into Anglo-Norman, and back again into Latin, Edmund's work undergoes a process of *mouvance* comparable to *Ancrene Wisse*, and that careful attention to the audiences of these translations, the terms used to describe them, and the ways in which the text is altered for them, shows both the development of pastoral concerns and the adaptability of the text.

Nicholas Watson picks up this thread, arguing that the translation and adaptation of Edmund's *Speculum* 'has much to teach us … about the continuing importance of early thirteenth century theological and pastoral categories to late medieval writers and readers in particular'. Watson argues that the *Speculum*'s chief importance lies in its combination of contemplative thought with the new pastoral theology of the early thirteenth century. Indeed, Watson suggests, the work 'aspires to vernacularization' with its shift in the presentation of the contemplative life. The Middle English translations reinforce the complexities of the audience(s) and the shifting definitions of *religiosi* and the life of perfection: some are addressed to professional religious; some include both lay and religious; yet others are addressed specifically to the laity. Once again, the adaptability of earlier pastoral literature to new audiences reflects the growth in the development of spirituality in England.

E. A. Jones is concerned with the production, readership and institutional context of texts of pastoral literature and spiritual direction. Examining texts associated with anchorites and hermits as both consumers of and dispensers of pastoral care, he shines new light on anchoritic texts, and raises interesting questions about the practical business of pastoral care. He also allows us to revise the definition of pastoral care, suggesting a wider context of spiritual direction, and moving away from concern with clerics providing pastoral care to lay people. Looking at the career of particular solitaries, Jones is able to show that 'the solitary life and the life of pastoral engagement figure as different stages in an individual's spiritual career' and continues, 'perhaps surprisingly', that it was 'also possible to pursue the two callings simultaneously' and concludes that while spiritual direction could be seen as a problem for solitaries, they could 'also be part of the solution to the problems of pastoral care in the late Middle Ages'.

The problems of pastoral care in a changing context are also addressed by Mishtooni Bose in her discussion of Thomas Gascoigne's *Liber Veritatum*; Bose argues that the reformist Gascoigne urged the importance of *prophetia comminationis*, a form of pastoral prophesy 'which typically took the form of the denunciation of lax mores and calls to repentance'. Through the close examination of one particular discourse, Bose argues that Gascoigne took on the voice of the biblical prophets, lamenting the decay of pastoral care in England and calling for a vigorous reform in which pastors return to their fundamental duty 'to evangelize, to provide testimony of God's judgements, and to make God's wishes manifest to his people through [their] words and through the example of [their] life'. Bose argues that rather than being polarized between orthodoxy and Lollardy (as argued by Kantik Ghosh), the fifteenth-century Church in which Gascoigne's thought was formed was far more complex and 'the English ecclesiastical establishment during this period was one that characteristically did its thinking in a variety of reformist modes'.

If Gascoigne was concerned to highlight the importance of lament and prophecy, Robert Hasenfratz argues that Robert Mannyng's *Handlyng Synne*, a translation of the *Manuel des Péchés*, focused on fear. The horrors of judgement day were illustrated in graphic, and terrifying, form. Hasenfratz explores the tradition of theological discussion of fear; in particular, anxiety about the efficacy of 'servile fear' – the fear of punishment and hell which seemingly dominates *Handlyng Synne* – led to the careful scholastic classification of varying levels of fear and their functions. But, Hasenfratz argues, in the process of adaptation and translation from high theology to Latin pastoral manuals to vernacular texts intended for lay audiences, 'carefully argued definitions and distinctions were inevitably elided, simplified, and adapted'. Illustrating this process through the works of Raymond of Penyafort and Thomas of Chobham, Hasenfratz shows that Thomas of Chobham replaced the potentially confusing categorization of fear with 'a powerful binary of love and fear'. However, he argues, '*Handlyng Synne* ... seems to push its readers and listeners away from sin and towards confession mainly by conjuring up a vivid and compelling form of servile fear, rather than pulling them towards God by love.' In its assumption that it was easier 'to strike fear than to inspire love in the hearts and minds of ... listeners' *Handlyng Synne* reflects a pessimistic view of lay capabilities.

A more positive form of the adaptation of theological and devotional subjects for lay readers is found in the text examined by Catherine Innes-Parker. Close attention to an English text known as *Þe passioun of oure lord* allows Innes-Parker to argue that it is a translation or, rather, a version of Bonaventure's *Lignum vitae*. By showing that 'much of the Latin text is expanded and its central metaphor is adapted in such a way as to radically alter its application expressly for a lay audience', Innes-Parker uses this example of a vernacular translation of a Latin text to illustrate the transition of pastoral literature, not just from one language to another, but from one usage and readership to another. *Þe passioun of oure lord*, in making the passion the central part of the text, adapts it to a devotional work capable of nourishing its lay readers through the consumption of the text in the act of reading. Innes-Parker argues that Bonaventure's assumptions about his more sophisticated readers were quite different: they approached the *Lignum vitae* in a more intellectual manner, while theological concepts are omitted or played down in the vernacular translation. The vernacular author is concerned to teach his readers about the liturgy and sacraments, but he also 'creates a close metaphorical tie between himself, the book, and the reader through the image of the cross, which he bears through composing the book, and they bear through reading the book which is, itself, the tree of the cross'. In this one example, we see something of the variation in pastoral literature produced in England in the Middle Ages.

While all the essays have a firm basis in their historical context, some from different periods make complementary points about the administration of pastoral care. The theoretical essays are illuminated by studies of specific manuscripts, and these manuscripts and texts, being produced in different institutional contexts (monastic, clerical, etc.) suggest interesting comparisons; the very act of collection enhances the individual papers. The ordering of the essays in this collection illustrates the development of pastoral literature and the growth of a lay and vernacular spirituality, but it also suggests intersections between texts written in different languages for different audiences. The collection is framed by two papers that focus on a particular audience and range from the early thirteenth century to the fifteenth century, suggesting the active pastoral concerns in both Latin and the vernacular for audiences of solitaries and of women throughout the period. Within that framework, essays on individual texts are ordered more or less chronologically, providing examples of recurring concerns for content and audience, and illustrating a growing movement towards the vernacular. The manuscript tradition itself is important in an understanding of this literature and its readership (as well as of the authors who produced it), and shows how the examination of specific texts can supplement and challenge our understanding of the literature of pastoral care.

The fact that this collection begins and ends with essays that refer to *Ancrene Wisse* shows how important the work of Bella Millett on that text has been. The wide range of texts discussed in this collection pays tribute to her pioneering studies of *Ancrene Wisse*'s place in the broader context of vernacular spirituality in England. Finally, this collection of essays on the literature of pastoral care pays tribute to Bella Millett's own 'pastoral' work, not only in the production and dissemination of knowledge, but also in the encouragement and inspiration of students and scholars whose work has been enriched by her writing and by her 'care'.

1

'Vae Soli': Solitaries and Pastoral Care*

E. A. Jones

> To glorify eremitism in general seems to me to be a dangerous thing, for each vocation to solitude is a problem of spiritual direction and aspirants should not be encouraged, without distinction, to seek it.[1]

Vae soli, says the Preacher: 'Woe to him that is alone, for when he falleth, he hath none to lift him up' (Eccles. 4. 10). The lament is perfect ammunition for anyone who wishes to emphasize the dangers of the solitary vocation in general, and in particular to highlight the problems it poses for a system of pastoral care.

The *locus classicus* is St Basil's argument for the superiority of the common life in the seventh of his Longer Rules.[2] He reasons that, whilst an individual may have one or more spiritual gifts, the result when a group of individuals pools their respective gifts is both a more complete realization of the Christian life, and greater than the sum of its parts: a *coenobium* of all the talents, perhaps. Set alongside this positive argument in favour of the life in common are two cautions against the solitary vocation. First of all, the solitary is too self-focused properly to fulfil the demands of charity. As he asks:

> Wherewith shall a man show humility, if he has no one in comparison with whom to show himself humble? Wherewith shall he show compassion, when he is cut off from the communion of the many? How can he practise himself in long-suffering, when there is none to withstand his wishes? ... Whose feet then wilt thou wash? Whom wilt thou care for? In comparison with whom wilt thou be last if thou livest by thyself?[3]

But the solitary is exposed to faults not only of omission but of commission as well – and when he offends in this regard the danger is acute, since he

---

*   I am very grateful for the assistance provided by Margaret Yoon in the research for this essay.

1   Quoted in 'L'Erémetisme dans la vie spirituelle et dans la vie religieuse', *La Vie spirituelle*, Oct. 1952, 278–88 (p. 278).

2   *Patrologia Graeca*, ed. J.-P. Migne (Paris, 1857–66), 31.927–34. Translated in W. K. L. Clarke, *The Ascetic Works of Saint Basil* (London, 1925), pp. 163–6.

3   *Ascetic Works*, trans. Clarke, pp. 165–6.

'will not even recognize his defects readily, not having anyone to reprove him and to set him right with kindness and compassion'. The problem for the solitary is identified precisely as one of spiritual direction:

> Such a guide it is difficult to find in solitude, unless one has already formed a link with him in community life. There happens to him in consequence what has been said: 'Woe to the solitary man, since if he fall there is none to raise him up.'[4]

Basil's arguments are influential and much-quoted, just as the verse around which he based his warnings against the dangers of solitude maintains an understandable attraction for apologists and legislators for various forms of the life in common. It may be more surprising to find *Vae soli* used in texts written for the encouragement and guidance of solitaries. In his ninth-century rule for Benedictine recluses, Grimlaic insists (perhaps counter-intuitively) that 'every effort be made that, if at all possible, there never be fewer than two or three solitaries at the same time'. He reasons: 'I know that the companionship of two solitaries is useful to those who are of the same will and purpose. On the other hand, I discern that in many cases to live the solitary life without any company is dangerous.' The catalogue of the dangers of solitude that follows is essentially Basil's, and Ecclesiastes 4. 10 is quoted as proof-text, directly following on from the familiar concern that solitaries 'will not easily recognize either their faults or their vices, since there will be no one to admonish and rebuke them'.[5] The lack of a spiritual guide similarly worries the author of the thirteenth-century rule for English recluses known as *Walter's Rule*.[6] How will the anchorite bewail the defects of his life when there is no one there to reprove him for them?[7] As he explains later, 'There is no one to oppose [recluses'] will, since they are themselves their own teacher and guide [ipsi sunt sibi doctor et pastor].'[8]

For a more challenging take on *Vae soli* we turn, almost inevitably, to Richard Rolle. The verse occurs in the context of his contention that 'the solitary life, and the hermit's, is superior to the communal or mixed life'. The arguments of those who have reckoned the coenobitic life superior are dismissed on the grounds that they are made from ignorance: 'they do not approve of the solitary life because they know nothing about it'. 'But,' he goes on,

---

4 Ibid., pp. 163–4.
5 *PL* 103.595. Trans. A. Thornton, 2007: www.anselm.edu/homepage / athornto/ grimlaicusweb.htm. Accessed 8 May 2008.
6 'Regula reclusorum angliae et quaestiones tres de vita solitaria' [Walter's Rule], ed. L. Oliger, *Antonianum* 9 (1934), 37–84 and 243–68 (pp. 53–84).
7 Ibid., Prologue, p. 53.
8 Ibid., cap. 10, p. 61 (my translation).

a worse mistake is to keep on denigrating the solitary life, and to abuse it. They cry, 'Woe to him who is alone!' They do not define 'alone' as being 'without God', but understand it to mean 'without company'. A man is alone indeed if God is not with him [Ille enim solus est cum quo Deus non est.][9]

This sounds like vintage Rolle – assertive, confrontational, and not a little wilful – but the argument is not without precedent. His editor noted a parallel in Hugh of St Victor's *De Arrha Animae*,[10] but the thought can be found closer to home, and closer to the core of this essay's subject-matter, in *Ancrene Wisse*. There, having evoked for his readers the dangers of swimming in strong winds and swift waters, the author expands:

> To wel we witen hu þe wei of þis world is slubbri [slippery], hu þe wind ant te stream of foundunge [temptation] aren stronge. Muche neod is þet euch halde wiþ bisie bonen [prayers] ant wid luue oþres honden; for, as Salomon seid, *Ve soli; quia cum ceciderit, non habet subleuantem*, 'Wa eauer þe ane; for hwen he falled, naued he hwa him areare [someone to lift him up.]' Nan nis ane þe haued Godd to fere [as a companion]; ant þet is euch þet sod luue haued in his heorte.[11]

In contrast to Rolle's, however, this assertion that to be with God is not to be alone is made in the context of a lengthy passage that emphasizes the value of mutual support and love, above all of one anchoress for another. This image, of hands extended in prayerful and loving support against the buffet-ings of the world, is a beautiful, and refreshingly non-hierarchical, image of pastoral care at work.

*

On 1 April 1421 in the Carmelite convent at Norwich, Emma Stapleton made her vow to live henceforth as an anchorite. Presiding was no less a figure than the prior provincial of the order, Thomas Netter, and he appointed as her tutors and guardians the prior of Norwich William Thorpe, the sub-prior Bartholomew Acton, and three other friars, Adam Hobbes, John Thorpe and Adam Hemlyngton.[12] These were men of some calibre. William Thorpe was

9   *The Incendium Amoris of Richard Rolle of Hampole*, cap. 13, ed. M. Deanesly (Manchester, 1915), p. 180; trans. C. Wolters, *The Fire of Love* (Harmondsworth, 1972), p. 82.
10 *Incendium Amoris*, ed. Deanesly, p. 180 n. 1, and see also *PL* 177.493 for another parallel in Hugh.
11 *Ancrene Wisse*, ed. B. Millett, Part 4, lines 1040–45 (pp. 95–6). Subsequent references to *Ancrene Wisse* will be given in the text.
12 R. Copsey, 'Thomas Netter of Walden: A Biography', in *Thomas Netter of Walden: Carmelite, Diplomat and Theologian (c. 1372–1430)*, ed. J. Bergström-Allen and R. Copsey, Carmel in Britain 4 (in press); A. K. Warren, *Anchorites and their Patrons*

an Oxford Doctor of Theology, and would succeed Netter as prior provincial. Hemlyngton and John Thorpe were also Doctors of Theology, of Oxford and Cambridge respectively, and authors of works of theology, philosophy and biblical commentary; Hemlyngton had been Master of the Carmelite School of Theology at Paris.[13]

Stapleton was a member of the spiritual as well as the material aristocracy of late medieval England. It would not be surprising if, when the daughter of Sir Miles Stapleton announced her vocation to the solitary life, her case was treated with more than the usual attentiveness. But what was 'the usual attentiveness' to the matter of a solitary's pastoral care? If 'each vocation to solitude is a problem of spiritual direction', then how (in theory and in practice) was that problem addressed and managed?

There are more reasons than the identity of this volume's honorand to begin an exploration of such questions with *Ancrene Wisse*. There the role of guide is allocated to the spiritual director or confessor: *meistre* or *schrift*, apparently without distinction.[14] It is often assumed that this *meistre* is identical with the author of the work but, as Bella Millett has pointed out, this is not certain.[15] Considerable authority is conferred upon the director. He is to advise the anchoresses on their observance of the Outer Rule, and his intimate personal knowledge of his charges allows him to make changes to it if he sees fit:

> For-þi schal euch ancre habben þe uttre riwle efter hire schriftes read [counsel], ant hwet-se he bit ant hat [commands] hire in obedience þe cnaweð hire manere ant wat hire strengðe. (Preface, 59–61)[16]

The anchoresses cannot be seen by anyone without his permission (2.118–19), nor can anyone eat in their presence (8.77); only he can authorize them to keep animals (8.91), to sell their handiwork or make purses for people or to give or receive any other gifts of handiwork (8.103–4, 167–8, 170–1), to

---

in Medieval England (Berkeley, 1985), pp. 213–14. Thanks to Johan Bergström-Allen for allowing me to see pre-publication text of the former.

13 A. B. Emden, *A Biographical Register of the University of Cambridge to 1500* (Cambridge, 1963), and *A Biographical Register of the University of Oxford to AD 1500*, 3 vols. (Oxford 1957–59), s. nn. Thorpe's *Sophismata* survive: see Sharpe, *Handlist*, s. n.

14 *Meistre* occurs more frequently than *schrift*. References to a *meistre* are, with a single exception, confined to the additions made to the Corpus manuscript as part of *Ancrene Wisse*'s updating for an expanding audience of solitaries. See *Ancrene Wisse*, ed. Millett, II.xxviii–xxix and n. 94. Millett argues that these additions are authorial. Two of the three references to *schrift* appear in the earliest version of the text, though that at 8.120 is an addition.

15 *Ancrene Wisse*, ed. Millett II.xxix and the note to 4.1108–14, II.179, where their identity is most strongly implied.

16 This is one of the apparently original uses of *schrift*.

employ 'uncundeliche lechecraft' [arcane medical practices] against illness (8.128–9) or to engage in fleshly mortification (8.120); and it is only with his advice that they can take a limited role in educating the young (8.200–1).

Much of the anchoresses' direction would doubtless have taken place during confession – a time for instruction and guidance as much as for the recollection of sins. An anchoress was to be confessed at least once a week (5.610–11). She should take the opportunity of a visit from a trustworthy priest to be confessed (2.311–26), but she should speak of fleshly temptations only to her own *schrift-feader* [confessor], 'oðer to sum lif-hali mon, ȝef ha mei him habben' (5.632–3). There is anxiety in that rider. Millett deduces from such comments that the anchoresses had previously been 'dependent for their immediate pastoral support on individual (and not very satisfactory) arrangements with the local clergy', and the role of *meistre* seems to have been developed in response to this situation.[17]

Aelred had also given careful consideration to the finding of a suitable confessor in his *De Institutione Inclusarum*:

Si fieri potest, prouideatur in uicino monasterio uel ecclesia presbyter aliquis senex, maturis moribus et bonae opinionis, cui raro de confessione et animae aedificatione loquatur, a quo consilium accipiat in dubiis, in tristibus consolationem.

[A priest should be provided, if this is feasible, by the neighboring monastery or church; an elderly man of mature character and good reputation. To him she may speak infrequently and solely for the purposes of confession and spiritual direction, receiving advice from him when in doubt and encouragement when depressed.][18]

Probably most anchorites would have turned for spiritual direction to the priest serving the church to which (in almost all cases) their cell was attached. But in the later period a significant number are found being granted licences to choose their own confessor. The private confessor was, perhaps, the medieval spiritual equivalent of the personal trainer: an essential overseer of training and development (or *askesis*) for the professional athlete, and a desirable accessory for the wealthy – and for aspirants to the lifestyle of either group. Such personal confessors are a feature of noble and gentry religion in the later Middle Ages. A typical example from among the *athletae* is John Lot, recluse at Lynn, who was licensed in 1497 to choose a confessor to hear his confession once a month.[19]

By the time that Lot was leading his enclosed life, *Ancrene Wisse* and the *De Institutione* were several centuries old (though, as we know, by no means

[17] *Ancrene Wisse*, ed. Millett, II.xxviii.
[18] Aelred, *De Instiutione*, cap. 6, p. 642; trans. Macpherson, 'Rule of Life' pp. 51–2.
[19] C. F. R. Palmer, 'The Friar Preachers, or Black Friars, of King's Lynn', *Archaeological Journal* 41 (1884), 79–86 (p. 84).

unread). Other rules and guidance texts for anchorites had been developed, but these are generally silent on the matter of spiritual direction. An interesting partial exception is the early fifteenth-century *Speculum Inclusorum*.[20] Whilst having nothing to say on the pastoral care of the recluse once enclosed, it does give careful attention to the process leading up to his enclosure, apparently with the dual audience of both the postulant himself and his spiritual advisors in mind.

> Ffirst, let hym schewe his purpos to to or þre persones to-gidere þat bien discret and good lyuers þat mowe diligently and bisily examyne his entent wiþ alle pertinent circumstaunces. And þoruȝ her assent & conseil, lat hym proue hym-self continuely al an hool ȝeer, lyuynge in alle þinges lik or moore streytly þan a reclus is holde to doo.

At the end of this probationary period,

> Ȝif he duelle and contynue in his desir as he dide byforn & þat þe conseil of discreet men conforme & assente vn-to hym by good and ripe avys [reflection] and deliberacion, þane lat hym stablissche his wil in this caas & knytte vp his purpoos & take þat lyf or make his avow þerto, trustynge in þe grace & mercy of his God.[21]

Who were these 'discret and good lyuers'? How were they chosen, and how appointed? Could they perhaps be related to the two *seniores* who lead the candidate to the altar, and accompany him during the first part of the service, in the liturgy for the enclosure of anchorites?[22] Did they maintain a mentoring role after enclosure had taken place? In which case, is this perhaps an example of the kind of relationship – begun before reclusion and continuing beyond it – that Basil envisaged as an ideal, albeit one that was difficult to achieve? These are the intriguing questions that the *Speculum* poses, but that, in our present state of knowledge, we may have to leave as unanswered speculations.

When we turn to the extant rules for hermits, we find texts that speak to a life of significantly less spiritual ambition than that of the anchorite, and this is reflected in the evidence for spiritual direction that can be gleaned from the surviving hermits' rules. The most basic are designed expressly for the

---

20 *Speculum Inclusorum auctore anonymo anglico saeculi xiv*, ed. L. Oliger, Lateranum n.s. 4/1 (Rome 1938); defective text of an English translation *Myrour of Recluses* ed. Harley. I am working on a new, parallel-text edition. For discussion, see my 'A New Look into the *Speculum Inclusorum*', in *The Medieval Mystical Tradition: England, Ireland and Wales*, Exeter Symposium VI, ed. M. Glasscoe (Cambridge, 1999), pp. 123–45.

21 *Myrour of Recluses*, ed. Harley, lines 200–1.

22 'Seriuicium recludendi', printed as an appendix to *The Pontifical of Magdalen College*, ed. H. A. Wilson, Henry Bradshaw Society 39 (London, 1910), pp. 243–4.

illiterate road- and bridge-mending hermits who predominate in the fifteenth and sixteenth centuries. They envisage the hermit meeting with a confessor two or three times a year, but otherwise the matter of spiritual guidance is not broached.[23]

Not all hermits' rules are as unforthcoming. The second chapter of the fifteenth-century *Cambridge Rule* opens with a striking 'Soli Deo debet heremita obedienciam facere' ('a hermit should render obedience only to God'). This uncompromising 'expression of individualism' was one of the passages that led Hope Emily Allen to admit the possibility that the 'Rule' might have been the work of Rolle, or at least something that he had read and been influenced by.[24] In fact, the author is less exceptionally anti-authoritarian than his opening makes him sound. The hermit is to seek out his bishop, or the patron of the place where he lives (if he is a prelate or a priest of good discretion), and notify him of his mode of living. If the latter finds anything that needs to be amended, 'he should willingly submit to his advice for Christ's sake'.[25] Quoting Aelred, the author goes on to recommend that the hermit should find a wise and mature priest to whom he might confess, and whom he should obey. The same priest may also dispense the hermit from some of the stricter injunctions of the rule, especially when he is engaged in heavy manual work.

The *Cambridge Rule* concerns itself significantly with the inward disposition of the hermit, and provides many authorities and inspiring texts relevant to his manner of living. The emphasis of the fifteenth-century *Rule of Celestine*, which incorporates some material from the Cambridge text, is much more decisively on the Outer Rule. It is extant in a Latin version – the text's original language – and three English versions which may be independent.[26] *Celestine* takes over from the *Cambridge Rule* the requirement to render obedience only to God, though one of the English texts perhaps nervously moderates this to 'ylke a hermeytt owght *ffyrst* to be buxum [obedient] to God

---

[23] See for example V. Davis, 'The Rule of Saint Paul, the First Hermit, in Late Medieval England', in *Monks, Hermits and the Ascetic Tradition*, Studies in Church History 22, ed. W. Sheils (Oxford, 1985), pp. 203–14 (p. 211).

[24] *Writings Ascribed to Richard Rolle* (New York, 1927), p. 327. The attribution is fanciful.

[25] 'Regulae tres reclusorum et eremitarum angliae saec. xiii–xiv', ed. L. Oliger, *Antonianum* 3 (1928), 151–90 and 299–320, at pp. 299–312; this from cap. ii, pp. 304–5 (translations mine).

[26] Latin text, 'Regulae tres', ed. Oliger, pp. 312–20 (his fourteenth-century dating is almost certainly too early); for the Middle English texts, see Jolliffe, *Check-List*, H. 10. I have a parallel text of all four versions in hand. A transcription of one of the English versions appeared in my 'Canons and Hermits: The Chapel of St Simon and St Jude in Coverdale', *Yorkshire Archaeological Journal* 76 (2004), 153–69.

Allmyghty'.[27] As in the earlier rule, the hermit should nevertheless notify his bishop or patron of his life and follow his advice.

Celestine is of particular value, however, for some evidence we have for the way in which it might have been used in a pastoral context. The latest of the Middle English texts is preserved in a commonplace book that belonged to John Gysborn, a canon of Coverham Abbey (North Yorkshire) in the first part of the sixteenth century.[28] During this period, a sequence of hermits lived in one end of the chapel of Saints Simon and Jude in Coverdale, a chantry chapel situated beside the River Cover a few miles above Coverham. The Coverdale hermit was 'a temporall and a poore man and did for the most part live by begging or of the Releife of the … Inhabitantes of Melmerby & Scrafton', the two nearby villages, and his main responsibility was to keep the chapel clean. He was subject to the monastery since 'the Abbots of Coverham (for the tyme beinge) … had the placinge and displacinge of the Hermyts'. Coverham also had spiritual responsibility for the chapel and the parishioners who used it as a chapel of ease: the abbot 'did comonly vse to send one of the Bretheren of the said monestery euery thursday and fryday yearly to say masse and service in the said Chapell'.[29] Putting this information together with the contents of Gysborn's manuscript is suggestive. The book bears witness to a dedicated engagement with the work of pastoral care. It includes a list of answers to the kinds of questions celebrants are frequently asked (such as 'Why is water blessed before mass, but bread after?'), material on the publishing of the banns, a range of prayers and invocations, a number of particular use in times of plague (against which there is also a handful of medicinal recipes) and no fewer than six forms of confession.[30] Joseph Gribbin comments: 'Gisborn was evidently preoccupied with hearing confessions'.[31] This is, of course, no bad thing in a pastor, and it is certainly tempting to think that among those whose confessions Gysborn heard was the hermit of the Coverdale chapel, and that – conscientious in this as in his other duties – he procured his copy of the *Rule of Celestine* in order the better to discharge his additional responsibility for the hermit's pastoral care.

*

27 Jones, 'Canons and Hermits', p. 167, my italics.
28 There were two John Gysborns at Coverham in this period; see ibid., p. 163. I am ignoring, for the sake of clarity, the fact that some of these details were under dispute during the Elizabethan lawsuit that allows us this glimpse of the hermits of Coverdale.
29 Ibid., pp. 163, 162.
30 Jolliffe, *Check-List*, E. 10, C. 34, E. 2 (which occurs twice, the first incomplete), C. 3, C. 16.
31 J. A. Gribbin, *The Premonstratensian Order in Late Medieval England* (Woodbridge, 2001), p. 163.

So far, then, we have followed Basil in considering solitaries as 'a problem of spiritual direction'. That phrase comes from my epigraph, which I have borrowed from Thomas Merton. He used it for a piece he wrote in 1965, when he was trying to persuade his superiors in the Cistercian order that the eremitic vocation should once again be recognized as a valid aspect of the monastic life.[32] Merton himself was finally granted his wish to take up permanent residence in the hermitage he had established in the grounds of the Abbey of Gethsemani (Kentucky) later that same year. He had spent the preceding ten years as Master of Novices – one of the most senior administrative roles in the monastery. Almost exactly six centuries previously, an identical career trajectory had been followed by John Whiterig, monk and novice-master at Durham in the later 1350s, who retired in 1363 to the Priory's cell on the island of Inner Farne, where he wrote the sequence of meditations that has come down to us.[33] For these two men, and for the others considered in the remainder of this essay, a simple picture of solitaries, on the one hand, posing pastoral problems and, on the other, pastors trying to solve them, will not suffice.

Merton and Whiterig's progression from monastic officer to solitary, from an outward-facing role concerned with the direction of others to the radical inwardness of the hermit, reminds us that the *Rule of St Benedict* sees the eremitic state as the logical, though not universal, culmination of the monastic life.[34] Merton seems to have nursed a solitary vocation from his earliest years in Gethsemani. For others, solitude may have come as a chance to see out in quiet contemplation the last years of a monastic career that had become caught up in the cares and business of high office. As Knowles puts it, these would be monks who, 'after a life of service with Martha, wished to end their days in seclusion and recollection with her sister'.[35] For example, Hugh de Lacy, second Abbot of Selby (North Yorkshire), who had worked at the building of the abbey with his own hands 'like a common workman', resigned his office around 1123 and went to live as a hermit on one of the monastery's nearby estates.[36] Likewise in 1531 John Grene relinquished his office as abbot of Leiston (Suffolk) and went to live as an anchorite at the chapel of St Mary on the marshy site by the sea where the abbey had origi-

---

[32] Thomas Merton, 'The Case for a Renewal of Eremitism in the Monastic State', in *Contemplation in a World of Action* (London, 1971), pp. 294–327. The translation I have used is his.

[33] *The Monk of Farne*, ed. H. Farmer and trans. a Benedictine of Stanbrook (London, 1961). Further work on Whiterig is currently being done by Barbara Mosse.

[34] *The Rule of St Benedict*, ed. T. Fry (Collegeville, MN, 1981), cap. 1.

[35] D. Knowles, *The Religious Orders in England*, II (Cambridge, 1955), p. 221.

[36] *The Coucher Book of Selby*, I, ed. J. T. Fowler, Yorkshire Archaeological Society Record Series 10 (Durham, 1891), p. 25.

nally stood.[37] Thomas Ringmer made the transition from the common to the solitary life by degrees. The one-time prior of the cathedral priory at Canterbury, he resigned in 1285 and joined the eremitically inspired Cistercians at Beaulieu. Within a few years, however, he had changed his habit again, and was living as a hermit in the Forest of Windsor.[38]

We know less about seculars: although it was normal for male anchorites to be priests, in very few cases do we have evidence of a career of pastoral responsibility that precedes the entry into the reclusory. A notable exception is John Dygon, who spent at least the last decade and a half of his life as the anchorite attached to Sheen charterhouse. He was an Oxford-trained lawyer and held benefices in Salisbury diocese and subsequently in London. Immediately prior to his enclosure in 1435 he was rector of St Andrew's Holborn. A scholar and scribe, Dygon may have been attracted to the solitary life, as Petrarch (a copy of whose epistle on the subject he owned) was, for the chance to pursue a quiet life of leisure and letters. But his ownership of copies of the Latin *Ancrene Wisse* and *Walter's Rule*, Fishlake's Latin *Scale*, and the earliest known English translation of Thomas à Kempis would seem to testify to a genuine interest in the spirituality of solitude.[39] We know nothing, however, of the spiritual life of William Bolle, rector of Aldrington (Sussex), who resigned his living in 1402 and was given permission to build himself a cell on the north side of the Lady Chapel of Chichester Cathedral, occupying a site 29 feet by 24 feet, where he was enclosed, and where he remained for at least another decade.[40]

A career that moves in the opposite direction to this may seem to us rather less natural: a life of solitary contemplation does not necessarily suggest itself as the best grounding for a role in pastoral care. But this would be to forget that such a sequence is precisely in accordance with the Gregorian model of the three lives, the highest of which is the Mixed Life of the bishop who takes the wisdom that he has acquired through contemplation back into the world where it can be applied for the benefit of others; and it would be to ignore the calibre of some of the men whose career it describes.[41] Well-known examples include Walter Hilton, who found his own brand of the mixed life

37 *The Register or Chronicle of Butley Priory, Suffolk 1510–1535*, ed. A. G. Dickens (Winchester, 1951), p. 59.

38 *The Historical Works of Gervase of Canterbury*, ed. W. Stubbs, 2 vols., Rolls Series 73 (London, 1879–80), II, 295.

39 R. Hanna, 'John Dygon, Fifth Recluse of Sheen: His Career, Books and Acquaintance', in *Imagining the Book*, ed. S. Kelly and J. J. Thompson (Turnhout, 2006), pp. 127–41.

40 E. Turner, 'Domus Anachoritæ, Aldrington', *Sussex Archaeological Collections* 12 (1860), 117–39. Turner misinterprets the documents, to have Bolle enclosed at Aldrington itself.

41 For the Gregorian mixed life, see the primary material translated in C. Butler, *Western Mysticism*, 2nd edn (London, 1926), pp. 176–86.

with the Austin canons only after a period spent as a hermit, and a pair of Carmelite friars. Richard Misyn – like Richard Rolle, two of whose Latin treatises he translated into English – lived as a hermit for some years following his return from university, but by 1435 he was prior of Lincoln, and in the last years of his life was absentee bishop of Dromore and a suffragan of the archbishop of York as well as holding several benefices; and Thomas Scrope (alias Bradley), who was also bishop of Dromore for a time as well as serving as a suffragan in Norwich diocese through the second half of the fifteenth century, had lived as a recluse in the Carmelite house at Norwich during the 1430s and 1440s.[42] The first two Confessors General of the Bridgettine Syon Abbey (founded 1415) were each summoned from their anchorholds to take on this significant pastoral responsibility – though the second of them, Thomas Fishbourne, proved better suited to the role than his predecessor, William Alnwick.[43] Most illustrious of all was the hermit-pope Celestine V, who – as the Middle English rule named after him puts it – 'was an heremyte and chosyn for hys holynes out of wyldernes to be pope, and afterwarde left the popase and returnyd ynto wyldernes ayend'.[44] Given this history, it is perhaps less surprising than it at first seems to find John Steward, the last hermit of the chapel of St James in Sandwich (Kent), being appointed, on the suppression of his chapel, vicar of St Mary's there.[45]

In these examples, the solitary life and the life of pastoral engagement figure as different stages in an individual's spiritual career. It was, however – and perhaps surprisingly – also possible to pursue the two callings simultaneously, though here the two principal solitary vocations diverge markedly. While most male anchorites were priests, by the late Middle Ages the priest-hermit was an exceptional figure. Indeed, when Thomas Blaksale was ordained priest in 1371, having proceeded smoothly enough through minor orders over the preceding couple of years, it was with the express condition that 'he reject the habit of hermit with which he is accustomed to be clothed, and do not use it more'.[46] Several scandalous instances further cement the strict separation of eremitic status and priestly ministry. In 1344, Archbishop Melton of York forbade Henry de Staunton, hermit and (*soi-disant*) priest, from preaching, hearing confessions and offering absolution,

---

[42] See the entries by J. P. H. Clark (Hilton) and R. Copsey (Misyn, Scrope-Bradley) in the *ODNB*, s. nn.

[43] See *Chronica Monasterii S. Albani*: V, *Annales monasterii S. Albani a Johanne Amundesham*, ed. H. T. Riley, Rolls Series 28/5, 2 vols. (1870–1), I, 27. Alnwick resigned after a year, 'taedio et senio confectus' [worn out with exhaustion and age].

[44] Bristol Reference Library, MS 6, fol. 137v. The ascription is quite fantastic.

[45] E. Hasted, *The History and Topographical Survey of the County of Kent*, 12 vols., repr. with intro. by A. Everitt (Wakefield, 1972), X, 201.

[46] *Registrum Simonis de Sudbiria diocesis Londoniensis, AD 1362–1375*, ed. R. C. Fowler and C. Jenkins, Canterbury & York Society 34, 38 (1927–38), II, 99. But cf. the example of John Shyrbourne, below, for whom no such stipulation was made.

after his (evidently charismatic) teachings had been found to contain several errors.[47] In 1311 the hermit of Cripplegate (London), Thomas de Byreford, had been found hearing confessions, ministering sacraments and sacramentals, preaching publicly, offering indulgences to those visiting his hermitage, parading images of the saints through the streets, receiving offerings, and burying the dead, all without licence. He was to desist immediately, on pain of excommunication.[48]

Hermits do, however, seem to have had a particular affinity with hospitals. In some cases, the hermit probably acted only as a collector for the hospital, and as such may have been indistinguishable from the other wandering beggar-hermits of the late Middle Ages. In some late fourteenth century instances, the grant of a hospital to a hermit may represent not the latter taking on a significant pastoral role, but merely the extinction of the hospital as a going concern.[49] But in 1417, John Shyrbourne was described at his ordination as hermit and Master of the hospital of St Anne in Colchester (Essex), and two other hermits are recorded as founders of hospitals: Nicholas Jurdan at Bicester (Oxfordshire) in 1352, and John Beket at Earl Soham (Suffolk) in 1466.[50]

Anchorites, as priests, had a wider range of pastoral roles open to them. We have already seen that they could benefit from the services of a personal confessor. There are also some notable examples of solitaries providing this key pastoral role. Margery Kempe's faithful confessor and 'principal gostly fader' was 'the ankyr at the Frer Prechowrys', a doctor of divinity and man of prophecy, to whom alone she dared show her revelations, 'for he cowde most skyl in swech thyngys'.[51] A little later, another Lynn anchorite, Richard

---

47 *The Register of William Melton, Archbishop of York 1317–1340*, III ed. Rosalind M. T. Hill, Canterbury & York Society 76 (1988), pp. 131–2.

48 *Registrum Radulphi Baldock, Gilberti Segrave, Ricardi Newport et Stephani Gravesend, Episcoporum Londoniensium*, AD MCCCIV–MCCCXXXVIII, ed. R. C. Fowler, Canterbury & York Society 7 (1910–11), pp. 141–2.

49 This was a common fate in the period following the Black Death. See W. J. Dohar, '"Since the Pestilence Time": Pastoral Care in the Later Middle Ages', in *A History of Pastoral Care*, ed. G. R. Evans (London, 2000), pp. 175–60 (p. 178).

50 *The Register of Henry Chichele, Archbishop of Canterbury, 1414–1443*, IV, ed. E. F. Jacob, Canterbury & York Society 47 (1947), p. 328; E. A. Jones, 'The Hermits and Anchorites of Oxfordshire', *Oxoniensia* 63 (1998), 51–77 (p. 53); *Calendar of Entries in the Papal Register Relating to Great Britain and Ireland: Papal Letters ...* XII, ed. J. A. Twemlow (London, 1933), p. 501.

51 *The Book of Margery Kempe*, ed. B. Windeatt (Cambridge, 2004), lines 1396, 528, 1612. On this anchorite, see further Windeatt's note to lines 528–30 on pp. 73–4. I am confining myself in this part of the essay to formal pastoral arrangements, and therefore to male anchorites. Anchorites in general, and female anchorites in particular, were also valued for their informal counsel. Margery's conversations with Julian of Norwich certainly belong, in a broader sense, in the field of pastoral care. On this topic, see further my 'Anchoritic Aspects of Julian of Norwich', in *A*

Francis, was the confessor of John L'estrange of Hunstanton, who left him 3*s*. 4*d*. in his will.[52] Successive anchorites of Westminster Abbey enjoyed moments of comparable intimacy with their kings. The fourteen-year-old Richard II spent the morning of 15 June 1381 at the abbey, where 'he spoke with the anchorite, and confessed to him, and remained with him some time', directly before his confrontation with the rebels at Smithfield.[53] Henry V spent a night of penitential crisis with a later recluse on the eve of his coronation. He remembered the Westminster anchorite at other key points in his life – on the occasion of his marriage and in his will – which suggests an ongoing relationship, though this is not otherwise documented.[54]

Private confessors catered to the spiritual needs of the few. We also find solitaries taking the more public role of penitentiaries. These were 'clerics of usually high reputation who were granted special faculties by the bishop to hear confessions and absolve even in cases of reserved sins'; they were employed especially in the second half of the fourteenth century when, due to the plague, the sacrament was under the twin pressures of increased demand for confession, and diminished numbers of priests to administer it.[55] John de Chorleton, a Dominican who was enclosed at Chester in 1363, was appointed penitentiary in the archdeaconry in 1364 and continued in the role for most of the rest of the 1360s.[56] Brother John Boner, a solitary perhaps living in the chapel on Stockport bridge, had held a similar role in 1361, and occurs in it again in the early 1370s.[57] William Tredewy, anchorite at Great Torrington (Devon), held the position of penitentiary in the deanery of Torrington for over thirty years, from 1395 to at least 1429.[58]

Others were able to carry on a kind of ministry without compromising the solitude of the cell. According to the *Speculum Inclusorum*, the anchorite is to divide his free time among prayer, meditation, edifying reading and manual work.[59] Above all other kinds of manual work, in the author's view,

---

Companion to Julian of Norwich, ed. L. H. McAvoy (Cambridge, 2008), pp. 75–87 (pp. 80–2).

[52] R. M. Clay, 'Further Studies on Medieval Recluses', *Journal of the British Archaeological Association*, 3rd ser. 16 (1953), 74–86 (p. 78 n. 1), where some of my other examples are also noted.

[53] *The Peasants' Revolt of 1381*, ed. R. B. Dobson, 2nd edn (Basingstoke, 1983), p. 163.

[54] C. T. Allmand, *Henry V* (London, 1992), pp. 63, 156n, 179. Henry's confessor was Thomas Netter.

[55] Dohar, 'Since the Pestilence Time', p. 181.

[56] *The Registers of Act Books of the Bishops of Coventry and Lichfield. Book 5, being the second register of Bishop Robert de Stretton, AD 1360–1385*, ed. R. A. Wilson, William Salt Archaeological Society, n.s. 8 (1905), pp. 21, 32, 42, 47.

[57] *A History of the County of Chester*, III, ed. B. E. Harris, VCH (Oxford, 1980), p. 127 n. 21.

[58] *The Register of Edmund Lacy, Bishop of Exeter, 1420–1455: Registrum Commune*, I, ed. G. R. Dunstan, Canterbury & York Society 60 (1963), pp. 352, 217.

[59] *Speculum Inclusorum* II, iii, ed. Oliger, p. 102.

the writing (*scriptura*) of holy and edifying reading seems especially meritorious, which, after the death of the writer – even perhaps to the Day of Judgement – will somehow make him live and gain merit by the edification and profit of each person who reads or hears his writing.[60]

The author – like the Carthusian legislators whose 'preaching with the hands' he is echoing – seems to have the copying of texts uppermost in his mind.

John Dygon, the anchorite at Sheen charterhouse, was a significant owner, copyist and indexer of books.[61] He can be linked to nineteen surviving manuscripts which fall broadly into two classes. We have already noted a collection of texts that share a pastoral interest in the anchoritic life (*Ancrene Wisse*, *Walter's Rule*, and the Latin *Scale*). These were perhaps for Dygon's own use – acting as his own *doctor et pastor*, as *Walter's Rule* puts it – but we should also note that, in five of the books associated with him, his name appears in the donation notice alongside that of Joan Grenewode, anchorite at St Botolph's without Bishopsgate (London). We do not know the nature of the relationship between Dygon and Grenewode, but it might have been one of (formal or informal) spiritual direction. Most of Dygon's other books reflect his priestly background: biblical commentaries and preaching material, and a copy of the eminently pastoral *Somme le roi*. His donations witness a continuing investment in the *cura animarum*. One of the volumes was intended for 'those students … wishing to preach the word of God' at Exeter College in Oxford, and three of the donations given jointly with Joan Grenewode were to go to her son Thomas, a priest.

A contemporary of Dygon's was John Wodfowl, hermit of the chapel of St Mary at Eldernall in Whittlesey (Cambridgeshire), and (unusually for hermits of this period) a priest. His will dated 1 January 1455 includes bequests of a number of books, including a *Manuel des Peches* to Thomas vicar of St Andrew's Whittlesey, who was one of his executors, and to the Praemonstratensians of Barlings a *Pupilla [oculi]* – John Burgh's digest (more focused, as it were) of William of Pagula's pastoral classic the *Oculus Sacerdotis*.[62]

The *Oculus Sacerdotis* also lies behind one of Richard Rolle's early works. The *Judica Me Deus*, after its opening of strikingly raw apologetics, is made up of core pastoral material taken from this source, including a form of confession and a model sermon on the last judgement.[63] It is addressed to

60 *Ibid.*, III, iii, p. 123; my translation.
61 See Hanna, 'John Dygon', *passim*, for this and what follows.
62 Will proved in Ely Consistory Court: Cambridge, Cambridgeshire Archives, VC 1:40.
63 *Judica Me Deus*, ed. J. P. Daly, Elizabethan and Renaissance Studies 92:14 (Salzburg, 1984); for analysis, N. Watson, *Richard Rolle and the Invention of Authority* (Cambridge, 1991), pp. 76–95. Despite some assumptions, there is no evidence that Rolle ever held any formal pastoral role in relation to Hampole nunnery.

a friend who is a priest, and thus, from the priest-*manqué* and vulnerably non-canonical hermit Rolle, a work of some presumption as well as defensiveness. In his last, calmer, works Rolle returns to a pastoral theme, pre-eminently with the Latin *Emendatio vitae* and the English writings: as Watson argues, with a single exception, 'all his English [prose] works ... are best seen as varieties of pastoral writing'.[64] Most notable among these is the last of them, the *Form of Living*, addressed to the newly enclosed anchoress Margaret Kirkby, and designed to teach her 'how þou may dispose þi lyfe, and rewle it to Goddes will'.[65] Containing material on sins and their remedies, temptations, (moderate) ascesis, and the love of God and contemplation, the *Form of Living* is both a sound pastoral manual and an invitation to a life of greater spiritual aspiration, and as such its popularity with a wider audience in the fifteenth and sixteenth centuries is not difficult to understand.

Less celebrated among solitary writers is the author of *Walter's Rule*. He reveals that he is in his sixties and in his nineteenth year as a recluse. Prior to his enclosure, he had spent thirty years in the cenobitic life.[66] He requires every recluse who has a copy of his work to keep the original for himself, and to copy it for the use of one or two recluses in his neighbourhood.[67] *Walter's Rule*, then, is written by a recluse for the guidance of recluses, while the *Form of Living* testifies to a hermit's direction of an anchorite: one solitary holding another's hand as they struggle together through a world of temptation and tribulation, in a textual version of the mutual support imagined in *Ancrene Wisse*.

My final and fullest example is the anchorite John Lacy. A Dominican, he was enclosed at the order's convent in Newcastle upon Tyne, being recorded there between 1407 and 1434.[68] He first appears ten years earlier, at his ordination as subdeacon and then as priest, as a member of the convent of Newcastle under Lyme (Staffordshire), which was (to judge by the language of his English writing) the area from which he originated.[69] He gave an English New Testament to the church of St John in Newcastle upon Tyne, and copied another work under the title 'Grace Dieu', which is thought to be Deguileville's *Pélerinage de l'âme*. Of particular interest in the present context, however, is the book that he wrote and extensively illuminated between 1420

---

64 Watson, *Richard Rolle*, p. 222.
65 H. E. Allen, *English Writings of Richard Rolle* (Oxford, 1931), p. 102.
66 Passages from 'Walter's Rule', ed. Oliger cap. 11, p. 63, and cap. 29, p. 81.
67 Cap. 29, p. 81.
68 Clay, 'Further Studies', pp. 75–8; J. B. Friedman, *Northern English Books, Owners, and Makers in the Late Middle Ages* (New York, 1995), p. 52.
69 Friedman, *Northern English Books*, p. 52; R. Hanna, *A Descriptive Catalogue of the Western Medieval Manuscripts of St John's College, Oxford* (Oxford, 2002), p. 129. Clay, Friedman and Hanna are, unless stated otherwise, my sources for the rest of this paragraph.

and 1434, now St John's College Oxford, MS 94. Both writing and limning are of professional quality,[70] though the manuscript as a whole is the product of a long process of accretion and insertion, more in the manner of a commonplace book.[71] It includes several references to Lacy himself and a half-page self-portrait showing him, tonsured and wearing his Dominican habit, looking out through the grille of his two-storey anchorhold at an image of the rood and Mary and John, whilst a scroll issuing from his mouth asks for mercy on his soul.[72] After his death, he intended the volume to go to Roger Stonysdale, a chaplain at the church of St Nicholas in Newcastle, for the term of his life; he was to bequeath it to another priest of the same church, and he to another, and so on for as long as the book lasted.[73] Like Dygon and Wodfowl, then, here was a solitary who had not forgotten the importance of the *cura animarum*.

Lacy called his book a 'primer' (*primarium*), and its first two-thirds are occupied with the Latin contents of the book of hours that that term usually designates. Following on from this material – but, by Lacy's insistence, indivisible from it – is a sequence of mostly English texts. These fall into three groups. First is a sequence of catechetic material familiar in *pastoralia* since the thirteenth century: a tract on the Ten Commandments, followed by lists of the seven deadly sins and the twelve articles of the faith. There follow two rather more spiritually ambitious texts, butted together to form a single treatise. The first is the Middle English translation of the Ps.-Jerome 'Epistle to Demetrias', known in five other fifteenth-century manuscripts, and providing a sensible and sensitive 'form of living' particularly well suited to those embarking on a non-regular vocation.[74] This is followed by four of Hilton's *Eight Chapters*, among which has been slipped an *exemplum* from the *Vitae Patrum*. The final group is concerned with the practice of confession, and includes a range of material in English prose, English verse, and Latin. The Pelagius/Hilton compilation might have been solely for Lacy's own use – though it would also have been useful in the kind of spiritual direction that Margery Kempe's confessor, another Dominican, was engaged in. But the confessional material – with which the *catechetica* should probably be included, since confession was often the occasion for instruction in such matters – seems to point to a public or semi-public role as confessor.

Did Lacy experience the various aspects of his anchoritic life as a contra-

70 A. I. Doyle, 'The English Provincial Book Trade Before Printing', in *Six Centuries of the Provincial Book Trade in Britain*, ed. P. Isaac (Winchester, 1990), 13–29 (p. 22).
71 Hanna, *Catalogue*, p. 128.
72 Colour reproduction in ibid., Plate IV.
73 Donation notice quoted ibid., pp. 129–30.
74 Discussed in my 'The Heresiarch, the Virgin, the Recluse, the Vowess, the Priest: Some Medieval Audiences for Pelagius's Epistle to Demetrias', *Leeds Studies in English* n.s. 31 (2000), 205–27.

diction? It is difficult to tell: his manuscript, while unusually self-referring, is not particularly self-revealing. But its last leaf is filled, in a smaller, less formal script, with a series of Latin *sententiae* – favourite quotations, apparently – on a range of topics (charity, temptations, and so on) but headed by a pair of contrasting definitions taken from Gregory's classic exposition of the two lives in the *Homilies on Ezechiel*, their juxtaposition highlighted by the use of large decorated initials (the only such examples in this final sequence):

> Actiua uita est panem esurientem tribuere, verbum sapiencie nescientem docere, errantem corrigere, ad humilitatis viam supervientem proximum reuocare, infirmitatis curam gerere, que singulis quibusque expediant dispensare, et commissis nobis qualiter subsistere valeant prouidere.
>
> Contemplatiua uero uita est caritatem Dei & proximi mente retinere, sed ab exteriore accione quiescere, soli desiderio conditoris inherere, ut nil iam agere[75] libeat, set, calcatis curis omnibus, ad uidendam faciem sui creatoris inardescat.

> [The active life is: to give bread to the hungry, to teach the ignorant the word of wisdom, to correct the erring, to recall to the path of humility our neighbour when he waxes proud, to tend the sick, to dispense to all what they need, and to provide those entrusted to us with the means of subsistence.
>
> But the contemplative life is: to retain indeed with all one's mind the love of God and neighbour, but to rest from exterior action, and cleave only to the desire of the Maker, that the mind may now take no pleasure in doing anything, but having spurned all cares, may be aglow to see the face of its Creator.][76]

It is a clear, even stark, statement – perhaps a self-conscious restatement – of the two lives, given some poignancy by the realization that, so far as we can reconstruct it, much of Lacy's form of living seems to have been situated not at one of these poles or the other, but in the ambiguous region between them.

*

We know that, after finishing his legal studies, Walter Hilton spent some time – perhaps four or five years – as a solitary. But the life left him unfulfilled, and around 1386 he entered the house of Austin canons at Thurgarton. As explanation for his decision John Clark offers: 'He was at heart a pastor and a "community" man'.[77] I hope this essay has shown that the two callings were not as completely or as straightforwardly opposed as that statement implies. Both St Basil and the anonymous author writing in *La Vie spirituelle* see the

---

[75] MS *agerere*.

[76] Fol. 153ra; abbreviations expanded silently and editorial punctuation supplied. Cf. *PL* 76.953. This translation from Butler, *Western Mysticism*, pp. 171–2.

[77] Clark, 'Walter Hilton', *ODNB*.

solitary life as a problem above all of spiritual direction. Although medieval texts recognize the potential problem, they – and, to an even greater extent, the lives of numerous hermits and anchorites – indicate that solitaries could also be part of the solution to the problems of pastoral care in the late Middle Ages.

2

Scribal Connections in Late Anglo-Saxon England

Elaine Treharne

> Much is due to those who first broke the way to knowledge,
> and left only to their successors the task of smoothing it.[1]

This paper aims to honour Bella Millett's quite outstanding contribution to early medieval textual studies[2] by focusing on the scriptoria of western England in the late Anglo-Saxon period. As Professor Millett has so convincingly illustrated in relation to the late twelfth and early thirteenth centuries, our understanding of the ways in which texts are produced, transmitted and used is much enlightened by recognizing broad networks of ecclesiastical and scholarly influence and exchange. In her work on *Ancrene Wisse* and the 'Katherine Group', Millett has asked us, effectively, to reappraise our apprehension of the regional locus of these texts' origin. Instead of seeing it as simply one of marginal and potentially geographically narrow significance we should consider the west of England in a European-wide complex of interconnections that functioned to spread important theological and scholastic innovations in the decades surrounding the Fourth Lateran Council. And while this brief paper can do little on the scale of Millett's research, I do hope to investigate the ways in which manuscripts are localized to particular scriptoria in late Anglo-Saxon England. I shall ask if we might not spread the net a little wider than the individual scriptorium – such as Worcester or Winchester – when considering particular attributions for vernacular manuscripts in the later eleventh century; and as I shall suggest, we might rather think of known centres of production as something more like the hubs of interconnecting networks of operation, or the lead partner in collaborative endeavours to manufacture codices with shared scholarly and theological agenda.

---

[1] S. Johnson, *Journey to the Western Islands of Scotland* (Dublin, 1775), 'Aberdeen', p. 31.

[2] This is to say nothing of her seminal work on English medieval prose for women, and her significant work on the links between medieval England and continental Europe's scholastic traditions. I should like here, too, to express my gratitude for her generosity and collegiality in her dealings with her students and fellow academics. She has long been an inspiration to me.

Any interest in medieval manuscripts starts, of course, with absence: the absence of so much *comparanda* upon which we might have built conclusions about origin. Although all medievalists are keenly aware of the loss of countless manuscripts, particularly during the turbulence of the Dissolution of the Monasteries between 1536 and 1542, John Leland's *Laboriouse Journey and Serche for Englandes Antiquitees* is a salutary reminder of what modern scholars are facing when they attempt to work with manuscript production and localization in the early medieval period. Undertaken while he travelled around Britain during the reign of Henry VIII and published with numerous interpolations and comments by John Bale in 1549, Leland's *Journey* describes the contemporary turmoil of early Reformation England. It furnishes us with significant, general, information about the libraries at which medieval books were to be found, about the ill-fortunes of many volumes, and a little about those which were extracted and saved by Leland. And while most scholars work with the better-known *Itinerary* of Leland, the effects of the Dissolution are dramatically narrated in the *Journey*, permitting a visualization of the permanent damage done to the nation's literary and intellectual history at this time.[3]

Indications of what was lost come in general terms from the *Journey*. Leland and his interventionist editor, Bale, tell us that:

> If there had bene in euery shyre of Englande, but one solempne lybrary, to the preseruacyon of those noble workes, and preferrement of good seruynges in oure posteryte, it had bene yet sumwhat. But to destroye all without consyderacyon, is and wyll be unto Englande for euer, a moste horryble infamy amonge the graue senyours of other nacyons. A great nombre of them whych purchased those superstycyouse mansyons, reserued of those lybrarye bokes, some to serue theyr iakes, some to scoure theyr candelstyckes, and some to rubbe their bootes. Some they solde to the grosser and sope sellers, & some they sent ouer see to the bokebynders, not in small nombre, but at tymes whole shyppes full, to the wonderynge of the foren nacyons ... I knowe a merchaunt man, whych shall at tyme be namelesse, that boughte the contentes of two noble lybraryes for .xl. shyllynges pryce, a shame it is to be spoken. Thys stuffe hath he occupied in the stede of graye paper by the space of more than these .x. yeares, and yet he hath

---

3   On John Leland and these two works (the *Journey* [*STC* 15445] and the *Itinerary*, finally published in the eighteenth century by Thomas Hearne), see, for example, J. Chandler, *John Leland's Itinerary: Travels in Tudor England* (Stroud, 1993, 1998); J. P. Carley, 'Leland, John (*c.* 1503–1552)', J. P. Carley, 'The Manuscript Remains of John Leland: "The King's Antiquary"', *Text* 2 (1985), 111–20; J. P. Carley, 'John Leland and the contents of the English Pre-dissolution Libraries: Lincolnshire', *Transactions of the Cambridge Bibliographical Society* 9 (1989), 330–57; and *ODNB*, s.v. 'John Leland', by J. P. Carley.

store ynough for as many yeares to come. A prodygyouse example is this, & to be abhorred of all men which loue their nacyon as they shoulde do.[4]

The image of a scrunched-up manuscript (of Bede or of Ælfric) being used as shoe-shining material is enough to induce an audible whimper, but it suggests, quite unambiguously, the very great gap in our knowledge caused by, among other things, the dispersal of manuscripts throughout Europe at this time, most to end up in a rubbish tip. Such a gap probably explains why so many Anglo-Saxon manuscripts (and later medieval ones too) remain unlocalized: there is insufficient evidence in many cases to make safe attributions. This applies even to the most famous of manuscripts, since, for example, it is all but impossible to locate the *Beowulf* manuscript, London, British Library, Cotton Vitellius A. xv, as there appear to be no other examples of the scribes' work and little comparable physical evidence to assist in localization.

The major progress that was made in the twentieth century in the scholarship of English manuscript production – a century that saw the firm acceptance of palaeography and manuscript studies into mainstream medieval studies – is in large part due to the publication in 1957 of Neil Ripley Ker's *Catalogue of Manuscripts Containing Anglo-Saxon*,[5] and the significant work of scholars, such as Kenneth Sisam, Julian Brown, Malcolm Parkes and David Dumville. In very recent years, too, thanks to electronic editions and digitization projects,[6] great advances have been made in our ability to work in increasingly detailed ways with manuscripts (often from remote locations). With all of these tools at our disposal, new research increasingly sheds light on the remaining knotty problems of Anglo-Saxon manuscripts, and especially their places of origin, which will tell us such a great deal about the intentionality of their compilers, the resources available to their creators, and the potential nature of their readers' interaction with the objects themselves.

---

4   *The laboryouse iourney [and] serche of Iohan Leylande, for Englandes antiquitees geuen of hym as a newe yeares gyfte to Kynge Henry the viij. in the. xxxvij. yeare of his reygne, with declaracyons enlarged: by Iohan Bale* (London, 1549), cited from Early English Books Online http://name.umdl.umich.edu.proxy.lib.fsu.edu/A05300.0001.001

5   Ker, *Catologue Containing Anglo-Saxon*. In a review of the *Catalogue* Kenneth Sisam prophetically commented: 'An editor will not be shirking his duty if, instead of trying himself to provide a palaeographical description of the Anglo-Saxon manuscripts he is working on, he refers to this *Catalogue* and checks the matters of fact he intends to use … Wanley's Catalogue has held the field for two centuries and a half, and it may be as long before Mr. Ker's *Catalogue* is replaced by another complete resurvey of the manuscripts that contain Anglo-Saxon', *RES* 10 (1959) 69–71.

6   One thinks here of Kevin Kiernan's *Electronic Beowulf*, Bernard Muir's editions of the Exeter Book (*Exeter Anthology of Old English Poetry* [Exeter, 2006]) and the Junius Manuscript (*Junius 11* [Oxford, 2004]), and the work of the Parker on the Web team at Corpus Christi College, Cambridge. I would also like to mention here Bella Millett's website on textual *mouvance*, which is an exceptionally useful and reliable pedagogic tool and an exemplary instance of accessible scholarship.

Accurate or feasible localization permits scholars to build theories about the impetus for manuscript production; the potential agenda and constructed audiences of manuscript compilers; the economy, material and physical resources of a writing office; and the nature and longevity of writing environments themselves. This is true of the entire medieval period, but the eleventh and twelfth centuries represent important periods where specificity in the localization of manuscripts helps explain the major changes in England in the character of book production.[7]

It is not surprising that the numbers of vernacular manuscripts decline after the Conquest, but rather than a wholesale diminution, there is a more complex response; relatively low levels of production in English were maintained from 1000 to 1200 in comparison with Latin books, followed by some major surges in the third quarter of the eleventh century (principally at Exeter and Worcester), and in the first and last quarters of the twelfth century (notably at Rochester and Canterbury). The English manuscripts' status and function also change during the period: in the post-Conquest era, for example, English books are less authorized but more politicized in that English is no longer a prestigious written medium, and yet the production of English manuscripts in a period of conquest and displacement is necessarily politically charged. English is often poorly resourced, with no *de luxe* or illustrated volumes (bar the Eadwine Psalter), but the efforts that went into adapting earlier, pre-Conquest texts for contemporary use suggest that the English language was highly valued for literary, historical, legal and religious works and records. Moreover, the production of English is surprisingly coherent, in that most manuscripts contain prose religious and legal texts sharing major similarities in scribes' attitudes towards the language of their exemplars.

English book production is, however, geographically dispersed, with books produced predominantly in both the eastern and western parts of southern England. For scholars, too, paradoxes emerge in the analysis of this material: we might read into some of these manuscripts a literary resistance to the Conquest, or, contrarily, a compliance with the needs of Norman prelates for materials in the vernacular of lay audiences; on the other hand we can perceive a contemporary and dynamic tradition, or, contrarily, an antiquarian and nostalgic impulse by old-fashioned monastic houses.[8] In reality,

---

7 Within this paper, I am focusing principally on books written in English, and by 'English manuscripts', I therefore generally mean books containing English texts. For this period generally, see R. Gameson, *The Manuscripts of Early Norman England (1066–1130)* (Oxford, 1999).

8 For an analysis of all of these trends, see, most recently, E. Treharne, 'Periodization and Categorization: The Silence of (the) English in the Twelfth Century', in *New Medieval Literatures* 8 (2007), ed. R. Copeland, W. Scase and D. Wallace, pp. 248–75. For Worcester, in particular, see M. Swan, 'Mobile Libraries: Old English

however, without specific historical and, particularly, locational siting, much of our context about the where, how and why of manuscript production is lost, and many of our hypotheses remain less well substantiated than we might wish.

The medieval priory of Worcester has been the centre of considerable attention for many decades.[9] This institution has many manuscripts attributable to it throughout the medieval period, and many more have subsequently been given a provenance of Worcester. Since its central role in early English and Latin manuscript production and collection is so fundamental to our overall understanding of monastic literate culture in the late eleventh and twelfth centuries, it is worth looking at the evidence for assigning manuscripts to this scriptorium, and thinking a little more about those with whom it may have had links, to see what new ideas can be added to the discussion.[10]

One of the interesting aspects of scholarship, perhaps specifically modern scholarship, is that a proliferation of research generates more related research,[11] and indeed, Worcester surely represents one of the most (if not *the* most) well-researched institutions, certainly from the Benedictine Reform period onwards. This attention is entirely understandable since so many manuscripts survive intact from the medieval library at Worcester, large numbers of which appear to have originated there, or at least to have an early provenance of Worcester.

Worcester's dominance in published research on the production of English manuscripts especially is of some significance in our estimation of book production in the eleventh and twelfth centuries in particular. For, given the gap in our knowledge of the sum of manuscripts produced in this period, so dramatically described by Leland, Worcester's survivals (many never having left the institution) increase its prominence as a manufacturer of codices, and, potentially, detract from our acknowledgement of the role of other scriptoria in that intellectual and divinely inspired endeavour. Moreover, there is always the possibility that numerous other books become centripetally associated

---

Manuscript Production in Worcester and the West Midlands, 1090–1215', in Scase, *Manuscript Geography*, pp. 29–42.

[9] For example, Franzen, *Tremulous Hand*; E. Mason, *St Wulfstan of Worcester c. 1008–1095* (Oxford, 1990); *St Oswald of Worcester: Life and Influence*, ed. N. P. Brooks and C. Cubitt (Leicester, 1996); R. M. Thomson, *A Descriptive Catalogue of the Medieval Manuscripts in Worcester Cathedral Library*, with a contribution on the bindings by M. Gullick (Cambridge, 2001); and Scase, *Manuscript Geography*.

[10] By scriptorium, I mean a writing office staffed with monastic or professional scribes functioning over a considerable period of time or even permanently at an ecclesiastical institution.

[11] Just as there is a canon of literature, there is also a canon of scholarship. It has often been commented upon that, in any given year, *Beowulf* attracts more criticism than the rest of the Old English corpus put together; if *Beowulf* represents the most discussed Old English literary work, then, for Anglo-Saxon scriptoria, Worcester is probably most well represented in scholarship to date.

with the Cathedral Priory scriptorium,[12] thereby increasing its reputation in modern scholarship as a producer of texts, when the phenomenon of late Anglo-Saxon writing environments was, perhaps, rather more complex and varied.

For Worcester, the issue of manuscript assignation is not only one of origin, but also, and very significantly, provenance too, since many codices are affiliated to that institution principally because of the Tremulous Hand's activities, which may have taken place there.[13] For an historical figure about whom we actually know so little, the Tremulous Hand's significance to late Old English studies and the cultural impact of the changes brought about by the Norman Conquest can hardly be overestimated. His shaky glossing and annotation in books is one of the major characteristics for assigning or associating a book's origin, and less commonly, provenance, to Worcester. This chain of association, despite the cautious and meticulous work of Franzen and Collier in their studies of him,[14] has become a process of incremental but indirect instantiation directly linking many English and Latin manuscripts with Worcester's library in the very late twelfth and earlier thirteenth centuries. And indeed, while many manuscripts, no doubt, are Worcester products,

---

12 This same effect happens with Christ Church, Canterbury, though here it is less noticeable, because the Christ Church library was so dramatically dispersed that we have lost many of the anchor manuscripts required to be sure about localization of others by association. Moreover, in the first half of the twelfth century, the 'prickly script' developed by Christ Church scribes was also used by St Augustine's scribes and scribes at Rochester. Manuscripts produced at any one of these places are often simply assigned to 'either' one 'or' the other. Similar dilution of scriptorial activity features in analyses of eleventh-century manuscripts too. For examples, see M. P. Richards, 'On the Date and Provenance of the MS Cotton Vespasian D.XIV, fols. 4–169', *Manuscripta* 17 (1973), 31–5, which argues for a Rochester origin; R. Handley, 'British Museum MS Cotton Vespasian D. xiv,' *Notes and Queries* 219 (1974), 243–50, which argues for a Christ Church, Canterbury origin; and E. Treharne, 'The Dates and Origins of Three Twelfth-Century Manuscripts', in *Anglo-Saxon Manuscripts and Their Heritage: Tenth to Twelfth Centuries*, ed. P. Pulsiano and E. M. Treharne (Aldershot, 1998), pp. 227–52.

13 See Franzen, *Tremulous Hand*; see also Thomson, *Descriptive Catalogue*; R. M. Thomson, *Books and Learning in Twelfth-Century England: The Ending of 'Alter Orbis'*, The Lyell Lectures 2000–1 (Walkern, 2006); R. M. Thomson, 'The Use of the Vernacular in Manuscripts from Worcester Cathedral Priory', in *Transactions of the Worcestershire Archaeological Society* 20 (2006), 113–19.

14 C. Franzen points out in 'The Tremulous Hand of Worcester and the Nero Scribe of the *Ancrene Wisse*', *Medium Aevum* 72 (2003), 13–31, that 'It has generally been assumed that he was working in Worcester because many of the manuscripts he worked on have Worcester connections, but we do not know exactly where he worked' (p. 13). Franzen does suggest that the Tremulous Hand was affiliated to Worcester, and perhaps even to the bishop's household. See also W. Collier, 'The Tremulous Worcester Hand and Gregory's Pastoral Care', in *Rewriting Old English in the Twelfth Century*, ed. M. Swan and E. Treharne, CSASE 30 (Cambridge, 2000), pp. 195–207.

and while that scriptorium is of immense significance in the transmission of vernacular texts, it is also the case that there are important nuances in manuscript production in this period to be found by paying close attention to less well-known manuscripts and to less-studied contemporary scriptoria and writing environments.

The 'scribal connections' of my title thus involve principally the Occam's Razor approach to palaeography that is practised so widely and often with good reason.[15] But it is as well to consider possibilities beyond the law of parsimony, and to look again at the ways in which, on occasion, manuscripts become affiliated to institutions. In relation to Worcester, again, an interesting example of its whirlpool effect is illustrated by scholarship concerning Cambridge, Corpus Christi College 322, datable to the second half of the eleventh century. This manuscript contains the Old English *Dialogues* of Gregory the Great, one of three copies potentially attributable to Worcester,[16] though it is principally the manuscript's provenance that ultimately creates this attribution.

In Ker's description of Corpus 322 in his *Catalogue*, with typical scholarly reservation when he was not sure, he gives no hint of the origin or provenance of this manuscript either in the description itself or in the introduction where he lists scriptoria and their potential attributions.[17] Subsequent scholars have worked hard to locate the manuscript; in his 1978 work on the Old English *Dialogues*, David Yerkes suggested a Worcester origin for Corpus 322, based on nine twelfth-century glosses copied into Corpus 322 from Cambridge, Clare College 30, a Latin manuscript of the glosses, datable to the eleventh century, and itself with a thirteenth-century Worcester provenance.[18] Christine Franzen in her work on the manuscripts inscribed by

---

[15] And often without good reason, as I rather embarrassingly demonstrate in my own article, 'Producing a Library in Late Anglo-Saxon England: Exeter, 1050–1072', *RES* 54 (2003), 155–72, where I attributed Wells's fragmentary copy of the *Benedictine Rule* (Ker, *Catalogue Containing Anglo-Saxon*, pp. 464–5) to Wells itself (p. 170). This erroneous attribution was kindly pointed out to me by Rohini Jayatilaka and I am glad to correct it here.

[16] See most recently on the *Dialogues*, David Johnson, 'Why Ditch the *Dialogues*? Reclaiming an Invisible Text', in *Source of Wisdom: Old English and Early Medieval Latin in Honour of Thomas D. Hill*, ed. C. D. Wright, F. M. Biggs and T. Hall (Toronto, 2007), pp. 201–16.

[17] Ker, *Catalogue Containing Anglo-Saxon*, pp. 106–7 and xliv, respectively.

[18] D. Yerkes, 'The Medieval Provenance of Corpus Christi College, Cambridge MS 322', *Transactions of the Cambridge Bibliographical Society* 7 (1978), 245–7. Clare College 30's Worcester 'provenance' is a Worcester origin (for Part I of this two-part composite manuscript, at least) in M. R. James, *A Descriptive Catalogue of the Western Manuscripts in the Library of Clare College, Cambridge* (1909), pp. 47–50. It is cited as of Worcester origin in the widely used unpublished thesis of E. A. McIntyre, 'Early Twelfth-Century Worcester Cathedral Priory with special reference to the Manuscripts Written There' (DPhil thesis, University of Oxford, 1978), pp. 17–18;

Tremulous Hand is cautious in her response to Yerkes, commenting: '[i]f CCCC 322 were still in Worcester in the thirteenth century, however, it seems odd that the tremulous scribe left no traces in it since the other two copies of the Dialogues ... were glossed by him'.[19]

Mildred Budny, building on this earlier scholarship in her *Insular, Anglo-Saxon and Early Anglo-Norman Art: Illustrated Catalogue*, points out in relation to Corpus 322 that it is

> Made in England, probably at Worcester; second half of the eleventh century. The presumed place of origin rests partly on the subsequent provenance, partly on the origin of the textual exemplar, which must have been associated with Wærferth's Worcester, and partly on the character of the script.[20]

This script she links with Cambridge, Corpus Christi College 391, pages 613–17 and 713–21. Corpus 391 is, of course, the well-known *Portiforium* of Wulfstan, a manuscript intimately linked with Wulfstan II of Worcester. Unfortunately, no plates of these precise folios are provided in Budny's *Catalogue* for comparison, but it is the case that the hand of Corpus 391, pages 613–17 and 713–21, bears some vague similarity to that of Corpus 322, particularly in the rotundity of the aspect, the elongated, curving descenders, the hooked long *s*, and the tall upstroke of *eth*. However, numerous dissimilarities – including the different forms of *a*, *f*, and *e* – suggest that the scripts are only linked to the same degree as Corpus 322's scribe might be linked with that of London, Lambeth Palace, Lambeth 489[21] or the later folios of Cambridge, Corpus Christi College 201, which shows a similar lack of interlinear space as Corpus 322; a similar rotundity of aspect; and the tall upstroke

---

and a Worcester origin is given in Gameson, *Manuscripts of Early Norman England*, p. 60, and in H. Gneuss, *Handlist of Anglo-Saxon Manuscripts: A List of Manuscripts and Manuscript Fragments Written or Owned in England up to 1100*, MRTS (Tempe AZ, 2001), p. 30. Neither of these lists explains how this localization was achieved. While the first part of this two-part manuscript clearly has Worcester affiliations, the second part containing the Latin *Dialogues* has a palaeographical likeness that links it to Worcester in McIntyre.

19 *Tremulous Hand*, p. 75. She goes on to point out that the Worcester booklist in Cambridge, Corpus Christi College 367 only mentions 'ii. englissce dialogas', when Corpus 322 would make a third version in addition to Oxford, Bodleian Library, Hatton 76 and London, British Library, Cotton Otho C. i, both Worcester manuscripts.

20 M. Budny, *Insular, Anglo-Saxon and Early Anglo-Norman Manuscript Art at Corpus Christi College, Cambridge: An Illustrated Catalogue* (Kalamazoo, 1997) I, 625–6. The fact that the Tremulous Hand did not work with Corpus 322 is not considered as significant evidence against the Worcester provenance by Budny.

21 See P. Robinson, *A Catalogue of Dated and Datable Manuscripts c. 888–1600 in London Libraries*, 2 vols. (London, 2003), II, Plates 2 and 3. Lambeth 489 is an Exeter homiliary, datable to Leofric's episcopacy.

of *eth*.[22] In turn, Corpus 201 may have originated in Winchester, though its localization is not certain, by any means.

Budny, in her detailed analyses of Corpus 322, is relatively confident that the manuscript bears close scrutiny with Worcester manuscripts, but there is still room for reasonable doubt in her discussion. At some point between the publication of Budny's immensely useful two-volume *Catalogue* and the publication of further *Catalogues*, however, the tentative ascription of Corpus 322 to a Worcester localization becomes much less 'possible' or even 'probable', and where there was doubt, there is now certainty about this manuscript's origin. Thus, in Gameson's *Catalogue* published in 1999, for reasons not provided, Corpus 322 is firmly assigned to an origin of Worcester.[23] In Helmut Gneuss's *Handlist*, published in 2001, more judicious caution is given in the 'Worcester? (prov. Worcester?)' description.[24] A more recent *Catalogue*, funded by the UK Arts and Humanities Research Council, and directed from the University of Manchester Department of English, has sought to describe and evaluate all individual vernacular scribal stints in the eleventh century. In so doing, it lists Corpus 322 among the manuscripts scrutinized. Here, however, the project's research reinstates the certainty of a Worcester origin for Corpus 322 but, as with Gameson, provides no evidence for this assertion.[25]

This example of the scholarly analyses of one manuscript, and not a manuscript that tends to attract a great deal of attention either, illustrates effectively a critical area in late Anglo-Saxon and twelfth-century English palaeography and codicology: namely, how manuscripts are localized to a particular scriptorium, and how often that particular scriptorium tends to be one of the large writing centres. One might thus argue that, despite notable lacunae in our extant corpus of manuscripts, looking again at scribal connections between writing centres might aid our understanding of the complexity of scribal cultures, the variety of centres of production, and the methods and resources behind the manufacture of English texts in this period.

As is widely accepted, of course, there were far more scriptoria than Worcester copying English in the eleventh and twelfth centuries, and the most commonly cited in scholarly literature on the period are Exeter, Rochester, Peterborough and Christ Church, Canterbury. These five in total represent only a small proportion of the number of scriptoria or writing offices functioning

---

[22] See Budny, *Illustrated Catalogue*, I, 475–87.
[23] Gameson, *Manuscripts of Early Norman England*, p. 63.
[24] Gneuss, *Handlist of Anglo-Saxon Manuscripts*, p. 36.
[25] www.arts.manchester.ac. uk/mancass/C11database / is the general database; www.arts.manchester.ac. uk/mancass/C11database/data/text_details.php provides the 'Scribe Location: Worcester' localization, even though 'no palaeographical images [are] stored for this hand' and no additional information, beyond a cursory description is given. This database is still being added to, I believe.

during the decades before and the century after the Conquest. Dr Orietta Da Rold, working for the project, 'The Production and Use of English Manuscripts, 1060 to 1220',[26] compiled a list of all the known scriptoria in Anglo-Saxon and Anglo-Norman England copying English materials, derived from a meticulous reading of Ker's *Catalogue*, which contains all the information from which to begin such an analysis.[27] From her list, there are seventy-five scriptoria or, at least, sites where writing took place, to which manuscripts can be assigned during the twelfth century. This number seems, perhaps, rather considerable to those who work principally on vernacular materials: it may be difficult to think of seventy-five possible locations for manuscripts when we consider early medieval England, but that is because, from *c.* 1050 to 1200, only seventeen of them in total, according to Ker, produced 'literary' material written in English that still survives: these are Abingdon, Barking, Bath, Bodmin, Bury St Edmunds, Christ Church and St Augustine's Canterbury, Durham, Ely, Exeter, Hereford, Peterborough, Rochester, St Paul's, Thorney, Winchester Old Minster and Worcester. We know of a handful of other places – like Glastonbury, Salisbury or Sherborne – where there was the capability to copy English materials, but what of all the other potential places like Westbury where Coleman of Worcester was prior? What of Crowland, Gloucester, Lincoln, Ramsey or Wells, for example? An interesting case in point here may be the reference by John Leland in his *Collectanea* to the survival of two books at Pershore, one of which is described as 'Elfrici grammatica Latinosaxonica decerpta ex Prisciano'.[28] This manuscript is not associated with any extant surviving copy of Ælfric's *Grammar*, and indeed, the manuscript at Pershore when Leland saw it need not have originated there, but it does suggest there are places scholars can look for vernacular manuscript provenance, and perhaps origin, other than the best-known and most often-cited centres of writing.[29]

---

26 www.le.ac. uk/ee/em1060to1220 / This is a five-year AHRC-funded project running from 2005 to 2010, directed from the Universities of Leicester and Leeds, and seeking to catalogue and analyse all the surviving English literary manuscripts from 1060 to 1220, including those with a tentative date of s. xi med.

27 See also N. Ker, *Medieval Manuscripts in British Libraries* (Oxford, 1969–). For a survey of manuscript production in the late eleventh and twelfth centuries, see O. Da Rold, 'English Manuscripts 1060 to 1220 and the Making of a Re-Source', *Literature Compass* 3 (2006).

28 *English Benedictine Libraries, The Shorter Catalogues*, ed. R. Sharpe, J. P. Carley, R. M. Thomson, and A. G. Watson, Corpus of British Medieval Library Catalogues 4 (London, 2000), pp. 325–6.

29 None of the fourteen surviving manuscripts and fragments (of which one is a series of extracts) of the *Grammar* is attributed to Pershore. In Gneuss, *Handlist of Anglo-Saxon Manuscripts*, p. 150, of the fourteen listed entries, only two are localized and these are to Exeter (Cambridge University Library, Hh. 1. 10) and Canterbury (Durham Cathedral Library, B. III. 32). London, British Library, Harley 107 originated in south-east England.

It may be, ultimately, that the evidence we need for the origin or provenance of the majority of early medieval manuscripts will never be forthcoming, and that the exceptional scholarship of Ker, Malcolm Parkes and
Helmut Gneuss, among many others, will prove to have taken us as far as
possible in relation to the localization of English manuscripts.[30] But still it has
to be a worthwhile endeavour to seek places of origin for the many unlocalized manuscripts,[31] since the information about resource, agenda, motivation
and potential audiences for English would be invaluable for a cultural reas-
sessment of the status of English in the later eleventh and twelfth centuries. Thus, in order to make some broad suggestions for future research, this
paper will turn now to a discussion about connections between institutions
during this period, trying to ascertain what kinds of intellectual and cultural
exchange took place. It will also seek to uncover if there are differences
between the movement of English books and contemporary Latin books,
since the production of the two languages seems to diverge markedly after
the Conquest, as one might indeed expect.

Throughout the history of early medieval book production there was
significant movement of books between institutions within England, the
British Isles and Europe in its broadest sense. Much of it is obvious: as a
result of an individual taking his or her books from place to place (the early
English missionaries spring to mind, of course); as a result of a known individual sending books to a colleague upon their request. The movement of
books is a consequence of donation or bequest, such as the donations of
Athelstan to Chester-le-Street, or the very notable bequest of Leofric to Exeter
Cathedral in or before 1072. In the case of Cnut and Emma's beautiful gift
to Wulfstan I of the York Gospels, executed at Christ Church, Canterbury in
the first two decades of the eleventh century, the book moved with Wulfstan
to his northern archdiocese, where he augmented the Gospels with homilies
and Cnut's letter. In this case, while the book was transported as a result of
its ownership by an individual, it may be as a consequence of a bribe that
Wulfstan had the book at all; that is, it took the presentation of the book by
Emma and Cnut to persuade him to consecrate Athelnoth as Archbishop of
Canterbury in 1020.[32] This commodification of the book might be paralleled
by the case of the Vercelli Homilies, which could, perhaps, have been made
over to Vercelli as a gift or payment by a clerical pilgrim en route to Rome.

---

[30] Ker, *Catalogue of Manuscripts*; Gneuss, *Handlist of Anglo-Saxon Manuscripts*; Parkes,
'Orrmulum'.

[31] In the AHRC-funded project, 'English Manuscripts 1060 to 1220', of the manuscripts we have catalogued to date, just over a third have a place of origin assigned
to them.

[32] The York Gospels are York Minster I. See T. A. Heslop, 'Art and the Man: Archbishop Wulfstan and the York Gospelbook', in *Wulfstan: Archbishop of York*, ed.
Matthew Townend, Studies in the Early Middle Ages 10 (Turnhout, 2004), pp.
279–308.

With many prestigious volumes, then, we are able to trace their movement; in the case of early missionary books, from their script and date, it seems relatively straightforward to deduce the ways in which these books travelled. The same might be said of a cultural conquest coming in the opposite direction: the importation of hundreds, if not thousands, of books into England as a consequence of the Norman Conquest and the imposition of Norman clerics and nobles in English religious and political institutions. Numerous scholars have investigated and explained the patterns of book movements in the late eleventh and early twelfth centuries, and especially between England and mainland Europe.[33] In relation to the commissioning of books for use in places other than the originating centre, R. M. Thomson has suggested that institutions such as Hereford and Worcester seem to have written books not only for their dependencies, but also for other houses in their local vicinities, making the question of consultancy and outsourcing an interesting issue even in this early period.[34] Indeed, Worcester's central role in gathering books suggests that it undertook this role of major research library seriously. Very recently, Dave Postles has shown how small houses that barely see the light of day in scholarship, such as Oseney Priory in Oxford – a small house of Augustinian canons – were able to access the learning and book collections of larger institutions,[35] in this case, again, at Worcester. There has, however, been little sustained investigation into the ways in which books written in English travelled between places and the motivations behind this phenomenon.[36]

Neither have we begun to put the jigsaw pieces of earlier medieval textual culture into the puzzle of medieval intellectual and manuscript culture in general. I think here of the notable shift in English vernacular textual production around *c.* 1170, when, seemingly from nowhere, Oxford, Bodleian Library, Bodley 343 (currently unlocalized, but generally assigned to the West Midlands) was copied in an innovative format, with extensive Latin and English texts. It was followed by the Lambeth Homilies (London, Lambeth Palace, Lambeth 487) and the Trinity Homilies (Cambridge, Trinity College, B. 14.52), both of which seem not to emerge from obvious (and mostly Benedictine), earlier centres of manuscript production, such as Worcester or Christ Church, Canterbury. During these latter decades of the twelfth century, too,

---

33 See, for example, T. Webber, 'The Patristic Content of English Book Collections in the Eleventh Century: Towards a Continental Perspective', in *Of the Making of Books: Medieval Manuscripts, Their Scribes and Readers. Essays Presented to M. B. Parkes*, ed. P. R. Robinson and R. Zim (Aldershot, 1997), pp. 191–205; and the Introduction in Gameson, *The Manuscripts of Early Norman England*, pp. 1–41.

34 Thomson, *Descriptive Catalogue*, passim.

35 D. A. Postles, 'Oseney Abbey: Studies on a House of Austin Canons, 1129–1348' (unpublished PhD dissertation, University of Leicester, 1975). This is now published at www.le.ac. uk/ee/pot/oseney/oseney.pdf

36 A very notable exception is Mary Swan's article, 'Mobile Libraries', cited above.

the *Ormulum* was produced by Orm, a canon in the Arrouaisian house at Bourne.[37] Bella Millett's extensive work on later twelfth-century texts like the Lambeth and Trinity Homilies, as well as her magisterial scholarship on the thirteenth-century *Ancrene Wisse*, suggest that scholars on English vernacular texts might fruitfully look beyond the scriptoria generally associated with late Anglo-Saxon books to localize these later works and their codices. In the case of *Ancrene Wisse*, for example, the earliest manuscripts seem to emerge from smaller, newer types of institution, belonging to orders like the Dominicans; that is, orders other than the Benedictines, who are responsible for sustaining English textual production throughout the post-Conquest period until the third quarter of the twelfth century or so. One of the major manuscripts of *Ancrene Wisse*, Cambridge, Corpus Christi College 402, itself remains unlocalized, though its later provenance of Wigmore Abbey is well known.[38]

In the later medieval period, from *c.* 1150 on, as the new religious orders proliferated in England, a multitude of smaller scriptoria such as Llantony and Buildwas (as well as the sustainedly larger centres, like Worcester and Canterbury, Salisbury and Durham), began producing manuscripts of fundamentally important Latin texts.[39] It is these latter centres that have attracted the majority of scholarly attention and concomitant manuscript localization.[40] Yet it is clear from the recent discovery of the Taunton Fragment (Taunton, Somerset County Record Office, DD/SAS C/1193/77) that during the eleventh century, too, there were other centres where writing took place outside the sphere of the major scriptoria that have been studied in depth to date.[41] The Taunton Fragment consists of four folios, once used for binding or wrapping, and containing alternating Latin and English homiletic texts that Aidan Conti has shown in his recent superb article are derived from the Angers Homiliary.[42] The Taunton Fragment, inasmuch as it does not seem to be the product of an identifiable major writing centre, might for this very reason be loosely allied with the slightly earlier Cambridge, Corpus Christi College 41 – the Old English translation of Bede's *Ecclesiastical History*, which contains written into its margins multiple texts, ranging from homilies and martyro-

---

[37] Parkes, '*Orrmulum*'.

[38] For all of this information on *Ancrene Wisse*, see *Ancrene Wisse* ed. Millett, II, xi–xxix, plus the references to Millett's earlier work cited therein.

[39] See, *inter alia*, Ker, *English Manuscripts in the Century after the Conquest*.

[40] For example, T. Webber, *Scribes and Scholars at Salisbury Cathedral*, Oxford Medieval Monographs (Oxford, 1992); *Canterbury and the Norman Conquest: Churches, Saints and Scholars, 1066–1109*, ed. R. Eales and R. Sharpe (London, 1995).

[41] The text is edited and commented upon by M. Gretsch, 'The Taunton Fragment: A New Text from Anglo-Saxon England', *Anglo-Saxon England* 33 (2004), 145–93. I do not find her suggestion that the scribe is a foreigner convincing.

[42] A. Conti, 'The Taunton Fragment and the Homiliary of Angers: Context for New Old English', *RES* 59 (published online June 2008, doi 10.1093/res/hgn073).

logical items to charms and sapiential literature.[43] Another manuscript, but one which seems to bear some concrete palaeographical affinities with the Taunton Fragment, is Cambridge, Corpus Christi College 140, an English copy of the West Saxon Gospels, written at Bath in the eleventh century.[44] The palaeographical similarities relate principally to the aspect and duct of the manuscripts which are broadly similar, especially in the case of the stint of the first scribe of the Gospels in Corpus 140, who copied the Gospel of Matthew, and the scribe of the Taunton Fragment.[45]

Given our present knowledge, it seems evident from the way in which these manuscripts have been written that they are not products of the dominant eleventh-century Anglo-Saxon scriptoria that are relatively well studied. Corpus 41 illustrates what seems to be a dramatic lack of available material resources, necessitating the copying of many texts into the margins of the Old English *Ecclesiastical History*; the Taunton Fragment demonstrates characteristics quite unlike other extant homiletic manuscripts, from its unusual spelling to its idiosyncratic Latinity. It is thus essentially negative evidence that provides us with something to work with here. Corpus 41, we know, was at Exeter when Leofric gave his books to the cathedral, but it probably came to him from elsewhere. He is perhaps the arch-collector in this period and seems to have acquired books from a number of institutions at the foundation of Exeter in 1050 to bolster his own library at speed. Not only did Corpus 41 come into his hands, but also Cambridge, Corpus Christi College 419 and 421, which possibly originated in Christ Church, Canterbury and contain a large collection of Old English homilies, mostly by Ælfric. How he obtained this pair of related volumes is unknown; recent work shows that these two volumes may have been regarded as companion volumes for other homiliaries actually produced in Exeter.[46] But this represents a rather strange context of production, since these Corpus manuscripts share phys-

---

43 See the very full description in Budny, *Illustrated Catalogue*, I, 501–24, where, relevant to this discussion, she proposes that Corpus 41 was made 'apparently in a provincial centre' (p. 508).

44 Budny, *Illustrated Catalogue*, I, 577–9.

45 Of particular note would be the frequent use of the *punctus versus*; the form of capital *G* with a rounded bow and tail that sweeps to the left; the enlarged initial *a*; the insular *g* with a narrow top to the shoulder extending into a broader finish on the ruled line; and the occasional very distinctive *nota* with an angled headstroke. These are not the same scribes, but the general similarities are notable. On the Gospels, see *The Old English Version of the Gospels*, ed. R. M. Liuzza, 2 vols., EETS OS 304, 314 (Oxford, 1994–2000).

46 See E. Treharne, 'The Bishop's Book: Leofric's Homiliary and Early Eleventh-Century Exeter', in *Early Medieval Studies in Memory of Patrick Wormald*, ed. N. Brooks, C. Karkov, J. Nelson, and S. Baxter (Aldershot, 2009), pp. 521–37; and, more importantly, see now E. Corradini, 'Leofric of Exeter and his Lotharingian Connections: A Bishop's Books, *c*. 1050–72' (unpublished PhD dissertation, University of Leicester, 2008).

ical characteristics with the homiliaries made in Exeter. Thus, rather than being obtained as companion volumes, or maybe *as well as* being companion volumes, it seems likely that they formed the *model* for Leofric's own homiliary, now extant as two volumes, London, British Library, Cotton Cleopatra B. xiii and London, Lambeth Palace, Lambeth 489.

These two volumes, copied in the 1050s or 1060s by Leofric's scribes, seem to have provided his key vernacular pastoral texts, probably inspired by the manuscripts Corpus 419 and 421 that he received from their original scriptoria. There is still a great deal of work to do on the influence of major scriptoria like Christ Church, Canterbury, and especially on the dissemination of English texts from one centre to another, and on the motivation for manuscript production at known writing centres. It is evident in this case of Exeter, though, that Leofric set up his writing office in 1050, with a clear design for Exeter's role in the production of manuscripts in both English and Latin. To achieve his goals, he required assistance from colleagues at other institutions to begin the process of book production: model books and texts to copy, scripts and layout to emulate and adapt. Exeter, for two decades, became an immensely prolific centre of English manuscript manufacture that all but ceased to function for decades after his episcopacy. The activity of the early decades of the second half of the eleventh century must, therefore, be regarded as indicating something like a writing office attached to the individual prelate, operating through the influence of that one prelate, rather than being an ongoing dedicated scriptorium like those at the other major centres, which operate throughout this period independent of an individual's instruction.

Interesting questions emerge from the brief glance at Exeter in the 1050s and 1060s, questions that are central to our understanding of the ways in which manuscripts written in English circulated, and libraries were built up in the eleventh and twelfth centuries. Did Exeter acquire Corpus 419 and 421 from another institution as a result of a request by Leofric to colleagues at these institutions? Were these books brought as gifts at Leofric's ordination as bishop? And did they send him books they owned, but which they felt were redundant? This might go some way towards explaining why Corpus 419 and 421 were considerably expanded at Exeter by the addition of extra homilies. Or were these books specially commissioned to act as exemplars, but also physical models, for his scribes to copy? This might explain why the books are of almost identical dimensions and *mise-en-page*. Were these indeed books that were meant only to be loaned, but which through the multiple expansions they underwent, became effectively Exeter's by default? Leofric and his scribes were certainly adept at adapting the material they inherited, suggesting that, in its original state, it was insufficient for the needs of the bishop and perhaps his canons.

It seems possible that Exeter also had access to material from Worcester, or, at least, had close contacts with Worcester, facilitating the copying of texts. The scant evidence that survives comes in the form of homilies again, this time associated with Wulfstan I, Archbishop of York, the great eleventh-century homilist and statesman. Thus, for example, once again in Cleopatra B. xiii, the fifth text, *De dedicatione ecclesiae*, was written by Wulfstan, and occurs in its entirety only in this manuscript, though it might have shared an exemplar with a manuscript from Worcester – Oxford, Bodleian Library, Hatton 114 – which itself includes only the last portion of the homily.[47] It might not be surprising for Worcester to loan or donate books to another western scriptorium in need of pastoral provisions, especially since Leofric and his contemporary bishops at Worcester seemed to share a similar pastoral agenda, one that included the vernacular at its heart. Indeed, Christ Church, Canterbury, set a solid example, with its role as manufacturer, donor and centralized provider of major English texts, like Ælfric's *Catholic Homilies*.[48] Yet, rather interestingly, current evidence might suggest that Worcester was rather more of a gatherer than a disperser of texts; rather more of a reference library than a lending institution, and from the geographical perspective, it must surely have been the most important repository of texts in the West of England through this early medieval period and into the thirteenth century.[49] It might be that this was the aim of successive precentors and bishops from Wulfstan I onwards: Worcester as the western English equal of Christ Church, Canterbury, in terms of its learning, spirituality and manuscript collection.

Worcester undoubtedly forms the core of an important regional network of affiliated monasteries. The evidence for this brings us back again to Cambridge, Corpus Christi College 140, in the form of a dismembered leaf, now Cambridge, Corpus Christi College 111, pages 56–7.[50] This manuscript, written at Bath according to the colophon of Ælfric the scribe,[51] contains not only the Old English Gospels, as discussed above, but also manumissions and other additions of the second half of the eleventh and earlier twelfth centuries. Corpus 140 and 111 is an immensely important manuscript for any number of reasons, but particularly because it is a rare witness to an eleventh-century west of England centre of writing that is neither Worcester nor Exeter. What is striking about this manuscript (apart from its first scribe's possible palaeographical links to the Taunton Fragment) is the similarity of the hand of pages 56–7 to the hands known from Worcester manuscripts,

47 *Homilies of Wulfstan*, ed. D. Bethurum (Oxford, 1957), pp. 249–50, lines 125–49. See further Treharne, 'The Bishop's Book'.
48 *Ælfric's Catholic Homilies, First Series: Text*, ed. P. Clemoes, EETS SS 17 (Oxford, 1997).
49 See Swan, 'Mobile Libraries' on the ways in which Worcester seems to have gathered material in the twelfth century.
50 For which, see E. Treharne, *The Ideology of Early English* (Oxford, forthcoming 2010).
51 'Ego Ælfricus scripsi hunc librum in monasterio Baðþonio et dedi Brihtwoldo preposito' ['I, Ælfric, wrote this book in the monastery of Bath and gave it to Briht-wold, the provost']. See Budny, *Illustrated Catalogue*, I, 579.

such as Oxford, Bodleian Library, Hatton 113 and 114, or Junius 121 in the second half of the eleventh century. As might be expected from hands copying manuscripts at the same time – in the second half of the eleventh century – broad similarities of letter formation exist, but here, with pages 56–7 of Corpus 111 there is evidence of what one might conceive of as sufficient similarity to merit the term 'regional script', suggesting, perhaps, trends in writing and decoration assignable to particular methods of training or a shared aesthetic in the copying of books.[52]

Rodney Thomson has discussed a similar phenomenon in relation to similarities between decorated initials in a number of twelfth-century west of England manuscripts and the style of contemporary sculpture,[53] and Anne Lawrence-Mathers has also drawn attention to the shared features of manuscripts in twelfth-century Northumberland,[54] so common trends in *mise-en-page*, script and decoration are well-attested features of artistic production. Corpus 111, as an additional text, shares some elements of script and *mise-en-page* with Worcester manuscripts of the same period (including Corpus 332). However, it is not just the script that is interesting in this example of *membra disiecta* from Corpus 140, for the text itself on pages 56–7 of Corpus 111 is the Confraternity Agreement initiated by Wulfstan of Worcester in 1077, seeking to formalize the relationship between Worcester and other English monastic houses; namely, and in the order of the text, Evesham, Chertsey, Bath, Pershore, Winchcombe, Gloucester, and Worcester itself. Emma Mason, in her reading of this important association, regards the 'values promoted by the agreement [as] those of the late Anglo-Saxon church', and she discusses the very real links between the houses that this agreement intimates.[55] It may be worth considering the possibility that these formal links extended to practical issues, such as scribal training, manuscript exchange, and the fostering of a cultivated identity of English Benedictine monasticism through deliberate use of a regional script-type. If this shared visual identity is indeed feasible, as it seems to be from comparing Corpus 111 with other, similarly

---

[52] This is similar to Ker's 'prickly script' identified in manuscripts of the first half of the twelfth century copied in Kent, and especially Christ Church and St Augustine's, Canterbury, and Rochester. See his *Manuscripts in the Century after the Conquest*, The Lyell Lectures (Oxford, 1960). What tends to happen to these manuscripts is that they are assigned by scholars to a localization of either Canterbury or Rochester. For the west of England at this time, see also McIntyre, 'Early Twelfth-Century Worcester Cathedral Priory'.

[53] Thomson, *Books and Learning in Twelfth-Century England*, p. 78, where he is discussing Hereford, and possibly Gloucester, manuscripts, and carvings at Kilpeck and other local churches.

[54] A. Lawrence-Mathers, *Manuscripts in Northumbria in the Eleventh and Twelfth Centuries* (Cambridge, 2003).

[55] Including the singing of masses for all the brothers of all the houses, and the required charitable acts of the abbots involved. See Mason, *St Wulfstan of Worcester*, pp. 197–200.

dated manuscripts from the region, then this clearly complicates our ability to assign manuscripts to one place within this network. Perhaps we might begin to think, then, of Worcester as more of a conglomeration of associated scriptoria and writing environments, than an individual (and, arguably, default) centre to which so many manuscripts are automatically attributed.

Such an explanation of a cultural network seems obvious in relation to texts, like Ælfric's *Catholic Homilies*, disseminated as an authorized set of materials for pastoral purposes. For English manuscripts, too, this is an analogous way to think about the movement of books, elements of script and production. It might also go some way towards accounting for the emergence of what appear to be new textual phenomena in the later twelfth century, when English books seem to emerge from smaller centres we are not yet equipped to identify. This may be less a case of gaps in our extant records, and more a case of looking in the wrong places for much of the time, focusing on large writing centres, such as Worcester, rather than seeing these as the hub of closely associated networks of production.

As Bella Millett has demonstrated throughout her exemplary scholarly career, it is always worth going back to ask again those crucial, primary questions at each new stage of research. Where was a text produced? Who might be responsible for its production? What are a work's or a manuscript's relationships to potential textual sources and broader cultural trends? We may not end up with the satisfactorily tied-up loose ends we might desire, but the advances that can made from the thorough re-examination of our primary sources and our methodologies are potentially limitless.[56]

---

[56] I owe a significant debt to the editors of this volume for their patience and careful scrutiny of the essay; to Mary Swan and Orietta Da Rold for our conversations and their comments; and to the volume's readers for their criticisms.

3

Gerald of Wales, the *Gemma Ecclesiastica* and Pastoral Care

Brian Golding

Gerald of Wales, who was proud of all his literary output, was clearly partic-ularly proud of the *Gemma Ecclesiastica*.[1] With typically false self-deprecation he wrote in the preface that if perhaps the work should cross the Anglo-Welsh border and fall into the hands of the great, and be seen by the eyes of the learned, he would prefer that they read what they knew already than that his Welsh readership should be deprived.[2] And in a famous passage in his autobiography he tells how when he visited Rome in 1199 he presented Pope Innocent III with six of his books – *libros* rather than *libras* (pounds) – and that the pope kept all the volumes at his bedside for about a month before distributing five of them to five of his cardinals who requested them, but he would not allow himself to be parted from the *Gemma*, which he loved above all the rest. By reciting Innocent's approbation it is as if Gerald was granting himself an *imprimatur* from the greatest of all medieval reforming popes. Yet, compared with many other of Gerald's works, notably the topographical, historical and autobiographical ones, the *Gemma* has received little attention from commentators. It was edited, and published in 1862, in the Rolls Series by J. S. Brewer who provided a lengthy introduction, and a translation with introduction by John Hagen appeared in 1979 as *The Jewel of the Church*.[3] As is the case with a work which can in many ways be seen as its sister volume, the *Speculum ecclesie*, there have been no major studies of the *Gemma*. Though it was apparently little read, when set within the context of Paris-inspired developments in pastoral theology, it is an important indicator of reforming preoccupations at a time of unprecedented concern for the spiritual well-being of clergy and laity alike, as typified in England by Thomas of Chob-ham's *Summa Confessorum*.

---

[1] Gerald's voluminous output is conveniently listed in R. Bartlett, *Gerald of Wales, 1146–1223* (Oxford, 1982), pp. 213–21.

[2] Gerald of Wales, *Gemma*, pp. 6–7.

[3] J. J. Hagen, *Gerald of Wales, The Jewel of the Church: a Translation of* Gemma Ecclesi-astica *by Giraldus Cambrensis* (Leiden, 1979).

The *Gemma* is the earliest of a trio of explicitly didactic works that also include the *De principis instructione* and the *Speculum ecclesie*.[4] It is probably to be dated to *c.* 1197 and the *De principis instructione* to some time before *c.* 1217; the *Speculum* was not completed till 1219 at the earliest. However, Gerald was certainly writing or planning both the *De principis instructione* and *Speculum* by the time of the first recension of the *Itinerarium Kambriae* of 1191, and as he was constantly reworking, adding to and embellishing all his works throughout his life, it is generally impossible to fix on a precise date for any of them. It has indeed been plausibly suggested that there was a later edition of the *Gemma*, part of whose text was incorporated into Gerald's *Speculum duorum*, one of his last works.[5] Some further, though questionable, evidence is found in the *De iure* where Gerald writes that he wrote the *Gemma* when he was in his seventies ('anno quasi septuagesimo').[6] If Gerald, who was born in 1146, was accurate then this would mean the *Gemma* was indeed a late work.

Gerald refers to the *Gemma* in two of his short pieces, the earlier, the *Catalogus brevior librorum suorum*, dating from *c.*1217 (though here again the date is uncertain), and the later *Epistola de libris a se scriptis*, addressed to the cathedral chapter of Hereford, which sets out to describe in chronological order all of his works. The *Catalogus* describes the *Gemma* as being for the instruction of the clergy concerning the greater sacraments and other matters necessary to know about, and as encouragement for them to lead a respectable life, both by word and example.[7] The *Epistola* characterizes it in very similar terms, as setting out the sacraments most necessary for salvation, as well as containing many chapters concerning clerical chastity using both suitable *exempla* and precepts.[8] Though Gerald usually refers to the *Gemma*, in his list of titles and their incipits in the *Symbolum electorum* it is styled the *De sacramentali instructione* ['Concerning priestly instruction'] and in the *Invectiones* he calls it the *Gemma sacerdotalis*.[9]

In the preface Gerald states that he has set out the questions to be addressed in brief chapter notes. Then he will deal with these questions in turn: the book is divided, he says, into *distinctiones* and chapter headings

---

4   A fourth work, now lost, the *De fidei fructu fideique defectu*, may well have also been primarily instructive in intent.
5   *Giraldus Cambrensis: Speculum Duorum or a Mirror of Two Men*, ed. Y. Lefèvre and R. B. C. Huygens (Cardiff, 1974), p. 102n.
6   *Giraldi Cambrensis: De iure et statu Menevensis ecclesie*, ed. J. S. Brewer (Rolls Series, London, 1863), pp. 372–3. For a sceptical view of Gerald's dating see *Speculum Duorum*, pp. xx–xxi and see also Bartlett, *Gerald of Wales*, p. 127, n. 16.
7   *Giraldi Cambrensis: Catalogus brevior*, ed. J. S. Brewer (Rolls Series, London 1961), I, 422.
8   *Epistola de libris a se scriptis*, ibid. p. 415.
9   *Invectiones*, ed. W. S. Davies, *Y Cymmrodor* 30 (1920), 232. It is also called this in an early catalogue of Lincoln Cathedral Library (see below, n. 19)

to make it easier and less tedious to use.[10] But, though the first *distinctio* is broadly concerned with the sacraments and the behaviour of the laity, while the second concentrates on the reform of the priesthood and senior clergy, especially as regards sexual morality and learning, it repeats some of what has already been said, as Gerald admits, and in fact the work is extraordinarily rambling and difficult to follow. There is little structure to the argument, themes are taken up, dropped, and then picked up again some chapters later. The opening chapters consider the Eucharist (and extreme unction) and how it should be administered, before moving to much briefer discussions of baptism and confession. The following eighteen chapters constitute a lengthy *excursus* devoted primarily to evil spirits and miraculous images that are sacrilegiously assaulted by Jews and others, accounts illustrated by many *exempla* drawn from the early Church. Gerald then returns to the themes of confession and penance, before once again reverting to the Eucharist, though these chapters are interspersed with chapters on specific sins of the laity such as unseemly behaviour in churches and churchyards, perjury and blasphemy. If there is a focus to the second *distinctio* it is on the sins of the clergy, both lesser and greater. It deals with sexual misconduct, gluttony and simony of all kinds, before closing with bitter criticism of episcopal excesses and the unsuitability for their post of many contemporary prelates.

While still in his late twenties Gerald had been appointed archdeacon of Brecon through the intervention of Archbishop Richard of Dover: his youth probably testifies to his ability, and certainly to the power of patronage, which lay behind so many archidiaconal appointments.[11] He retained this office till his resignation in 1204. Gerald took his new duties seriously, and was concerned to protect archidiaconal prerogatives, complaining that bishop Geoffrey of St Davids on occasion made episcopal visitations too frequently, infringing the archdeacon's rights.[12] Indeed, even prior to his appointment, Gerald had carried out some archidiaconal functions as archiepiscopal legate in the diocese of St Davids, insisting on the payment of tithes, protecting church property and enforcing clerical chastity.[13] And it was his action, perhaps not entirely disinterestedly driven by a desire for priestly

---

[10] *Gemma*, p. 7. The *Speculum ecclesie* and the *De instructione principis* are likewise divided into *distinctiones*.

[11] *Giraldi Cambrensis: De rebus a se gestis*, ed. J. S. Brewer (Rolls Series, London, 1861), p. 27. Gerald's appointment whilst still a young man was by no means unusual. On this and archdeacons in general during the first half of the twelfth century see M. Brett, *The English Church under Henry I* (Oxford, 1975), pp. 201–11.

[12] *Speculum Duorum*, pp. 270–3. For Gerald's career as archdeacon see ibid. pp. xlix–lii.

[13] For the judicial activity of archdeacons at a parochial level see B. Kemp, 'Archdeacons and Parish Churches in England in the Twelfth Century', in *Law and Government in Medieval England and Normandy: Essays in Honour of Sir James Holt*, ed. G. Garnett and J. Hudson (Cambridge, 1994), pp. 341–64 and *Twelfth-century*

celibacy, in suspending the archdeacon of Brecon for living with his mistress that led to his own appointment. This issue of clerical celibacy came to be the defining issue of Gerald's reform programme for the secular and regular clergy alike. As archdeacon Gerald held visitations of rural deaneries; he tells of one conducted shortly before he left for Lincoln at which he heard that he had been defrauded by the bishop of money intended for the archdeacon's income.[14]

In his self-compiled compendium or *florilegium* of extracts that he considered his choicest works, the *Symbolum electorum*, Gerald includes three letters addressed to his officials and clergy, as well as an archidiaconal sermon preached at a synod held at St Davids. These demonstrate his concerns and preoccupations, as well as revealing him as a sympathetic and thoughtful archdeacon. In the first letter he tells his officials not to deny ecclesiastical justice to anyone nor to exploit anyone.[15] Simony was totally forbidden. Yet Gerald recognized the realities of local political patronage. His men were to show deference to William de Braose and his wife, and if they did do anything contrary to Church law, they were to be warned to improve their behaviour, as Gerald had personally instructed before he left, rather than be placed under interdict or other sentence which might provoke them. If they did prove incorrigible then their case was to be passed to the bishop. William was a supporter of Gerald; he was also one of the most powerful Anglo-Norman barons in south Wales – it was not good to alienate him.

Every church was to be visited annually and checks made whether services were properly conducted and whether there were suitable chalices, books, holy water stoups and other necessary ornaments. If lacking, the clergy were to be severely punished since they had been frequently warned about this many times. Gerald ends by asking his officials, when holding their rural chapters, to ask each priest to say a mass for Gerald's dearest friend, master Peter de Leche, archdeacon of Worcester, who had recently died,[16] as well as a mass of the Holy Spirit for himself, and their prayers for their own understanding and observance of Holy Scripture.

These activities were common to any conscientious archdeacon: where Gerald is unique is in apparently setting down a programme for reform and Christian living for his clergy.[17] By the time Gerald wrote the *Gemma*,

---

Archidiaconal and Vice-Archidiaconal Acta, ed. B. R. Kemp, Canterbury & York Society, 92 (2001).

14 *Speculum Duorum*, pp. 246–9.

15 *Giraldi Cambrensis: Symbolum Electorum*, ed. J. S. Brewer (Rolls Series, London, 1861), pp. 251–2.

16 Peter died in or before 1198. See *John le Neve: Fasti Ecclesiae Anglicanae 1066–1300: II Monastic Cathedrals*, compiled D. E. Greenway (London, 1971), p. 105.

17 On archdeacons in general see above n. 13 and A. H. Thompson, 'Diocesan Organization in the Middle Ages: Archdeacons and Rural Deans', *Proceedings of the British Academy* 29 (1947 for 1943), 153–94 and J. Scamell, 'The Rural Chapter in England

however, he was far from his clerical flock. His time since appointment as archdeacon had been punctuated by long absences, in Paris to study, in Ireland and England on diplomatic business, and in Wales itself as administrator of the St Davids diocese and preaching the crusade in the company of Archbishop Baldwin of Canterbury. Gerald reports how it was necessary to appoint a general official to look after his interests and the needs of the archdeaconry while he was absent at the schools.[18] Now he was in Lincoln, and it was almost certainly here that he began the *Gemma*. Though absent from his clergy, Gerald's time in Lincoln gave him access both to leading scholars – his friend, William de Montibus, the chancellor, in particular – and to an academic library where he would find many of the authorities he cites and uses in the *Gemma*.[19] For the *Gemma* was informed not only by Gerald's practical experiences as a senior secular cleric and ecclesiastical administrator, especially as archdeacon, but also by the theoretical awareness obtained in the Paris schools, and perhaps as important, but less easy to document, by his time at the secular cathedrals of Hereford and Lincoln. Gerald had become a canon of Hereford, probably sometime after 1186 and most likely through the good offices of bishop William de Vere, and perhaps as a response to the request of another friend, the canon Simon de Freine, who had written to him urging him to come to Hereford where all the liberal arts were studied.[20]

How much time Gerald actually spent at Hereford is unclear, but he was possibly there between 1194 and 1196.[21] What is certain is that in 1196 he went to Lincoln, since he was unable to travel as he wished to Paris in order to resume his studies because war had broken out between kings Philip Augustus and Richard I.[22] There were very good reasons to go there. Lincoln was, as Gerald recognized, one of the great powerhouses of scholarship in England at the end of the twelfth century: 'he knew that the science of theology flourished here more soundly and healthily than anywhere in England'; here master William de Montibus, 'the best of teachers', who had been known to Gerald when William taught at Mont Ste Geneviève in Paris,

from the Eleventh to the Fourteenth Century', *English Historical Review* 86 (1971), 1–21.

18 *Speculum Duorum*, pp. l, 248–51.
19 Though R. M. Thomson (*Catalogue of the Manuscripts of Lincoln Cathedral Chapter Library* (Cambridge, 1989), pp. xv–xvi) has cautioned against an inflated view of the scholarship at Lincoln, pointing out that its library was hardly substantial, and suggesting that the cathedral's reputation for learning rested on the influence of individual chancellors, such as William de Montibus, rather than on the institution.
20 See *Fasti: Hereford*, pp. 69, 89 and R. W. Hunt, 'English Learning in the Late Twelfth Century', *Transactions of the Royal Historical Society* 4th ser., 19 (1936), 36–7.
21 See Bartlett, *Gerald of Wales*, p. 58, n. 1.
22 *De rebus a se gestis*, p. 93 and see Dimock's comments in *Giraldi Cambrensis: Topographica Hibernica*, ed. J. F. Dimock (Rolls Series, London, 1867), p. liii, n. 2.

was cathedral chancellor.[23] Indeed it is likely that Gerald had been taught by him in Paris. William was not the only Paris-educated scholar associated with both Lincoln and Hereford. In the early 1190s the young Robert Grosseteste was 'on the fringe' of the household of bishop Hugh of Lincoln and later entered the household of bishop William de Vere at Hereford. While it is not certain that Gerald and Robert ever met, Gerald certainly knew of Robert and thought highly of him, for he wrote to bishop William urging his further promotion. Unfortunately, William died in 1198 and Robert's hopes of advancement in this diocese were quashed.[24]

Another scholar from Paris was also part of this circle: Gerald's contemporary, Stephen Langton, may, as a local boy, have received his first education at Lincoln cathedral school; he may, and again this is conjectural, have studied under William de Montibus in Paris.[25] What is much more certain is that he met Gerald whilst in Paris, and they were almost certainly together as students of Peter the Chanter who was to be the greatest influence on their pastoral theology. Gerald thought highly of Langton. He was a defender of the *libertas ecclesie* and agreed with Gerald that monks should not be made bishops. Gerald refers to a conversation he had with Langton at Guildford, shortly before he heard that the archbishop was going to Rome and was seriously considering resigning his office and becoming a hermit or a Carthusian. This prompted Gerald to write a long letter to Langton to dissuade him from such a step.[26] Langton was also the dedicatee of several of Gerald's works, the *De iure et statu Menevensis ecclesie*, the *Speculum ecclesie*, as well as later editions of the *Itinerarium* and *Descriptio Kambriae*, and, very appropriately, the *vitae* of two Lincoln bishops, Remigius and Hugh of Witham.[27]

During his studies at Paris Gerald had studied both canon law and theology, and the influence of Gratian (who though never himself a Paris master was yet the dominant legal authority there), Peter Lombard and a number of other Paris scholars, of whom Peter the Chanter is by far the most important, permeates his work.[28] Peter the Chanter was undoubtedly the most influential of all the Paris masters who were setting out a new theology for a new age at the end of the twelfth and beginning of the thirteenth centuries.[29]

---

23 For William de Montibus's life and work, see Goering, *William de Montibus*. He discusses the schools of Lincoln and William's teaching there, pp. 42–57.

24 For Grosseteste's early career see R. W. Southern, *Robert Grosseteste: the Growth of an English Mind in Medieval Europe* (Oxford, 1986), pp. 63–8; *Symbolum Electorum*, I, 249.

25 F. M. Powicke, *Stephen Langton* (Oxford, 1928), pp. 9–10.

26 *Epistola ad Stephanum Langton*, ed. J. S. Brewer (Rolls Series, London, 1861), pp. 401–7.

27 For Gerald's dedications see Bartlett, *Gerald of Wales*, pp. 60–2.

28 Gerald was in Paris between *c.* 1165 and 1172 and again from 1176 to 1179.

29 See the wide-ranging and magisterial study by Baldwin, *Masters, Princes and Merchants*.

While it is not absolutely certain that Gerald actually studied under Peter, who became chanter of Paris cathedral in 1183, he was very well acquainted with his work. He explicitly acknowledged his debt to Peter in the *Speculum duorum*, where he refers to his *Verbum abbreviatum* as Peter's *summa*, and elsewhere speaks highly of him, describing him in the *Speculum ecclesie* as 'not only an eminent theologian, but also a moral philosopher distinguished for his teaching of good conduct'.[30] Not just Gerald, but also Stephen Langton, Thomas of Chobham, Robert of Courson and Robert of Flamborough, all of English background, were greatly indebted to Peter the Chanter, and in particular to his largest and most significant work, the inappropriately titled *Verbum abbreviatum*, which survives in more than ninety manuscripts.[31]

Gerald's use (to put it at its mildest) of the *Verbum* has long been recognized. Interestingly, however, he only once mentions Peter by name in the *Gemma*, and then to explicitly criticize his view that a priest going to celebrate mass again on the same day should not rinse the chalice.[32] Was this, perhaps, to deflect any criticism he might have incurred for having followed Peter so closely in this work? Sanford and Boutemy both demonstrated the *Gemma*'s substantial reliance on the *Verbum*.[33] My own debt to these scholars is considerable and will be acknowledged here, I hope, with rather more care than Gerald used toward Peter. It is not only in the *Gemma* that Gerald employed the *Verbum*; there are substantial borrowings (again seldom acknowledged) in the *Speculum ecclesie*, and to a lesser extent, in other works such as the *Speculum duorum*. Boutemy calculated that something like an eighth of the *Gemma* is copied from the *Verbum*.[34] However, such borrowings are not indiscriminate throughout the text, though there are some scattered echoes everywhere, but rather, as both Boutemy and Sanford pointed out, it is only certain, lengthy sections of the work that derive extensively from the *Verbum*.[35] These are the closing three chapters (49 to 51) of the first *distinctio* and chapters 22 to 34 of the second *distinctio*.

On one major question Gerald differs from Peter. The latter paid compara-

---

[30] *Speculum Duorum*, p. 148; *Giraldi Cambrensis: Speculum ecclesie*, ed. J. S. Brewer (Rolls Series, London, 1861), p. 62.

[31] For these men's relationship to Peter see Baldwin, *Masters, Princes and Merchants*, I, 19–36, 41–3.

[32] *Gemma*, p. 126.

[33] E. M. Sanford, 'Giraldus Cambrensis' Debt to Petrus Cantor', *Medievalia et Humanistica* 3 (1945), 16–32; A. Boutemy, 'Giraud de Barri et Pierre le Chantre: une source de la *Gemma Ecclesiastica*', *Revue du moyen age latin* 2 (1946), 45–62. Though they wrote at about the same time they were seemingly unaware of each other's work. The 'long version' of the *Verbum* has recently been edited by M. Boutry, *Petrus Cantoris Parisiensis. Verbum Abbreviatum. Textus Conflatus* (CCCM 196, Turnhout, 2004) and see also *PL* 205.

[34] Boutemy, 'Giraud de Barri', p. 61.

[35] Ibid., esp. pp. 57–62 and Sanford, 'Giraldus Cambrensis' Debt', esp. p. 20.

tively little attention to the question of priestly sexual incontinence, an issue on which Gerald is at his most vociferous, and, indeed, most radical, going so far as to make a tentative suggestion that a married clergy might be permitted if properly supervised. Gerald denied that early decretals permitted clerical marriage but said that individual clerics, especially those in minor orders, might seek such permission from the papal curia. Acknowledging that the Eastern Church did allow priestly marriage and that there was no biblical prohibition, but that the early Western Church fathers had only urged celibacy to promote greater purity, he argued that a general council of the Church would be necessary to permit marriage, saying that Pope Alexander III was reported to have gained consent for such a measure, unanimous save for the opposition of the papal chancellor.[36]

Though, as we have seen, Gerald undoubtedly thought highly of the *Gemma* and seems to have anticipated a wide readership for it, it is very unusual amongst Gerald's works in that it is not explicitly dedicated to a patron, actual or potential. Here at any rate Gerald, though he always looked for approbation – in the preface he refers to his work as being worthy of his clergy's praise and gratitude for his compilation – seems not to be overtly seeking favour. Gerald sets out his reasons for writing the *Gemma* in the preface, which is addressed to his clergy and officials: but were these the intended audience? It was, he says, his duty as archdeacon, though absent in the body, to set out their ecclesiastical duties concerning which they frequently used to question him whilst he was with them, together with detailing matters that it was most necessary they should know. This would demonstrate his loving care for his flock and that he had not abandoned them though distant from them. The text was also, he says, written solely for the benefit of the Welsh clergy in a plain unadorned language that could be readily understood.[37] If we take Gerald's stated intentions at face value then the *Gemma* is the first work of pastoral care produced for the Welsh clergy.[38] It

---

36 *Gemma*, pp. 186–7.
37 In fact there is little or no observable difference in style or language between the *Gemma* and Gerald's other didactic works.
38 It was not until the late thirteenth and early fourteenth centuries that pastoral works appeared in the Welsh vernacular: Gruffudd Bola translated the Athanasian Creed for Efa, ferch Maredudd ab Owain, and the more comprehensive, and slightly later, collections of the *White Book of Rhydderch* and the *Book of the Anchorite of Llandewibrefi* contain a number of pastoral texts, whilst a translation of substantial portions of Raymond of Penyafort's *Summa de Poenitentia et Matrimonio* was probably already in circulation at this date. For these developments see G. Williams, *The Welsh Church from Conquest to Reformation* (Cardiff, 1976), ch. II, especially pp. 92–4; H. Lewis, 'Credo Athanasius', *Bulletin of the Board of Celtic Studies* 5 (1929–31), 193–203 and for Efa, C. Lloyd Morgan, 'More Written About Than Writing? Welsh Women and the Written Word', in *Literacy in Medieval Celtic Societies*, ed. H. Pryce (Caergrawnt, 1998), pp. 149–65; I. Ll. Foster, 'The Book of the Anchorite', *Proceedings of the British Academy* 36 (1950), 197–226; J. E. C. Williams, 'Medieval Welsh

is ironic that the second (the *De modo confitendi*) was produced by the Cistercian monk, Cadwgan of Llandyfei, who became bishop of Bangor in 1215, a man for whom Gerald had nothing but deep dislike and contempt (though even he praised his skill in Irish and Welsh).[39] Cadwgan was certainly a noted scholar; he is described in the *Chronica de Wallia* as 'vir mire facundie et sapientie' ['a man of remarkable eloquence and wisdom'], and as bishop he wrote three works: the tract on confession, a book of prayers and a commentary on a verse of the psalms, while Leland attributes homilies and a *Speculum Christianorum* to him.[40]

The most important modern full-length study of Gerald, Robert Bartlett's *Gerald of Wales, 1146–1223*, published in 1982 and reissued twenty-five years later, primarily interprets the *Gemma* within two matrices. First, Bartlett sees Gerald as a reformist churchman caught in tension between the need to maintain the *libertas ecclesie* against lay encroachments and interference at the same time as he himself was enmeshed within lay patronage and influence. Secondly, he sees Gerald's ecclesiastical programme for both Wales and Ireland as one element in Gerald's own ideology, born from the colonizing drive of the Anglo-Norman invaders amongst whom his own family was so important.[41] A little earlier, in 1978, F. X. Martin had written: 'the *Gemma* … is embroidered with such a variety of examples and incidents (supposedly true) that it is a veritable tapestry of clerical life, good, bad, and indifferent, in *Wales*' (my italics).[42]

Yet there are problems with such readings. There is, in fact, surprisingly little indication in the main body of the work that Gerald was writing

---

Religious Prose', *Proceedings of the Second International Congress of Celtic Studies 1963* (Cardiff, 1966), 65–97; I. Williams, 'Penityas', *Bulletin of the Board of Celtic Studies* 7 (1933–35), 124–6.

[39] See J. Conway Davies, *Episcopal Acts and Cognate Documents relating to Welsh Dioceses 1066–1272* (Historical Society of the Church in Wales, 4, 1948), II, 553–7; *Welsh Cathedrals*, pp. 3–4; J. E. Lloyd, *A History of Wales*, 2 vols., 3rd edn. (London, 1939), II, 688–9; F. G. Cowley, *The Monastic Order in South Wales, 1066–1349* (Cardiff, 1977), pp. 48, 122–3.

[40] See J. Goering and H. Pryce, 'The *De modo confitendi* of Cadwgan bishop of Bangor', *Medieval Studies* 62 (2000), 1–27; T. Jones, '"Chronica de Wallia" and other documents from Exeter Cathedral Library MS 3514', *Bulletin of the Board of Celtic Studies* 12 (1948), 35; J. Leland, *Commentarii de Scriptoribus Britannicis*, 2 vols. (London, 1709), I, 251; C. H. Talbot, 'Cadogan of Bangor', *Cîteaux in de Nederlanden* 9 (1958), 18–40; Cowley, *Monastic Order*, pp. 153–4; C. J. Holdsworth, 'Learning and Literature of English Cistercians, 1167–1214, with special reference to John of Ford' (unpublished PhD dissertation, University of Cambridge, 1960), p. 28.

[41] Bartlett, *Gerald of Wales*, pp. 27–45.

[42] F. X. Martin, 'Giraldus as Historian', in *Expugnatio Hibernica: The Conquest of Ireland by Giraldus Cambrensis*, ed. A. B. Scott and F. X. Martin (Dublin, 1978), p. 269. See also D. Walker, *Medieval Wales* (Cambridge, 1990), p. 75: 'in his vignettes of Welsh ecclesiastical life … he was capable of warm and perceptive observation of the simple virtues of local clerical life'.

with a specific Welsh readership in mind. Generally, indeed, he is far more concerned with the Welsh church and its shortcomings in his other works, notably the *De iure et statu Menevensis ecclesie*, and his last completed text, the *Speculum ecclesie*. As Bartlett pointed out, in the *Descriptio Kambrie* Gerald noted and condemned portionary churches and the inheritance of benefices, both practices (as Bartlett recognized) by no means confined to the Welsh Church. Again in the *De iure* Gerald set out a programme for Archbishop Stephen Langton, exhorting him to visit Wales in order to eradicate these vices, together with that of concubinage.[43] It is therefore the more surprising that, though Gerald does have a great deal to say about clerical concubinage, an issue with which all contemporary moral theologians were engaging, there is nothing in the *Gemma* on either portionary churches or inheritance.

These were sins of the clergy: as far as the laity were concerned Gerald was most critical of Welsh marriage customs and especially the practice of incest, and the fact that there was no clear distinction between legitimate and illegitimate children in inheritance custom.[44] Yet again on these shortcomings, apparently so characteristic of the Welsh laity, there is hardly anything in a work avowedly intended for their pastoral care. On incest there is nothing at all, and only in a chapter on illicit gift giving to the clergy, not a chapter dealing with marriage law, does Gerald refer to the sin of receiving money to permit marriage within the second or third degree, divorce or marriage with the daughter of one's godfather or godmother. It should also be noted that Gerald seems to suggest here that the sin is to marry within two or three degrees, not the far more draconian, and ultimately unrealizable and unenforceable, seven degrees, reduced to four degrees by the 1215 Lateran Council.[45] But there is something else. This passage is taken *verbatim* from the *Verbum abbreviatum*: it is not linked to a Welsh context at all.

Moreover, Gerald makes very few references to practices specific to the Church in Wales. In what is probably the first mention in Anglo-Latin literature of cider he condemns the practice of its being used rather than wine in the Eucharist, a custom which may well have been more common in Wales than England.[46] Once he refers to pilgrims 'in your country' visiting the shrine of St Eluned and there dancing and miming the secular labours they have sinfully performed on feast days, but he develops this account in much more detail in the *Itinerarium Kambrie*.[47] He writes that the Welsh have less respect for oaths taken on the Gospels than they do for those taken on relics of the saints, such as their bells and staffs, and that they were very prone to

43 *De iure*, pp. 113 B 6. See Bartlett, *Gerald of Wales*, pp. 34–5.
44 Bartlett, *Gerald of Wales*, pp. 38–42.
45 *Gemma*, pp. 326–7.
46 Ibid., p. 124.
47 Ibid., pp. 162–3.

perjury.[48] It is only here and in the immediate following chapter where he condemns the modern Welsh contempt for excommunication, whereas they used greatly to fear it, that he addresses the Welsh parish clergy directly.[49]

Neither are his *exempla*, hagiographic or moral, usually drawn from a Welsh milieu. St Dogmael and other Dyfed hermits are likened for their flesh-denying practices to those of the northern English hermit-saint Godric of Finchale whose *vita* Gerald explicitly knew, and whose ascetism is described in much more detail.[50] He tells the story, which may or may not be apocryphal, of Enoch, an unchaste monk of Whitland, which he had already used in the *Itinerarium*, and was to recycle in the *Speculum ecclesie*.[51] Another, concerning punishment visited on a labourer who worked on St Lawrence's day, is located in Dyfed.[52] Generally, however, his *exempla* derive from a wide chronological and geographic range – from the early Church, to contemporary or near-contemporary western Europe, to Gerald's own experiences whilst a student in Paris. A number are drawn, as Gerald notes in the preface, from *vitae* of the Church fathers, both in the East and West, and especially from Gregory, since few of these texts, he writes, were known to the Welsh clergy.[53] Some relate to well-known contemporaries, including leading members of the aristocracy and royalty such as Richard de Clare ('Strongbow'), Ralph de Fayence, the uncle of Queen Eleanor of Aquitaine, or Louis VII of France, as well as notable churchmen such as Gilbert of Sempringham, John Comyn, archbishop of Dublin or Hugh of Witham, bishop of Lincoln. Some are very firmly localized, such as Holy Trinity Church, Dublin (i.e. Christ Church Cathedral), St Mary's Church, Canterbury, Holy Cross Church, Chichester, Stanway parish church in Gloucestershire and Boissy-en-Drouais near Chartres. Such *exempla* may or may not be fictional – none can be corroborated from other accounts – but they were clearly intended to be received as Gerald's own record of recent notable events and miraculous happenings. It is also surprising, as Boutemy noted, that in a work apparently intended for

---

48 Ibid., pp. 157–8. Gerald had earlier made the same point, in greater detail, in the *Itinerarium Kambrie* (p. 27). See also *Speculum Duorum*, p. xxxviii and n; and Bartlett, *Gerald of Wales*, pp. 35–6.

49 *Gemma*, pp. 157–60.

50 Ibid., pp. 214–16.

51 Ibid., pp. 245–6.

52 Ibid., p. 162.

53 Ibid., p. 6. Similarly in the opening chapter he refers to his quotations from Gratian (which make up the bulk of his first two chapters), since his readers may well not have access to these canons in Wales. ('Sed quoniam in partibus illis canonum copia non habetur ipsa capitula ex quibus solutiones elicere potestis uobis quoque scripta transmisimus').The lack of medieval library catalogues from Welsh religious houses makes it impossible to test Gerald's assertion, though it is inherently likely. Augustinian Llanthony, with which Gerald had close ties, may well be an exception. See also F. G. Cowley, *The Monastic Order in South Wales, 1066–1349* (Cardiff, 1977), pp. 143–6.

parish priests and the lesser secular clergy so much attention is also focused on the faults of the higher clergy, and that prelates, both collectively and as individuals, (for example, Archbishop Hubert Walter) are bitterly criticized.[54]

The *Gemma Ecclesiastica* is not a coherent work of moral and spiritual reform: it is an unstructured hodge-podge, self-consciously learned, containing much that was irrelevant to the experiences of its avowedly intended audience; it certainly does not appear 'fit for purpose'. Though its genre is *pastoralia*, beyond that it is impossible to categorize: it certainly cannot be located within the schematic diagram of pastoral literature provided by Leonard Boyle.[55] Indeed, there is no evidence that the *Gemma* was ever read by the Welsh clergy: their very illiteracy of which Gerald complains would have precluded a wide readership. Nor is the *Gemma* alone amongst Gerald's works in its shapelessness and difficulty of characterization: the *Speculum ecclesie* also falls into no obvious genre and has no coherent structure, though its general anti-monastic thrust is clear.

So, if the *Gemma* did not come directly into the hands of the Welsh clergy, who did see it? As we have seen, Gerald presented a copy to Pope Innocent III: another was apparently sent to Hereford since in a letter of 1198 or 1199 Gerald wrote that he had sent a copy of his *Symbolum electorum* to 'our chapter of Hereford' and that he would soon send a copy of a useful work, the labour of his autumn years, the *De sacramentali instructione*, since, though in England masters do not teach at harvest time, good pupils nevertheless do not rest from their studies.[56]

A third copy was presented to Lincoln Cathedral. In the collection of letters that he assembled sometime between 1208 and 1216 relating to his bitter quarrels with his nephew, Gerald fitzPhilip, and with William de Capella, Gerald preserved a letter which has no obvious connection with these disputes and which was addressed to his old friend and mentor, William de Montibus.[57] It is a pained response to criticisms that William had made, either verbally or in a now lost letter, of Gerald's Irish works, which the author had presented as a

54 A point made by Boutemy, 'Giraud de Barri', pp. 46–7, n. 4, who suggests that this criticism was intended to excite the interest of Pope Innocent III.
55 L. E. Boyle, 'The Fourth Lateran Council and Manuals of Popular Theology', in *The Popular Literature of Medieval England*, ed. T. J. Heffernan (Knoxville TN, 1985), p. 38.
56 *Symbolum Electorum*, letter xxiii, pp. 268–71. For the *Symbolum* see Bartlett, *Gerald of Wales*, pp. 218–19. Gerald went on to say that he intended to send the chapter copies of all his works. Though none of Gerald's works remain in Hereford cathedral library, there is evidence that Gerald did customarily send copies, for in the *De libris a se scriptis* he writes to the Hereford chapter asking for the return of his *Speculum ecclesie* which he had sent the previous year, and he is also known to have sent them a volume containing his *Topographica Hibernica* and the *Expugnatio* (*Epistola de libris a se scriptis*, ed. J. S. Brewer (Rolls Series, London, 1861), p. 409.)
57 *Speculum Duorum*, pp. xli, 168–75. See also R. B. C. Huygens, 'Une lettre de Giraud le Cambrien à propos de ses ouvrages historiques', *Latomus* 26 (1965), 90–100.

single volume to Lincoln Cathedral, on the grounds that some of the material was indecent, and more generally that Gerald should devote himself to theological, not historical, works. Gerald presented a vigorous defence and then wrote that if it was theological works that William wanted then he should look more kindly on the *Gemma* which, together with his *vita* of Remigius (the first Norman bishop of Lincoln), he had presented some years earlier to the cathedral. Unfortunately this letter cannot be closely dated. If Dymock was right in suggesting that there was a now lost first recension of the *vita* dating from *c.* 1198, then it is likely that Gerald gave the *Gemma* to the cathedral library shortly after its completion.[58]

All three presentations, therefore, were probably made *c.* 1198–99. This timing may be significant: Bishop Peter de Leia, bishop of St Davids, died in July 1198. Gerald was elected as his successor a year later, only for the election to be overruled by King John. It was during the subsequent appeal to Rome that Gerald presented Pope Innocent III with the copy of the *Gemma*. Prior to the *Gemma* Gerald had written works of cosmography, topography (which were also informed by a deep interest in natural history) and history as well as some hagiography. There was as yet nothing explicitly theological, an omission which (as we have just seen) could still inspire criticism even after the *Gemma* was written. Perhaps it was written with one eye at least on the author's reputation as he sought promotion, an addition to the publications in his *curriculum vitae*. By his own admission Gerald had earlier had ambitions for an English bishopric, spurning Welsh dioceses for their poverty and uncivilized flock.[59] Thwarted by political considerations and personal animosities in the mid-1190s, only then does he seem to have turned his hopes to St Davids.[60] This is not to accuse Gerald of cynical self-advertisement; for all his faults he truly did believe in the need for reform within the Church and his career as archdeacon demonstrated his commitment to ecclesiastical administration.

There is one final, poignant and perhaps significant, irony. For all of Gerald's pleasure and pride in the *Gemma*, and his hopes for its influence, it survives in a single manuscript, now London, Lambeth Palace Library MS 236.[61] Though Brewer raised the possibility that this manuscript might have

---

[58] *Giraldi Cambrensis: Vita S. Remigii et Vita S. Hugonis*, ed J. F. Dymock (Rolls Series, London, 1877), pp. x–xx: the contemporary catalogue of Lincoln Cathedral's books lists three donations from Gerald, the *Topographica Hibernica*, the *Vita Remigii*, and the *Gemma Sacerdotalis* (ibid., appendix C, p. 168).

[59] *Investiones*, p. 213, and see also Richter, *Giraldus Cambrensis*, pp. 89–90.

[60] He had earlier been nominated for the bishopric in 1176 but had turned it down, *De rebus a se gestis*, pp. 41–2.

[61] See M. R. James, *A Descriptive Catalogue of the Manuscripts in the Library of Lambeth Palace: The Medieval Manuscripts* (Cambridge, 1932), pp. 381–3. This manuscript also contains some of Gerald's poems, his two letters to Archbishop Stephen Langton

been that presented to Innocent III this is extremely unlikely.[62] Thus we have knowledge of only three, perhaps four, copies of the work. This should be compared with the over 100 surviving manuscripts (including fragments) of Thomas of Chobham's *Summa Confessorum*, a work which continued in popularity throughout the Middle Ages, and was even printed in two editions at the end of the fifteenth century.[63] There are over twenty copies of a vernacular Welsh pastoral work of the late thirteenth century, *Yn y modd hwn*.[64] Peter the Chanter's *Verbum Abbreviatum* also survives in more than 100 manuscripts. Gerald of Wales was extraordinarily prolific: he was also largely unread. Other than the Welsh and Irish texts, the *Topographica* and *Expugnatio Hibernica* and the *Itinerarium* and *Descriptio Kambriae* virtually none of his works survive in more than one manuscript. Only four manuscripts of the *Speculum ecclesie* are known: it is doubtful if many additional manuscripts of his other works existed but have now been lost.

The *Gemma* may have been the favourite bedtime reading of the greatest reforming pope of the Middle Ages, but it remained a little-known work. It was rapidly superseded, even if it initially had a wide readership, which seems unlikely, by other pastoral texts in both Wales and England. Its author, too, failed in his attempt to become bishop of St Davids and died in 1223, probably in Lincoln. He had resigned his archdeaconry in 1204. Yet it would be far too negative to see the *Gemma* as an unsuccessful work of an unsuccessful man. Joseph Goering has questioned the ready assumption that the audience for the new genre of *pastoralia* comprised 'the simple priests in their parishes' and observed that most parish priests continued to be of very modest education – indeed they were not expected to display academic ability, but other, more 'practical' values.[65] Certainly, the well-known example of the clergy associated with Sonning (Berkshire) and its dependencies in 1222 reveals a woeful ignorance not only of the basics of grammar, but of the texts and the singing of essential liturgical prayers;[66] and it is within the framework of Goering's analysis that the *Gemma* should be set. As both he and others (notably Boyle) have emphasized, though the Lateran Council undoubtedly acted as a catalyst for the production of pastoral literature, such works were already available prior to 1215.[67] They were experimental in form

and that to the chapter of Hereford. James considered that the manuscript was 'prepared under Giraldus's own supervision'.

[62] See *Gemma*, p. x.
[63] Chobham, *Summa Confessorum*, pp. lxxvi–lxxxviii.
[64] Williams, *Welsh Church*, p. 93.
[65] Goering, *William de Montibus*, pp. 59–63.
[66] *The Register of S. Osmund*, ed. W. H. Rich Jones 2 vols. (Rolls Series, London, 1883), I. 304–6.
[67] See, especially, L. Boyle, 'The Inter-Conciliar Period 1179–1215 and the Beginnings of Pastoral Manuals' in *Miscellanea Rolando Bandinelli Papa Alessandro III*, ed. F. Liotta (Siena, 1986), pp. 45–56.

and content, incoherent and unsystematic early prototypes of the ordered literature of the following generation, as they felt their way in giving voice to new needs and requirements.

Moreover, the concerns of the Council were first articulated by the pastoral theologians of late twelfth and early thirteenth century western Europe. So, while the writings of Gerald and others may not have directly influenced the reform programme promulgated at the Fourth Lateran Council, they created the environment for legislation at both papal and episcopal levels. Many of the concerns raised in the *Gemma* and other of Gerald's works foreshadow those of Pope Innocent III, while these shortcomings and the organizational structure necessary to address them that Gerald had highlighted were emphasized by the Council. Amongst its canons are rulings on ecclesiastical discipline; annual visitations whereby abuses would be reported to the diocesan synods, a system that clearly required active archidiaconal intervention of the sort that Gerald practised and taught; diocesan preaching; triennial visitation of monastic houses on the Cistercian model, which Gerald had advocated in the *Speculum ecclesie*, though he gives this much less prominence in the *Gemma*; dissolute and drunken clergy; the purity of churches and their fittings; annual confession and communion by the laity; the appointment of an educated clergy, without secular intervention; exploitation by episcopal procurations; simony. This is by no means an exhaustive list of contemporary pastoral issues found in Gerald's work.

All writers on the *Gemma Ecclesiastica* have taken Gerald's description of its function and audience at face value. According to J. Conway Davies, whose lengthy article on Gerald remains the best biography, the *Gemma* 'was a manual written for the clergy of his archdeaconry', while Rees Davies, the finest of Welsh medieval historians, wrote that it 'was written specifically to instruct the clergy of St Davids in the rudiments of theology'.[68] Yet, as I have tried to show, if that was the prime intention of the *Gemma* it cannot be said to have succeeded. Paradoxically it is only when this assumption is challenged that the importance of the *Gemma* in the development of pastoral literature appears. Undoubtedly Gerald's experiences as archdeacon taught him much of the spiritual and moral shortcomings of priest and people, but as important an inspiration was the teaching of the schools, and it was for the approbation and use of scholars like himself, rather than an ill-educated parish clergy, that the *Gemma* was primarily intended. Through such works, reformist values might ultimately permeate down to the parochial bedrock of ecclesiastical life, but that process was left to the following generation.

---

[68] J. Conway Davies, 'Giraldus Cambrensis, 1146–1946', *Archaeologia Cambrensis* 99 (1947), 276; R. R. Davies, *Conquest, Coexistence, and Change; Wales 1063–1415* (Oxford, 1987), p. 194.

4

Time to Read: Pastoral Care, Vernacular Access and the Case of Angier of St Frideswide

Jocelyn Wogan-Browne

The question of whether equipping audiences with an internalized penitential vocabulary and opening up pastoral reading to them does not simultaneously render them independent of their instructors is an area of concern in vernacular *pastoralia*. As a result, clerical writers, whether anxious to keep their vernacular audiences more dependent or more autonomous, tend to articulate explicitly and copiously the rationale and aims of their work and the common interests, as they see them, of themselves and their audiences. *Pastoralia* are always potentially texts of writerly as well as readerly self-awareness and often surprisingly innovative. Bella Millett has recently shown, for example, that a group of late twelfth and early thirteenth century English homilies, far from being a dying flicker of Anglo-Saxon tradition, is much more likely to have its true context in response to concern at diocesan level with meeting the need for vernacular *pastoralia*. These homilies, she argues, use older as well as newer material, but are fundamentally a fresh response and redeployment of existing homiletic tradition.[1] Alongside these developments in English writings, there are a number of francophone writers in the multilingual culture of late twelfth and thirteenth-century England

---

[1] B. Millett, 'The Pastoral Context of the Trinity and Lambeth Homilies', in Scase, *Manuscript Geography*, pp. 43–64. *Ancrene Wisse* itself, is of course, as Millett herself and Cate Gunn have shown, partly to be understood within the context of *pastoralia*. It is also an outstanding example of ideas from institutional clerisy articulated and renovated in response to a lay audience (Gunn, *AW From Pastoral Literature*, esp. pp. 31–126). I thank Jean-Pascal Pouzet and Tony Hunt for the opportunity to try out some of the material here at their conference on medieval exegesis and vernacular commentaries at Paris III-Sorbonne in 2007, Dr Pouzet for a most helpful reading of it and the editors of this volume for perspicacious and meticulous editing. To Bella Millett I am indebted, as we all are, for magnificent editing and scholarship and also for much scholarly and personal generosity over the years. Her remark to me long ago that 'the *Katherine*-Group and *Ancrene Wisse ought* to have been in French' has been an abiding stimulus to work and thought.

who also seek newly effective ways to present pastoral teaching to those in their spiritual care.[2]

Shortly before Lateran IV, a canon named Angier working in the Augustinian priory of St Frideswide at Oxford composed a French verse translation of Gregory the Great's *Dialogues* in some 20,000 lines of rhyming couplets, completed, according to his own inscription, on 29 November, 1212.[3] The *Dialogues de saint Grégoire* are extant in a single, almost certainly holograph manuscript, Paris, Bibliothèque nationale, MS f. fr. 24766, a small thick quarto, without illustrations, but decorated with blue and red, and occasionally green capitals and flourishings, as well as rubrics and other kinds of marking-up.[4] Angier identifies himself in his Latin colophon as 'Brother A.

---

[2] See N. Watson and J. Wogan-Browne, 'The French of England: The *Compileison*, *Ancrene Wisse*, and the Idea of Anglo-Norman', in *Cultural Traffic in the Medieval Romance World*: *Journal of Romance Studies* 4.3, special issue, ed. S. Gaunt and J. Weiss (winter 2004), 35–58; J. Wogan-Browne, '"Our Steward, St Jerome": Theology in the Anglo-Norman Household', in *Household, Women, and Christianity in Late Antiquity and the Middle Ages*, ed. A. Mulder-Bakker and J. Wogan-Browne (Turnhout, 2005), pp. 133–66.

[3] 'Explicit opus manuum mearum quod complevi. ego frater .A. subdiaconus. sancte Frideswide servientium minimus. anno verbi incarnati .m .cc .xii. mense .xi. Ebdomada .iiij. feria .vi. In vigilia sancti Andree apostolici, anno conversionis mee .vii°.' (Paris, MS BN fr. 24766, fol. 151vb/6–11). For the probability of the date's being actually 1213, see M. D. Legge, 'La date des écrits de Frère Angier', *Romania* 79 (1958), 512–14. Orengo accepts Legge's date for the *Dialogues* but not her conclusion that Angier made a second mistake in the inscription to his *Vie de saint Grégoire* (R. Orengo, 'Le Dialogue de Saint Grégoire le Grand traduit par Angier: Introduction et Edition' (unpublished thesis, Faculté des Lettres, Unversity of Zurich, 1969), pp. 30–1).

[4] The only edition is that of Orengo (n. 3 above). For a more accessible edition of Angier's 'accessus' i.e. his prologues, introductions, etc see T. Cloran, *The Dialogues of Gregory the Great translated into Anglo-Norman French by Angier* (Strasbourg, 1901). In addition to the inscriptions of Angier's authorship, there are many features of the manuscript which argue for its holograph status: the same hand copies all the elements mentioned in the introductory apparatus (the text, the inserted Latin chapter rubrics, their French translations in the *bas-de-page* and the notations of participants in the dialogue). In the main text, the ink of the Latin rubrics and their French translations changes its shade in tandem. Some guide letters remain faintly visible within subsequently painted and lightly flourished capitals, suggesting that Angier did not do these himself (though for the production of script and ornament by the same scribe in near-contemporary monastic practice, see J. G. G. Alexander, 'Scribes as Artists: The Arabesque Initial in Twelfth-Century English Manuscripts', in *Medieval Scribes, Manuscripts and Libraries: Essays Presented to N. R. Ker*, ed. M. B. Parkes and A. G. Watson (London, 1978), pp. 87–116). There are also some Latin marginal and *bas-de-page* notes and comments added by a subsequent reader, especially towards the end of the *Dialogues*. Otherwise everything in the manuscript seems the highly integrated production of a single writer. Moreover, as Orengo argues, traces of an initial medieval quire numbering ('iii' on fol. 32v, 'v' on fol. 48v *et seq.*) indicate that the first quire (into which the introductory material up

the subdeacon, the least of the servants of St Frideswide' (fol.151rb/8–9) and in the French text itself as 'the old sinner Angier, seven years young in the cloister' (fol. 151rb/1–2).[5]

Angier's work is of interest here for his creation of a vernacular *accessus* to the authority and spiritual benefits of the classic pastoral figure of Gregory the Great. *Accessus* is a term that has been used both strictly and loosely since Alastair Minnis highlighted its importance, and may embrace formal prologues describing the origins and procedures of a text, schematic guides to content such as chapter tables and manuscript layout and, more generally, levels and modes of access and the conception of access informing any text and its presentation.[6] In its vernacular incarnations, *accessus*, together with the intensified development of textual finding-aids in the thirteenth century so productively placed before us in the work of Richard and Mary Rouse, is sometimes conceptualized as a scholastic preoccupation which enters the vernacular by a process of 'trickle down'.[7] Angier's work suggests that developments of *accessus* and other forms of textual articulation are equally likely to take place on the manuscript page when clerical writers imagine and address their vernacular audiences, who may well, even at this early date, be conceived as readers as well as hearers.[8] Angier's desire to make textual

to the end of the table of chapters is carefully fitted, often in a more compressed version of the text hand) was added after the copying of the main text, rather than being copied first and directly continued on into the main text as would have happened if the extant manuscript were a copy rather than the holograph itself ('Le Dialogue', p. 11). The addition of the *Vie de saint Grégoire* two years after the main text in a new quire beginning at fol. 153r can also be better explained as the subsequent addition of the author, rather than as a copyist's treatment of the two texts (at the end of the *Dialogues*, the second half of fol. 151rb and its verso together with fol. 152 at the end of the final quire are left blank).

5   'Li vieil pecchierre Angier / De set anz ioeure onqors cloistrier', fol. 151rb/1–2) and see n. 3 above for the Latin colophon. For a reproduction of fols. 150v and 151r see P. Meyer, '*La Vie de saint Grégoire le Grand*, traduite du latin par Frère Angier, religieux de Sainte-Frideswide', *Romania* 12 (1883), 145–208 (between pp. 152 and 153). The name Angier may reflect an origin in Angers, France, and the language of the text shows continental traces from Anjou (M. K. Pope, *Étude sur la langue de Frère Angier* (Paris, 1904)). In quotations i/j and u/v are normalized, abbreviations silently expanded, and the usual grammatically disambiguating accents added, together with modern punctuation: quotation is by folio, column and line number from the manuscript (which allows for ease of reference to Cloran, who numbers lines by folio and column, not sequentially).

6   A. J. Minnis, *Medieval Literary Theory of Authorship: Scholastic Literary Attitudes in the Later Middle Ages* (Aldershot, 2nd edn, 1988). For the major types of late twelfth century academic prologues, see pp. 15–25 and for prologues to holy writings, pp. 46–63.

7   R. H. and M. A. Rouse, *Preachers, Florilegia and Sermons: Studies on the* Manipulus florum *of Thomas of Ireland* (Toronto, 1979), pp. 1–42, who point out vernacular uses of such aids by de Pizan and Chaucer, pp. 213–16.

8   The classic study of thirteenth-century reading is B. Millett, 'Women in No Man's

access, and not just textual content, vernacular – to put *accessus,* as he says, *'en rumanz'* and so allow audiences to find their own pathways through texts – informs every aspect of the manuscript realization of his composition. It also prompts his extended authorial meditation on the relation between clerical providers and the audiences to whom the reading choices made possible through *prolegomena* and finding aids are opened up.

This concern with aiding the reader's access is sustained throughout Angier's presentation of the *Dialogues.* In his prologue to the final book, for example, Angier reminds his audience that just as it was in 'the first prologue at the head of the first *Dialogue*' ['al premier prologe / Al chief del premier dialoge', fol. 108vb/21–2], the inspiration of his work in this last book remains St Gregory himself and the common good ['lu commun prou', fol. 108vb/10]. That is why, Angier reiterates, he wants to serve, through his French reworking, an audience of readers and hearers ['les litrés e les auditours'] who cannot follow the work without help (fol. 109ra/2). The most immediately striking feature at the beginning of Angier's text is his extensive provision of prolegomena to the *Dialogues* as a whole (see Table 4.1) as also to their four individual books. He also includes an initial table of chapter titles for the entire *Dialogues* (fols. 3v–8r, Latin with accompanying French translations) and, between the *Dialogues'* internal divisions into books, adds two substantial digressions, one on the value of rhetoric and Horace's 'utility versus pleasure' distinction at the end of Book I (fol. 32v) and one on the merits of prose and verse at the end of Book II (fol. 61v). So thoroughly is the work introduced and discussed that it does not seem too much to say that an entire vernacular poetics of introduction and access is created by Angier around his translation of the *Dialogues.*[9]

A preoccupation with explicitness, articulation of structure, and accessibility would be compatible with the instruction of novices or the provision of vernacular *pastoralia* for the use of Augustinian priests (something Angier himself later became).[10] A slightly earlier Augustinian holograph, the *Ormulum,* probably composed in the Arrouaisian Augustinian house at Bourne in Lincolnshire, has been argued to serve just such purposes: in Orm's case a specially developed orthographic system accompanied by various kinds of marking-up may have been devised to help francophone canons preach from an English text to anglophone audiences.[11] Nothing

Land: English Recluses and the Development of Vernacular Literature in the Twelfth and Thirteenth Centuries', in *Women and Literature,* pp. 86–103.

[9] Even the addition of the *Vie de saint Grégoire* (fols. 153ra–174ra) could be thought of as commentary on the *Dialogues.* For the text, see Meyer, *'La Vie de saint Grégoire le Grand'.*

[10] Angier's explicit to the *Vie de saint Grégoire* is dated to 'conversionis mee anno .ix°. sacerdocii .ii°.' (fol. 174ra), see Meyer, *'La Vie de saint Grégoire le Grand',* p. 192.

[11] See M. Worley, 'Using the *Ormulum* to Redefine Vernacularity', in *The Vulgar Tongue: Medieval and Post-Medieval Vernacularity,* ed. F. Somerset and N. Watson

TABLE 4.1: ANGIER, *LES DIALOGUES DE SAINT GRÉGOIRE*:
PARIS MS BN FR. 24766

First quire
[fol. 1 largely cut away, but on its stub remains part of a hymn (*Ave Maria* in red)].
1   fol. 2r **Invocatio** [*Veni creator*: Latin stanzas alternated with French translations; alternating red and blue capitals, slightly smaller script, fitted into the page]
2   fol. 2v **Oratio ad Trinitatem** [*Beau sire deuz. rois glorious autisme* 'Fair lord God, glorious and highest king': French stanzaic verse; slightly smaller script to fit the page]
3   fol. 3r **Incipit introductio in librum sequentem** [*Quiqe tu soies. lais. ou clerz.* 'whoever you are, layperson or cleric': French rhyming couplets]
4   fols. 3v–8r **Capitula**: Latin and French in alternate columns, red chapter numbers (left for Latin, right for French) and alternating red and blue capitals.
[fol. 8v blank]

Second quire
5   fol. 9r–10v **Incipit prefatio Fratris A. in Librum Dialogorum** [*Qui autre en droite voie ameine*: 'Whoever wants to lead another into the right path …': French rhyming couplets]

excludes Angier's *Dialogues* from comparable uses as a text designed to help fellow clergy in pastoral work (though in Angier's francophone case the potential multilingualism of Orm's text is absent).[12] But Angier explicitly envisages a lay as well as a religious audience, and persistently provides for all his audiences both as hearers *and* readers. The *Dialogues* address them-

(University Park PA, 2003), pp. 9–30. It is possible, though purely speculative, that Angier was aware of the pre-Conquest tradition of vernacular access to Gregory. Among the extant witnesses to the Old English translation of Gregory's *Dialogues*, two eleventh-century manuscripts, London BL MS Cotton Otho C i, vol ii and Oxford, Bodleian Library MS Hatton 76 were glossed by the Worcester scribe known as the Tremulous Hand in the early thirteenth century: see Ker, *Catalogue Containing Anglo-Saxon*, nos. 182 and 328. In the Hatton MS a French inscription of the late twelfth or early thirteenth century occurs beside the manuscript's text of the ps.-Apuleian *Herbarius* (fol. 74r): see further Franzen, *Tremulous Hand*, p. 69. For an excellent recent study of francophone clerical interest in Old English, see J. Frankis, 'Languages and Cultures in Contact: Vernacular Lives of St Giles and Anglo-Norman Annotations in an Anglo-Saxon Manuscript', *Leeds Studies in English* 38 (2007), 101–33.
12   The Augustinians, like the Benedictines, used French alongside Latin within their cloisters: see further M. Richter, *Sprache und Gesellschaft im Mittelalter* (Stuttgart, 1979), pp. 148–57 (esp. pp. 149–50), also pp. 78–94. For monastic *regulae* in French, see Dean and Boulton, *Anglo-Norman Literature*, nos 710–15, and for an Anglo-Norman rule in use at Leicester (one of the largest Augustinian houses), see T. Hunt, 'An Anglo-Norman Rule of St Augustine', *Augustiana* 45 (1995), 177–89 (a trilingual manuscript, see p. 179). Ralph Hanna notes that the Augustinians were forbidden English conversation and enjoined to use French and Latin as late as their statutes of 1325 and 1334 (R. Hanna, *London Literature 1300–1380* (Cambridge, 2005), pp. 159–60 and 213, n. 13).

selves from the beginning to 'lais ou clerz' (*Introductio*, fol. 3ra/1), and their inscribed audience is saluted as 'seingnors e dames, laie gent' (*Prefatio*, fol. 9vb/26).[13] Angier's work may not have been intended for mediation to lay audiences solely through readings by clerics, but also as an example of text layout suitable for patrons' own copies (especially if, as discussed below, St Frideswide's ran a scriptorium specializing in vernacular texts). In his *Prefatio* (no. 5 in Table 4.1 above) Angier lays out something like a proto-scholastic *accessus* in the vernacular. He describes (i) his work's origins ['charité me fait commencer', fol. 9vb/30]; (ii) its purpose ['nostre commun profit', fol. 9vb/34]; (iii) its author (Gregory, fol. 10ra/21); (iv) the author's authority (the Holy Spirit, fol. 10ra/17); and also (v) explains the work's name and mode of proceeding (fol. 10ra/28–36). His terms are not as formalized as scholastic *accessūs* (including those offered to lay readers in the vernacular) would later become, with their fully developed 'Aristotelian' causes for composition (formal, efficient, material and final) as used in the later thirteenth century.[14] On the other hand, they are not as formidable as the terms offered in the mid-twelfth century to Lady Aëliz de Cundé by her chaplain Sansun de Nanteuil

---

13 Since the address to 'seingnors et dames' is in the *Prefatio* on fol. 9v, near the beginning of the first quire of the main text, and the address to 'lais ou clerz' is on fol. 3r in the subsequently added introductory quire, a lay audience was envisioned as one possible audience throughout. On the controversy as to how far Augustinian canons were monastic and how far involved in pastoral care, see J. C. Dickinson, *The Origins of the Austin Canons and their Introduction into England* (London, 1950), pp. 224–41 and for a summary of recent scholarship, A. D. Fizzard, *Plympton Priory: A House of Augustinian Canons in South-Western England in the Late Middle Ages* (Leiden, 2008), pp. 5–7, and 63–4. The very fact that Angier and Orm in their holographs seem to be working out systems for wider use testifies to the importance to them of preaching and the reception of doctrine. The dates of their manuscripts (1170–80 and 1213–16 respectively) contrast with an earlier exposition of the Augustinian rule dated to 1141, which seems purely monastic in its specification of 'reading, expounding, and preaching the Word of God before the brethren, and practising for divine worship by reading as well as singing' ['Uerbum Dei coram fratribus legere, exponere, predicare, ministeriumque diuinum tam legendo quam canendo preuidere'] and 'preparing parchments for the scribes, writing, illuminating, ruling lines, scoring music, correcting and binding books' ['pergamenam scriptoribus preparare, libros scribere, illuminare, regulare, notare, emendare, atque ligare'] (*The Bridlington Dialogue*, ed and tr. by a Religious of CSMV (London, 1960), pp. 154, 154a). By the late twelfth century, given the increased involvement of canons in towns (see n. 19 below), the situation may have been very different.

14 On 'Aristotelian' prologues, see Minnis, *Medieval Literary Theory of Authorship*, pp. 28–32, 82–84. For an Aristotelian five-fold scheme of author, title, subject matter, form and purpose composed in 1267, see *La Lumere as lais* I, ed. G. Hesketh, ANTS 54–5 (London, 1996), vv. 531–614 (the Prologue is edited (from a nunnery manuscript not used by Hesketh) and translated by C. Hume in *The French of England: Vernacular Literary Theory and Practice, c. 1100–1500*, ed. J. Wogan-Browne, T. Fenster, D. W. Russell, forthcoming). See also H. E. Allen, 'The *Manuel des pechiez* and the Scholastic Prologue', *Romantic Review* 8 (1917), 434–62.

in his commentary for her on the *Proverbes de Salemon*. In Sansun's commentary, words such as 'ethimologie' and 'entituler' sprinkle the Prologue and the Argumentum, and a division of classical and divine genres of writing is laid out, together with an account of the linguistic transmission of the Bible. This learned framing of the text is partly offered in tribute to the patroness's prestige but also suggests the indispensability of her chaplain. Far from equipping his audience for their own reading as Angier does, Sansun presents the learned clerk as an intimate of an elite household: the most authoritative presence in his prologue's account of Biblical textual tradition is St Jerome, envisaged both as a steward serving spiritual bread and as a jewel-keeper polishing pearls for a noble magnate.[15]

Angier by contrast wants access for an inclusive and varied group of readers or hearers. He offers the *Dialogues* as a compendium of everything the reader, whether *'lais ou clerz'*, needs *or desires* for salvation:

> Car sans labor e sanz delai,
> Quanq'as mestier t'enseingnerai:
> Icest livre present lirras
> Ou trovras quanqe desirras
> De sens, de mours, e de vertu,
> Od quanq'apent a ta salu. (*Introductio*, fol. 3ra/7–12)

> [... for without trouble and delay I will teach you whatever you need. You will read this present book where you will find whatever you desire in the way of wisdom, moral behaviour and virtue, together with whatever is relevant to your salvation.]

At the same time, the *Dialogues* and their manuscript are to be entered upon with quasi-liturgical solemnity and careful, ritualized preparation: the *Introductio* is prefaced (see Table 4.1 above) by the invocation of the *Veni creator* hymn in French (fol. 2r) and by the French and Latin verse *oratio* to the Trinity (fol. 2v). In this, Angier is like those other monastic narrators, the Prioress and the Second Nun in Chaucer's *Canterbury Tales*, whose invocations and devotions so carefully conduct their audience to their tales. But even more than the Prioress's prayer or St Cecilia's 'bisynesse', Angier's *Introductio*, with its care to explain the value of his table of chapters, emphasizes concern with the disposition of time on his audiences' part (fols. 3v–8r). He offers, in effect, a vernacular exegesis of the textual and spiritual importance of *ordinatio*:

> E si seit qe n'aies laisir
> De lu parlire ou paroïr,
> Cest conseil feras soulement
> Si l[e] savras tot a ton talent.

---

15 *Les Proverbes de Salemon, by Sanson de Nanteuil*, I, ed. C. Isoz, ANTS 45 (London, 1988), vv. 101–90. See also Wogan-Browne, '"Our Steward, St Jerome"', pp. 139–44.

Des presenz chapitres notez,
Si com en ordre sont nombrez,
Quelqe tu voudras eslirras
E pues el livre lu querras.
Pues quant lu chapitre esleu
Avras parlit e entendu -
Si bien te siet e il te plaise
E ensemble as loisir e aise -,
Tot en meisme la maniere
Un autre chapitre regiere
[fol. 3rb]   Porras eslire e porvoier,
Dont ton quer puesses apaier.
Einsi trovras legierement
Sanz tei grever tot prestement
Quanqe te plaist oïr ou lire,
Quel ore tis quers lu desire.
    E si tis sens tant par est durs
Qe li latins lui seit oscurs,
En romanz en la marge escrit
Trovras quei li chapitre dit.
Einsi q'apertement verras
Tot mot a mot e pas por pas
Quanqe tu querz, sanz destorber,
A ton cors e t'alme sauver.

(Introductio, fol. 3ra/21–35b, fol. 3rb/1–13)

[And if it should happen that you do not have leisure to read or hear it all the way through, you have only to take this advice, and you will know it all according to your desire. From among the chapters noted, numbered in order as they are, you will choose whichever you wish and then seek it in the book. Then when you have thoroughly read and understood the chosen chapter – as it suits and pleases you and if you have both leisure and ease –, just so in the same way you will be able again to choose and examine another chapter with which you can delight your heart. Thus you will easily find ready to hand and without wearying yourself whatever it pleases you to read or hear, at whatever hour your heart desires it.

And if your intellect is so obdurate that it finds Latin unclear, you will find written in the margin in the vernacular what the chapter says, so that you can clearly see word by word and step by step and without hindrance whatever you seek to save your body and soul.]

For Angier, then, everyone must be able to find what they need according to their own determination and structuring of their reading time.[16] The audi-

---

[16] Although *Introductio*, fol. 3rb/6–9 (quoted above) sounds very like a reproach

ences who are here shown the user-value of textual *ordinatio* are not conceived of as dependent on what a reader may select for the content to which they have access, but as audiences who are *expected to wish to choose for themselves*. In this context, the business of textual navigation becomes imbricated, as reading had always been in the monastic day, with the deeply serious issue of the audience's organization of their time between active and contemplative living. Rather than any more modern sense of 'leisure reading', *'laisir'* (v. 32 above) is monastically inflected *otium*, conceived within a salvific use of time. It matters that readers can pursue particular chapters and themes according to their needs and spiritual programmes, with and without direct pastoral guidance, and irrespective of the specific mode of reading employed (a novice, a priest or clerk studying for themselves or mediating the *Dialogues*

to monastic novices, it cannot, given the preceding address to 'lais ou clerz' (fol. 3ra/1), represent the only audience for this table of chapters. The table is very carefully designed and written: over fols. 3v–8r, the Latin is regularly in col. a, the vernacular in col. b; there is a new line and number for each chapter, Latin and French are kept as closely equivalent as possible on the page, and highlighted with alternating red and blue capitals. Moreover, the table covers all four books of the *Dialogues*. Even the briefest sampling of precedent layouts suggests that this not an automatic or regular development. In the case of two twelfth-century Latin manuscripts of the *Dialogues* from Exeter Cathedral, for example, Oxford, Bodleian Library, MS Bodley 230 gives the *capitula* at the start of each of the first three books (fol. 1r, 21r, 42v–43v), but not at the beginning of Book Four, fol. 75r. (This last book is not rubricated into chapters, but presented as a continuous treatise, though still with Gregory and Peter's names marked, suggesting that unless, as with Books One to Three of the *Dialogues*, material is very obviously structured as separate *vitae* and anecdotes, *capitula* were by no means standard. Or a *capitula* table may simply have been lacking in the examplar.) In MS Bodley 190, on the other hand, there are no *capitula* for Book One, but *capitula* for Books Two to Four (fols. 26v–27r, 53r–v, 94r), set out with several chapters to a line rather than in list form. In the thirteenth century no one pattern seems to have been standard and Angier's layout remains outstandingly careful, clear, and helpful: compare for instance, Bodleian MS Auct. D 2. 7 (s. xiii), where the *Dialogues* are introduced by a prose invocation of the Trinity and an exchange between Gregory and Peter the Deacon, followed by *capitula* treated as running prose in the text block and distinguished only by small red capitals (fols. 117r–118r). Although Gregory and Peter continue to be distinguished in red and blue and rubrics given for chapters, the chapter numbering within the rubrics quickly becomes incorrect and then ceases. In this manuscript, the *Regula* or *Cura Pastoralis*, another potential influence on layout, is without initial *capitula* (fol. 185r). A much more careful manuscript, MS Bodley 116 (s. xiii), where the *Cura Pastoralis* is bookmarked, has its initial *capitula* distinguished by red and green capitals and set within continuous prose with red and blue roman numbers in the outer margins (fols. 1r–2r), with the chapter numbering maintained throughout the text. In MS Bodley 534 (s. xiii), a *capitula* table is present for the *Cura Pastoralis* but again written as continuous prose within the text block (fol. 21r). (These manuscripts are all among those discussed and provenanced by N. R. Ker, 'Thomas James's Collation of Gregory, Cyprian, and Ambrose', *Bodleian Library Record* 4 (1953), 16–30, see p. 24, nos. 7, 8, 9, 12.)

to those under spiritual direction; a layman or woman hearing their priest or clerk or reading for themselves, etc.). In the performative reading demanded by the work of salvation, being able to turn to the needed chapter at will is no merely pragmatic convenience, but as essential for lay audiences as it is for religious.

In addition to the table of chapters, this intense awareness of the reading process is supplemented by care about the manuscript page and its hierarchies for these newly independent readers:

> me plout
> De totes les vertuz les titres
> Destincter par divers chapitres,
> E nis le nom de la persone
> – La ou l'une l'autre araisone –
> De diverses colours noter:
> Car tost porreit li litré errer
> S'il n'eust sein qui li moustrast
> Quoi de quoi qui vers qui parlast.   (*Prefatio*, fol. 10rb/13–21)

> [... it has pleased me to pick out the titles of all the miracles in the different chapters and even to note in different colours the name of each person where he speaks to the other. For the reader could too easily go wrong if he did not have a sign that would show him anything about what is being said by whom against whom.]

When reading may be independent of a chaplain or other cleric, it is especially important that questions, objections and *correct* answers are clearly and unambiguously *readable* as well as audible, and the speaking personae of the *Dialogues* are indeed carefully marked up in the text with marginal indications to show whether Gregory or his deacon and interlocutor Peter speaks. So too, as earlier promised in the *Introductio*, the reader finds the Latin chapter rubrics translated into the vernacular in the margin ('en romanz en la marge escrit', fol. 3rb/8, quoted above), and immediately visible and legible in their separateness and red ink as a vernacular finding device.[17] Everything

---

[17] The translated rubrics begin on fol. 16r with the translation of Book I, ch. 6 (only Latin rubrics are given on fols. 11r–15v for Book I, chs. 1–5). Since the promise that they will be translated is made in the *Introductio* on fol. 3r, this is further confirmation of the arguments for the manuscript's holograph status discussed in n. 4 above, in particular that the first quire with its introductory materials was added later into the manuscript than the main text. The subsequent provision of the introductory first quire and of *in situ* French translations of chapter rubrics in the main text must be the fruit of continuing thought on how best to provide for the work's audiences. In addition (a feature on which all scholars have so far commented but none have been able to explain), the verse lines of the *Dialogues* are almost all marked with up to four light accents per line in red (as opposed to black accents distinguishing the letter *i* from other minim strokes, which also occur). I initially speculated that

possible is done to make the text searchable and usable by readers, who, in consequence of this very concern, have to be entrusted with the exercise of their own choice and discretion in what they do with these holy writings. Angier himself points out that lay choices may be spiritually safer than clerical: one of his images for clerical and lay knowledge is a comparison of the elephant and the lamb as swimmers in the river of Holy Scripture. When tempted to use his greater power to dive down further into specialist knowledge, the elephant can drown (in heresy) where the lamb gets safely through (*Digressio* II, fol. 63ra/20–34 to fol. 63rb/1–5).

The particular lambs with whom Angier may have had a pastoral relation are not known, but as subdeacon and priest, Angier's duties must have taken him from his priory into the town at whose heart it was situated. The priory of St Frideswide had the advowsons of seven parish churches in central Oxford as well as a number of outlying ones: they also had the right to an annual fair in Oxford.[18] They seem to have been more pastorally and less university-oriented than their neighbours, the Augustinian canons of Oseney Abbey.[19] The St Frideswide canons are generally thought to have had only one author, Robert of Cricklade, prior from *c.* 1141–75, who composed commentaries, a *Speculum fidei*, and accounts of St Frideswide and Becket.[20] But the canons may have been more active in *vernacular* literary production.[21] If Wathelet-

---

these might be indications for the reading of the lines (given that at this date even individual reading is as likely to be aloud as silent and will still involve forming the syllables with the mouth), a form of guidance to the greater influence of stress in the francophone couplet in a partly anglophone context. After further inspection of the manuscript, the accent marks now seem to me to fit better with the progress of a corrector of the text rather than as indications for reading the lines. Moreover, since the other features of the manuscript's layout are mentioned in the introductory materials, Angier's omission of any comment on these red accents probably indicates that they are to be seen as marks of text-checking, not as an aid to the reading of the text.

18 VCH, *Oxford* II (1907), p. 99.

19 Augustinian priories were extensively patronized by royalty and court administrators early in the twelfth century (Dickinson, *The Origins of the Austin Canons*, pp. 125–30), but by the late twelfth century were the objects of anti-monastic satire, alongside their rivals the Benedictines: see D. Postles, 'The Austin Canons in English Towns, *c.* 1100–1350', *Historical Research* 66 (1993), 1–20.

20 Robert's successor Prior Phillip wrote an account of the 1180 *translatio* of St Frideswide, but nothing else is known: Sharpe, *Handlist*, pp. 437 (Philip); 532–3 (Robert of Cricklade). At least thirty manuscripts are extant from Oseney: D. Postles, 'The Learning of the Austin Canons: The Case of Oseney Abbey', *Nottingham Medieval Studies* 29 (1985), 32–43 (p. 37); T. Webber and A. G. Watson, *The Libraries of the Augustinian Canons,* Corpus of British Medieval Library Catalogues 6 (London, 1998), pp. 403–5.

21 On canons and vernacular literature see J.-P. Pouzet, 'Quelques aspects de l'influence des chanoines augustins sur la production et la transmission littéraire vernaculaire en Angleterre (XIIIe–XVe siècles)', *Comptes Rendus de l'Académie des Inscriptions & Belles-lettres*, I (2004), pp. 169–213.

Willelm and Walpole are right in identifying Angier's manuscript and three constituent booklets from the 'Edwardes' manuscript as from the same scriptorium, St Frideswide's was producing a romance (the oldest extant text of *Gui de Warewic*, BL Addit. 38662); a chronicle (the continental version of the *Pseudo-Turpin Chronicle* patronized by Renaud de Beaujeu, BL Addit. 40142); and a *chanson de geste* (the *Chanson de Willelm*, BL Addit. 38663) in the early thirteenth century.[22] The patrons of *Gui de Warewic* may be associated with the d'Oilly family of nearby Wallingford castle (who were the founding family of Oseney Abbey), but St Frideswide's *chanson de geste* production need not have been exclusively for secular audiences. It was not unusual for monastic houses to own copies of such works: they are too strongly associated with historiography to be an inappropriate presence in either baronial or religious households.[23] Angier opposes reading Gregory's text to reading or hearing *chansons de geste*: the *Dialogues* are not to be less dear to the audience than Roland and Olivier (fol. 10ra/9–10), in the way that 'les fables d'Artur de Bretaigne / E les chançons de Charlemagne' (fol. 9va/29–30) are more cherished than the Gospels. These are standard *topoi* illustrative of overlap rather than separation in the texts of lay and clerical audiences: for the socio-economically privileged, francophone reading is as much a shared as a differentiating literary culture, and was well established, as Geoff Rector has shown, in the substantial corpus of insular francophone psalters of the

---

[22] J. Wathelet-Willem, *Recherches sur la* Chanson de Guillaume (Paris, 1975), I, 46–9: R. N. Walpole, *The Old French Johannes Translation of the* Pseudo-Turpin Chronicle: *A Supplement* (Berkeley, 1976), p. 169. The manuscripts' painted capitals are the same across the four texts: the flourishing varies as to the proportion of green as against red and blue but is in the same English earlier thirteenth century style found in a number of Augustinian and Benedictine scriptoria (I am grateful for the opportunity to use D. M. Callard's hand-painted typology of capitals in the Bodleian Library on this point: see on this resource Alexander, 'Scribes as Artists', p. 90). The hands are very similar (though Angier has an extra stroke upwards from the lower chamber of his 'g' where the other three close it more tightly and the bowl is more compressed). Ink, aspect, layout (allowing for differences appropriate to rhyming couplets, *laisses*, prose) are also similar, though among the three pieces of secular literature, no text is marked-up for access in the manner of the *Dialogues*.

[23] See H. Blurton, 'From *Chanson de geste* to Magna Carta: Genre and the Barons in Matthew Paris's *Chronica majora*', *New Medieval Literatures* 9 (2007), 117–38. On the Oseney Augustinians and *chanson de geste*, see Andrew Taylor, 'Can an Englishman Read a *Chanson de Geste*?' in *Conceptualizing Multilingualism in Medieval Britain to 1250*, ed. E. Tyler, Studies in the Early Middle Ages (Turnhout, forthcoming). I am grateful to Dr Taylor for a pre-publication copy of this essay. It is worth remembering that the earliest manuscript of the *Chanson de Roland* was bequeathed to Osney Abbey as late as the early fourteenth century: see A. Taylor, *Textual Situations: Three Medieval Manuscripts and their Readers* (Philadelphia, 2002), pp. 3–4, 56–7, 59.

twelfth century.[24] Like other Augustinian canons, Angier must have been familiar to some extent with vernacular literature and its patrons and audiences, especially given his order's early pastoral engagement with the elite as well as with humbler ranks.

In the *Dialogues*, consideration of audience includes extensive articulation of Angier's own role as provider of access. His two substantial digressions on the role of rhetoric and the respective merits of verse and prose (p. 65 above) are perhaps the most immediately striking fruits of this concern, and deserve separate study for what they reveal of the developing role of the author in this period. But equally noteworthy is Angier's meditation on his role and responsibility in relation to his audiences under the rule of charity (the opening precept of the Augustinian rule). Playing on 'proe' (profit, advantage, merit, virtue), 'profite' (benefit, advantage) and 'proesme' (neighbour), Angier reviews his own occupation and its place in the spiritual economy:

> Qui autrui voelt edefier
> Soi meisme entent heriter,
> Car qui a autre en bien profite,
> Molt li rent Deu bien sa merite.
> … Donc est li proeu tot asez mien
> Quanq'a mon proesme faz de bien,
> E d'autre part moie est la perte;
> Si mal li faz sanz sa deserte.   (*Prefatio*, fol. 9ra/13–16, 21–4)

> [Whoever wants to edify other people inherits his own intention, for God well repays the merit of any who enables others to profit in goodness … thus the benefit is all mine when I do good to my neighbour and on the other hand the loss is mine if I do him harm without his deserving it.]

Angier will subsequently argue that, beyond the corporal acts of mercy, the most important occupation under the regime of charity is that of drawing the sinner away from sin and reconciling him with his creator (fol. 9vb/24–5). But first he brings a new inflection to this pastoral relation by making the translator-cleric the good merchant to the soul and pondering his intellectual and spiritual capital:

> Hoem qui est sage marcheant
> Son avoir craest en despendant,
> Car quant plus despent en son proeu
> Plus li est sis avoir croeu;
> E hoem qui bien e largement
> Son sen e son savoir despent

---

24 G. Rector, '*En sa chambre sovent le lit: Otium* and the Pedagogical Sociabilities of Early *Romanz* Literature (*ca.* 1100–1150)' (forthcoming).

Plus li craest e plus i gaaingne,
Car miez le set quant plus l'enseingne.
Avoir souz terre empire tost
E sens s'en fuit s'il est rebost;
Avoir, quant l'en le baille, amende,
E savoir voeit qu'om le despende.
Avoir, quant est perdu, revient
E sens perist s'oem trop le tient:
Donc est li sens miez retenuz
Quant largement est despenduz.   (*Prefatio*, fol. 9rb/1–16)

[A man who is a wise merchant increases his wealth in spending it, for when he spends more to his profit, his wealth has grown greater for him; and a man who well and generously expends his wisdom and his knowledge increases it and wins more, for he knows it better the more he teaches it. Wealth in the ground quickly depreciates and wisdom goes away if it is left to rest; wealth, when one uses it, increases, and wisdom demands that one expend it. Wealth, when it is lost, comes again, and wisdom perishes if one withholds it too much: so wisdom is better retained when it is freely expended.]

The merchants are not simply a literal reflection of Angier's life in a busy market and university town. Discourses we tend to image by specific social estates – merchants for counting, knights for fighting – do not necessarily have one to one correspondence with these social classes. Parallels between wealth and wisdom draw on a long Solomonic tradition.[25] In comparing their respective ways of multiplying, Angier is chiefly preoccupied with the modes of reproduction for the spiritual capital of grace, and with a lengthy argument that grace does not expend itself, but rather is reproduced and increased through circulation. Angier's mercantile figure for clerical–lay translation is part of an increased preoccupation with enumeration and taxonomy (itself given long-established authority by Gregory's attention to diversity in his *Regula pastoralis*):[26]

Mais marcheanz sont molt divers:
Li uns est francs, li autre sers,

---

[25] See II Chron. 1. 10–12, also Eccles. 7. 11–12, Prov. 8. 20–21, and J. Nelson, 'Wealth and Wisdom: The Politics of Alfred the Great', in *Kings and Kingship*, ed. J. Rosenthal (Albany NY, 1984), pp. 31–52 (pp. 34–7). For some later developments, see J. Kaye, 'Money and Administrative Calculation as Reflected in Scholastic Natural Philosophy', in *Arts of Calculation: Quantifying Thought in Early Modern Europe*, ed. D. Gimp and M. R. Warren (New York, 2004), pp. 1–18.

[26] Over thirty subdivisions of the preacher's audience (by gender, age, occupation, type of sin, etc.) are treated by Gregory in his *Regula pastoralis*, cap. 23–59 (Grégoire le grand, *Règle Pastorale*, ed. B. Judic, Sources Chrétiennes 381 (Paris, 1992), pp. 116–20).

Li uns dedenz, l'autre dehors,
Li uns del alme, l'autre del cors,
Li uns fait tresor temporal,
E li autre celestial;
A l'un est sis tresor durable;
A l'autre veins e feible e lable.
Qui vent le pis por le meillour
Molt par est donc fel tricheour,
Car molt est plein de tricherie
Qui por lanterne vent vessie;
E cil rest trop fol marcheant
Qui a son oes le meins vaillant
Eslit, car molt est nice e vain
Qui prent la paille e laist le grain.   (*Prefatio*, fol. 9va/1–16).

[But merchants are very varied: some are generous, others close-fisted, some work indoors, others outdoors, some are merchants of the soul, others of the body, some create temporal wealth, and others heavenly: one has enduring treasure, and another's is vain, weak and transitory. For this reason anyone who sells the worse for the better is a great deceiver, for someone who sells a bladder for a lantern is full of trickery; and someone who chooses what is worth less for his profit is a crazy merchant, for anyone who takes the chaff and leaves the grain is extremely foolish and soft-headed.]

The intensified late twelfth and early thirteenth century perception of *ordo*, occupation and estate is in part a newly alert perception of varied audiences and in part a new perception of the power of quantification and taxonomy. As Thomas Lentes remarks of the high Middle Ages, 'a veritable arithmetic of salvation incorporated ever broader groups of the faithful and became more firmly entrenched as the written word gained in significance'.[27] When Angier uses occupational figures other than the merchant for the work of the translator, such as the soul-physician, for instance, he again stresses the physician's variety of clients and treatments and enumerates a whole taxonomy of cure. Regions, patients, temperaments and treatments vary, so that a physician must make his mixtures for various temperaments: the English and the Normans are different in their natures, and what cures one will kill the other ('faire ses confections / As diverses complexions … Li englois e li normant/

---

27 T. Lentes, 'Counting Piety in the Late Middle Ages', in *Ordering Medieval Society: Perspectives on Intellectual and Practical Modes of Shaping Social Relations*, ed. B. Jussen, tr. P. Selwyn (Philadelphia, 2001), pp. 55–91; on the heuristic status of estates schemes, see O. G. Oexle, 'Perceiving Social Reality in the Early and High Middle Ages', *loc. cit*, pp. 92–143 (esp. pp. 117–19); on attitudes to merchant's practices, O. Langholm, *Merchants and the Confessional: Trade and Price in the Pre-Reformation Penitential Handbooks* (Leiden, 2003), esp. chs. 1 and 14.

Sont de diverse qualité' [*Prefatio* to Bk II, fol. 62va/10–11, 17–18]). Angier moves between traditional exegetical metaphor (as also in the case of the merchant selecting grain from chaff, quoted above) and its newly intensified realization in the particularities and diversities of occupational identity.

The merchants, then, arrive in Angier's prologue not so much as a response to social change, but as part of his pastoral awareness of textual communities as occupationally diverse and his complementary awareness of his audience's need for a more explicit and self-determined calculus of how to spend their reading time. Angier's meditation on whether learning ('wisdom') is to be shared seems entirely appropriate to the potentially conflicting Augustinian emphases on monasticism *and* pastoral mission and also to the church's wider anxieties about outreach at the time of the Fourth Lateran Council. Whether doctrinal wisdom and institutional knowledge is diluted or multiplied if made accessible was a real question: Angier demonstrates the productive mixture of anxiety and control with which clerisy responded to the demands of vernacular readers. His bravura performance of access in all the dimensions of *accessus* – text and its introduction and manuscript layout – suggests how strongly lay needs and audiences influenced the clerical culture of which lay people were important patrons. Like his greater contemporary, the writer of *Ancrene Wisse*, Angier also shows that the clergy was prepared to respond and innovate in meeting lay demand, creating new roles and figures for its own authorial positions in tandem with freshly imagining its audiences.

5

Lambeth Palace Library, MS 487: Some Problems of Early Thirteenth-century Textual Transmission

Ralph Hanna

Among her many important contributions, our honorand has recently reminded us of the cultural importance of Lambeth Palace Library, MS 487.[1] Although its texts have been available since the early years of the Early English Text Society (see n. 5), this volume, mainly composed of homilies, has been long neglected. Here, I want to extend Bella Millett's findings and to argue that, beyond its innovative homiletic techniques, the book offers some broader purchase on the circulation of English texts in the earlier thirteenth century.

Although the shape and contents of the Lambeth manuscript should be well known, I will begin with a description. Although generally accurate, the great M. R. James's Lambeth catalogue did not examine or report the volume with the care customary in many of his descriptions. As my discussion will show, he was particularly inattentive to the contents, most especially those in Old English, and to the collation (as will emerge below, an important feature in assessing the volume). While many of these deficiencies have been remedied in Jonathan Wilcox's recent description, Wilcox is dedicated to explaining Old English items and scants the Middle English. There is a need both to consolidate and to dynamize the production information to be derived from the manuscript.[2]

---

1 Bella Millett, 'The Discontinuity of English Prose: Structural Innovation in the Lambeth and Trinity Homilies', in *Text and Language in Medieval English Prose: A Festschrift for Tadao Kubouchi*, ed. J. Fisiak et al. (Frankfurt, 2005), 129–50; and 'The Pastoral Context of the Lambeth and Trinity Homilies', in Scase, *Manuscript Geography*, pp. 43–64.

2 See M. R. James and C. Jenkins, *A Descriptive Catalogue of the Manuscripts in the Library of Lambeth Palace*, 5 parts (Cambridge, 1930–32), pp. 673–6. James is, generally speaking, accurate in indicating incipits, explicits, and the extent of the texts, although the report is flawed by a number of minor mistranscriptions. The presentation looks as if the material has been taken directly from James's rough notes, not a finished copy. Perhaps because both of his initial speed in moving through the collection and of a fifteen-year hiatus between research and publication, James

Lambeth 487 is on vellum, the manuscript proper 68 folios (numbered fols. 1–67, but fol. 1 followed by fol. 1a). It is, like many of its contemporaries, a small book, overall 180 mm x 120 mm, the current pages now *c.* 130 mm wide but virtually all with modern vellum repair strips pasted to the original edges. Some prickings survive, under the vellum repairs, and all pages are bounded and ruled, generally all the way across the sheet, in brown crayon. The writing area, always above top-line, varies; it is usually a narrow single column, 145 or 155 mm x 80 mm, in 27 to 29 lines to the page.

The original manuscript is written in very early textura; the hand responsible for items 1–18 is fairly similar to that of the later added text 19, although that is smaller and more tightly spaced. A loose note in the back of the book, signed 'J. P. G[ilson]' and dated 1923, says only a broad dating 1185–1225 is possible. This is generally true, the earlier date provided by the appearance of biting (regular in the sequence -*de*-, many touching curved strokes in similar contexts) and the later by universal writing above top-line.

More precise opinions have been offered, and vary. Malcolm Parkes reminds me that Humphrey Wanley declared the book 'Temp. Ricardi I'. Similarly, N. R. Ker indicated in print that the book might predate 1200, and was more emphatic in correspondence reported in Sarah M. O'Brien's unpublished Oxford DPhil thesis. James says merely 'Cent. xiii early'. Wanley reproduced the hand twice, its only published appearance until Wilcox's recent facsimile.[3] The first of his copies is considerably less descriptive of the hand than the second, and Malcolm Parkes suggests to me that Wanley had in fact carried his visual memory of another manuscript of homilies, Cambridge, Trinity College, MS B.14.52 (335), into his reproduction of the Lambeth manuscript (for the relation of Lambeth 487 to the Trinity manuscript, see further below).

The closest analogy to the script I know is hand A of British Library, MS Royal 17 A.xxvii (responsible for fols. 1–8v, 11–45v/5); although some features of the Lambeth manuscript are more closely approximated by the other scribes of that book ('Katherine Group' texts). The Royal manuscript is customarily (and unhelpfully) dated 's. xiii in.', with a suspicion, on the basis of contents, that it is a work of the 1220s. Among published dated manuscripts, the vocabulary of letter forms (although scarcely of duct) most proxi-

---

was unable to give this, his last extensive catalogue, the same care he showed elsewhere. See also Wilcox, *Anglo-Saxon Manuscripts in Microfiche Facsimile*, VIII, gen. eds P. Pulsiano and A. N. Doane, MRTS 219 (Tempe AZ, 2000), pp. 72–8.

[3] See Ker, *Catalogue Containing Anglo-Saxon*, p. xix; S. M. O'Brien, 'An Edition of Seven Homilies from Lambeth Palace Library MS 487' (unpublished DPhil thesis, University of Oxford, 1985; BodL, MS DPhil C.6009), p. 1. Study of the MS has probably been retarded by the absence of facsimiles; Wanley's pen-and-ink reproductions appear at George Hickes, *Linguarum vett. septentrionalium thesaurus*, 2 vols. (Oxford, 1703–5), 1, pt. 3, the last plate before 145, figures vi (fol. 3) and vii (fol. 24v).

mate to Lambeth 487 seems to me the hand of the 1202 Rochester booklist in BL, MS Royal 5 B.xii. I suspect one cannot do better than Ker and James and would incline to an equivocal dating, e.g. 'around or just after 1200'.[4]

However, certain aspects of the textual presentation and decoration may be of aid in dating for Lambeth 487; for example, the scribe frequently (although far from universally) introduces items with headings in red. But he has also left unfilled two-line spaces for initials at the start of the texts. This implies that he would have used a contrasting colour for them, but in their absence, one cannot tell whether they would have been green (or another colour, a twelfth-century usage) or blue (nearly universal after 1200). More tellingly, red also appears within the texts; the scribe, although he uses his normal text hand for them, routinely sets off Latin biblical lemmata in this way, perhaps a datable feature.

Lambeth 487 currently includes nineteen items (there was once a twentieth, a single leaf loose in the volume), eighteen of them the work of the original scribe[5] (see Table 5.1).

TABLE 5.1

Sisam's section A1
1. Fols 1–3: a unique homily for the 1st Sunday in Advent.
2. Fols 3–9: Wulfstan, 'Be godcundre warnunge' ed. as homily 19, Dorothy
   Bethurum, *The Homilies of Wulfstan* (Oxford, 1957), pp. 251–54 (a reference only
   to this copy, 'somewhat condensed in Middle English', at p. 355)
3. Fols 9–15v: a unique homily for Lent.
4. Fols 15v–18v: a unique homily for a Sunday.
5. Fols 18v–21v: a unique homily on Jeremiah in the pit.

Sisam's text transitional between A and B
6. Fols 21v–25: a verse explication of the Pater Noster, in couplets, *Index of Middle
   English Verse* 2709 (both this text and item 18 below written in the manner
   customary in Old English verse manuscripts, as prose).[6]

Sisam's B
7. Fols 25–27v: roughly = 'The Trinity Homilies', i.e. those of Cambridge, Trinity
   College, MS B.14.52 (mentioned above), here homily 4, 'Credo' (MS pp 9–16),

4   For Hand A of the Royal MS, see the frontispiece to *Seinte Katerine* …, ed. S. R. T.
    O. d'Ardenne and E. J. Dobson, EETS SS 7 (1981). The Rochester list ed. as B.79
    in *Corpus of British Medieval Library Catalogues* IV, 497–526. See the facsimile, A. G.
    Watson, *Catalogue of Dated and Datable Manuscripts c. 700–1600 in the Department of
    Manuscripts, the British Library*, 2 vols. (London, 1979), II, plate 115.
5   The full contents are reproduced, in MS order, in *Old English Homilies I*, I, 3–189;
    O'Brien re-edits selected items in her thesis. I have divided the contents to follow
    the linguistic distinctions outlined by Celia Sisam, 'The Scribal Tradition of the
    Lambeth Homilies', *Review of English Studies* ns 2 (1951), 105–13, discussed more thor-
    oughly below.
6   Ed. Carleton Brown and Rossell Hope Robbins (New York, 1943).

ed. Morris, *Old English Homilies of the Twelfth Century … Second Series*, EETS os 53 (1873), pp. 15–23.

8. Fols 27v–30v: a unique Middle English homily.

Sisam's section A2

9. Fols 30v–37v: Ælfric, *Catholic Homilies, first series,* homily 22, 'In die sancto Pentecosten', ed. Peter Clemoes, EETS ss 17 (1997), pp. 354–64 (this copy collated as Xi).

10. Fols 37v–45: 'De octo uitiis et de duodecim abusiuis gradus [sic?]' , an eleventh-century redaction of Ælfrician materials, also in Cambridge, Corpus Christi College, MS 178, pp. 73–88, whence printed as an appendix to the Lambeth texts, Morris, EETS os 29 (1867), pp. 296–304.[7]

Sisam's section A3

11. Fols 45–47: a homily on the Passion?, including an extract from Ælfric, *Catholic Homilies, first series,* homily 14, 'Dominica palmarum', ed. Clemoes, pp. 295–97 (lines 164–92) (this copy collated as Xi).

12. Fols 47–49: a further unique homily on the Passion?

13. Fols 49–51v: roughly = Trinity Homilies 26, 'De sancto Laurentio' (MS pp. 109–13), ed. Morris, pp. 153–59.

Sisam's B resumed

14. Fols 51v–54: a unique Middle English homily.

15. Fols 54–56: roughly = Trinity Homilies 32, 'Sermo in Marcum 8:34' (MS pp. 143–47), ed. Morris, pp. 203–9.

16. Fols 56–57v: roughly = Trinity Homilies 30, 'Estote fortes in bello' (for the feast of St Nathaniel [?]; MS pp. 132–37), ed. Morris, pp. 185–93.

17. Fols 57v–59v: roughly = Trinity Homilies 17, 'De sancto Iacobo' (MS pp. 104–9), ed. Morris, pp. 145–53.

18. Fols 59v–65: 'The Poema Morale', incomplete, *Index* 1276, ed. in parallel with the Trinity text, Joseph Hall, *Selections from Early Middle English,* 2 vols (Oxford, 1920), 1:30–47. Only eleven written lines appear on fol. 65, with the remainder blank, and the next (added) item begins on the (originally blank) verso.

Text(s) added later

19. Fols 65v–67: 'On wel swuðe god ureisun of god almichti', ed. W. Meredith Thompson, *The Wohunge of Ure Lauerd and Other Pieces,* EETS 241 (1958), 1–4 (with the only other copy, Cotton Nero A.xiv, fols 123v–26v, following at 5–9). The text ends precisely at the foot of fol. 67 (the verso blank, as that of fol. 65 was originally).

20. Hickes found in this MS the now lost one-folio fragment, 'The Battle of Finnesburh', ed. Bruce Mitchell and Fred C. Robinson, *Beowulf: An Edition* (Oxford, 1998), 212–15.[8]

As Betty Hill reports, M. L. Samuels places the scribe's language along the Hereford-Shropshire border. R. M. Wilson's suggestion that Lambeth 487 is

---

[7] See Ker, pp. 60–61 and cf. J. C. Pope, *The Homilies of Ælfric: A Supplementary Collection,* Volume I, EETS 259 (1965), 63–64.

[8] On the last two items, see Betty Hill, 'Early English Fragments and Manuscripts: Lambeth Palace 487, Bodleian Library Digby 4', *Proceedings of the Leeds Philosophical and Literary Society, Literary and Historical Section* 14 (1972), 269–80, who cogently dates item 19 *c.* 1240 or later (contemporary with the Nero MS). The scribe writes below top line and uses both wynn and *w.*

a Lanthony book should be rejected; Wilson offered this view simply on the basis that the manuscript is 'western' and that many books from Lanthony (secunda), in north Gloucestershire, are preserved at Lambeth Palace.[9] The volume includes no explicit signs of medieval provenance but appears in the earliest (1612) catalogues of the Lambeth collection, presumably as part of the donation of the founder, Richard Bancroft; it had the earlier shelf marks C.O.12 and Q.185.

James made a complete dog's breakfast of the collation.[10] The scribe uses neither catchwords nor signatures, but James cannot have examined the sewings, even in the most rudimentary way. The manuscript may be described as a sequence of six quires, the first three of rather uneven dimensions: i[12] (fols. 1, 1a, 2–11) ii[14] iii[18] iv–vi[8]. These units thus end at fols. 11, 25, 43, 51, 59, 67 (not James's 10, 26, 42, 52, 58, 67). On fol. 11v, the last ruled line on the page has been left blank, perhaps implying that the volume was copied from loose provided quires and that its shape imitates that of the archetypal materials, a possibility to which I now turn.

Here two inconsistent features of the production, variations in scribal language and those variations in page format I have mentioned above, provide key information. The book is the product of *literatim* copying brilliantly reconstructed in Sisam's study. In her account, the manuscript joins two sources, each relying on a separate graphemic system. One of these exemplars (A/X) was in late Old English and included the Wulfstan and Ælfric materials as well as anonyma; the second exemplar (B/Y), shared with 'the Trinity Homilies' (Cambridge, Trinity College, MS B.14.52 [335]), used a Middle English system. In addition to the prose, this second exemplar also included the 'Poema Morale'.

Sisam divides the manuscript into a series of linguistic segments (106–8), indicated in Table 5.1 above. Her Type A (the Old English) includes two blocks, items 1–5 and 9–13. Sisam further subdivides these as A1 = items 1–5, A2 = items 9–10 (undiluted representation of Ælfric) and A3 = items 11–13. Sisam' s Type B includes the two blocks following upon the chunks derived from A, items 7–8 and 14–18. In Sisam's account, item 6, the versified *Pater Noster*, displays rather mixed language. Sisam argues this represents the carryover of engrained Type A copying habits, gradually replaced by the Type B language of the scribe's exemplar.

9 See Betty Hill, 'The Twelfth-Century *Conduct of Life*, formerly the *Poema Morale* or *A Moral Ode*', *Leeds Studies in English* ns 9 (1977), 97–144 (pp. 108–9); Wilson, 'The Provenance of the Lambeth Homilies, With a New Collation', *Leeds Studies in English* 4 (1935), 24–43 (p. 39). Wilson's view is also rejected by Hill, 'Early English fragments', 278 n. 5.

10 One unfortunately repeated feature of this catalogue. Cf. the described collation of MS 491 at *Descriptive Catalogue* 681 with that provided, following alternation of vellum and paper leaves and the evidence of watermarks, 'The Scribe of Huntington HM 114', *Studies in Bibliography* 42 (1989), 120–33 (pp. 130–1).

As I indicate above, the writing area and *mise-en-page* of Lambeth 487 varies. In contrast to the usual single column, 145 or 155 mm x 80 mm, in 27 to 29 lines to the page, two substantial variations, a quire each, occur:

(a) fols. 44–51v: **160–3** mm x 80 mm, in **32 lines** (fol. 51r, with change of ductus, has 31 lines and fol. 5lv, in a rather sprawly style, only 27 lines); and
(b) fols. 52–59v: 155 mm x **90–5** mm, in **27 lines** (only 26 on fol. 59r).
In addition, fols. 65v–67, with the added item 19, differ from the remainder. This scribe uses a writing area 150 mm x 90 mm, in 29 lines. But since involving an added text, this variation is not germane to the original production.

It is instructive to align these variations with the texts (and associated languages) of the volume. The odd fols. 44–51 form quire 4. The head of this codicological unit falls rather late in item 10, and its end at the juncture of item 13 with item 14. The quire thus provides, in the main, Sisam's A3 materials, and its end thus falls at the juncture of Sisam's A and B languages.[11] The second deviant page format is similarly limited to the immediately following quire 5. This includes the second chunk of Type B prose, and its end coincides with the opening of item 18, the verse 'Poema Morale'.

This rough coincidence of contents, scribal languages, quire bounds, and variable page-formats does not seem likely to be accidental. In Sisam's showing, the manuscript combines two discontinuous sources, and the scribe switched between them. But these discontinuities also correspond to shifts in procedure in producing the book. One can construct a narrative of the book's production by coordinating all this information.

If one applies this kind of thinking to the head of the volume, the odd shapes of the first three quires begin to appear motivated. The scribe apparently began by imagining only a rather small book, perhaps a couple of quires total and completely given over to inherited Old English materials (Sisam's A1). He copied these consecutively, and on reaching the end of his first quire, saw that a slightly expanded version of the same format (fourteen leaves, rather than twelve) would accommodate the remainder of the materials currently to hand. Such expanded quires elsewhere typically mark the endings of production units; English scribes often produce relatively large

---

[11] I would note, however, one anomaly, suppressed, *argumenti causa*, Sisam, 'The Scribal Tradition', p. 110 n. 3. Although the language here is associated with the Old English derived Type A, item 13 is a Middle English homily shared with Trinity. This might imply that the A exemplar was a good deal later than Sisam's estimate of *c.* 1130 and that it had already assimilated some Middle English texts, cloaked in an earlier spelling system congruent with Old English materials. Such a conclusion might also explain the mixed language of the other text appearing at a point of A/B transition, item 6, the Pater Noster poem.

quires to finish the ends of texts economically.[12] These materials appear to have included Sisam's linguistically transitional item 6; just as later in the manuscript, verse texts, even if presented continuously, rather than by the line, follow the larger blocks of prose. The original impulse behind Lambeth 487, then, the first two quires, presented Sisam's A1 + item 6, and the scribe need not have, while copying them, contemplated any further work.

However, the scribe later saw reason to extend the volume. This involved the provision of the eighteen-leaf quire 3, a format designed to handle a large block of material. The scribe planned this unit to present two disparate groups of texts; one imagines texts not available to him previously. The quire pretty neatly includes his first access to Sisam's B materials, and it concludes with a pair of Ælfrician texts (Sisam's A2).

The subsequent quire 4, in relation to the *mise-en-page* common elsewhere in the volume, is decidedly packed. The writing area expands vertically to accommodate more lines per page than occur anywhere else in the book. On this basis, the eight-leaf quire 4 represents an effort at finishing off the available A material (here Sisam's A3) within a single, and at this point in the production, uniquely brief unit. The scribe's manipulation of the writing space was well planned and successful, so much so that, as he approached the end of the quire, he realized he might conclude his copying prematurely, without exhausting the full space he had initially planned. Hence, in the last two pages, he begins to space out the writing, and conveniently ends near the foot of the verso of his last leaf. One implication of this behaviour is that he did not have to hand, nor had he considered using, the subsequent portions of B material that now fill the remainder of the book.

Quire 5, devoted to concluding the prose materials that constitute Sisam's type B (items 14–17) neatly within eight leaves, shows a different form of textual compression. Unlike the preceding quire, the scribe returns to the twenty-nine-line format usual at the opening of his work. But he increases the amount of copy within the text-block by expanding the length of his writing line. This technique implies that he intended again to end his copying here; he either did not have, or had not determined that he present within this manuscript, 'Poema Morale'. That text came to hand or was reserved for the now-final eight-leaf quire 6. That this unit is a full one of eight leaves presupposes that the scribe knew the rough dimensions of the full poem. Although he ultimately copied only about 70 per cent of the 'Poema Morale' into the opening five and a bit leaves of the quire, he would have needed most of the remaining space, now with an added text, to reproduce the full poem.

Thus, Lambeth 487 has been pieced together out of (at least) two pre-existing books. Neither appears to have been continuously available to the

---

[12] See Hanna, *Pursuing History*, particularly pp. 30–4 (a discussion that equally notices the option of unusually small text-concluding quires, a feature that appears in Lambeth Palace 487, quire iv, discussed two paragraphs below).

scribe, who seems originally to have undertaken his work on the assumption that there was only one source, Sisam's A(1). This he supplemented sequentially as additional interesting exemplars became available.

In this regard, the possible provenance of the exemplars might be considered telling. The scribe's Old English – Sisam hypothesized from a book of *c.* 1130 – might well have relied on local West Midland sources such as Worcester. But his other sources would diminish one's assurance that he did so.[13] The Type B materials, including the 'Poema Morale', are best known from books from the south-east. If the Lambeth scribe (and his community) were able to import those exemplars from across the country, one cannot have a great deal of certainty about the source of their Old English materials.[14]

I return here to a point I made in passing above. At the end of Lambeth 487, in a different later hand, appears the *Wohunge Group* text, 'On wel swuðe god ureisun of god almichti'. This, as I have indicated, is known elsewhere from a single copy, in British Library, MS Cotton Nero A.xiv (like the Lambeth addition, *c.* 1240), where it follows *Ancrene Wisse*. In this book, the text has also been added in a later hand, on additional leaves at the end of the larger text. I do not think the belated provision shared by both manuscripts is just an accidental convergence, but typical of the production of a good many earlier thirteenth century books, as a look at a further manuscript containing *Ancrene Wisse* and contemporary with both Nero and the Lambeth addition, will indicate.

This is British Library, MS Cotton Titus D.xviii. The manuscript, again in a single hand, contains the texts listed in Table 5.2 (I intersperse with them a notation of the MS quiring).[15]

---

[13] The Corpus Christi MS of item 10 was in Worcester during the period. Cf. further Bodleian Library, MSS Hatton 113+114 and Junius 121, both of s. xi³/⁴ and with parallel Ælfric texts. See Ker, pp. 391–9, 412–18. But cf. Susan Irvine's discussion of the antecedents of another West Midland volume of s. xii², Bodleian Library, MS Bodley 343, *Old English Homilies*, EETS 302 (1993), passim, esp. the summary pp. l–liv; for this book, see Ker, pp. 368–75.

[14] On the Trinity Homilies, see Margaret Laing and Angus McIntosh, 'Cambridge, Trinity College, MS 335: Its Texts and Their Transmission', *New Science out of Old Books: Studies in Manuscripts and Early Printed Books in Honour of A. I. Doyle*, ed. Richard Beadle and A. J. Piper (Aldershot, 1995), pp. 14–52, with references to a variety of past discussions. For the scribal language of the seven other, almost completely south-eastern, copies of 'Poema Morale' (a staple in thirteenth-century miscellanies), see further Hill's report of Samuels's opinions, as above n. 6. But notice the considerably later (s. xiii³/⁴) western copy in Oxford, Jesus College, MS 29.

[15] See *The English Text of the Ancrene Riwle, BM MS Cotton Titus D xviii*, ed. Frances M. Mack EETS 252 (1963), pp. ix–x, a particularly skimpy account, without reference to the foliation of the texts or the dimensions of the quires.

TABLE 5.2

Quires i^{10} ii^{12} iii^{12} (-5) iv^{12} v^{12} (-10) vi^{10} vii^{12} viii^{16} [the text ends on the fourteenth leaf
of quire viii]
1. Fols 14ra–105ra: *Ancrene Wisse*

Quire ix^8 (-2) [the text ends on the original sixth leaf]
2. Fols 105va–12va: 'Sawles Ward'

Quire x^8 xi^{12} [item 4 ends on the eleventh leaf of quire xi, with part of 133ra and all of
133rb blank]
3. Fols 112va–27ra: 'Hali Meiðhad'
4. Fols 127rb–33ra: 'Þe Wohunge of ure Lauerd'
Quire xii^{14} (-14, probably blank)
5. Fols 133va–47vb: 'Seinte Katerine'

This extensive volume joins together members of all three sets of texts E. J.
Dobson wished to associate with Wigmore spirituality. In addition to *Ancrene
Wisse*, the volume has three of the five 'Katherine Group' texts and one of the
Wohunge Group.[16] But a closer look at the manuscript will show its resemblance
to Lambeth 487, as a gathering of separable fragments. Although all three
groups of texts are represented, their combination in the book can scarcely be
considered preplanned or the result of a non-problematic single acquisition
of all items as some formed canon dispersed from a single centre. First of all,
like Lambeth 487, the Titus manuscript shows variation of language. Except
for five short bits, perhaps contributed to its exemplar by a second scribe,
items 1 and 4 are written in the language of the south Cheshire border, whilst
items 2, 3 and 5 retain stronger evidence of 'AB language', associated with
Herefordshire. Additionally, relicts show item 4 as of a different source from
the remainder, with relict forms typical of the language of that area where
Derbyshire, Lancashire, and the West Riding join.[17]

Moreover, the quiring evidence, like that of Lambeth 487, would suggest
this manuscript developed as a series of accretions. Originally, it was only
to include *Ancrene Wisse*, as indicated by the reasonably consistent quiring
of this text, with two tens but otherwise invariably in twelves. However,

---

16 Most pregnantly, E. J. Dobson, *The Origins of* Ancrene Wisse (Oxford, 1976).
Dobson follows and builds extensively upon J. R. R. Tolkien's classic demonstra-
tion of the similar languages ('AB') in Cambridge, Corpus Christi College, MS 402
(*Ancrene Wisse*) and Bodley 34 ('Katherine Group'); see '"Ancrene Wisse" and "Hali
Meiðhad"', *Essays and Studies* 14 (1929), 104–26.

17 See Laing and McIntosh, 'The Language of *Ancrene Riwle*, The Katherine Group
Texts and Þe Wohunge of Ure Lauerd in BL Cotton Titus D XVIII', *Neuphilologische
Mitteilungen* 96 (1995), 235–63. I here offer qualifications to Laing and McIntosh's
various explanations of Titus's language as reproduced by the scribe from a single,
always available source.

the final quire containing this text is unusually large, a sixteen; just as the scribe of Lambeth 487, this book producer sought to conclude his work efficiently and presumably believed, for some time, that he had completed the manuscript by copying this text. Instructively, whatever their prevalence in *Ancrene Wisse*, Titus thereafter only returns to twelve-leaf quiring once (quire xi). The remainder of the volume shows a variety of quire-sizes, testimony to piecemeal acquisition of texts. Moreover, the lengthy ending quire of *Ancrene Wisse* is only the first of a series of stops and starts that indicate that the extent of the volume changed, and changed continuously.

Following *Ancrene Wisse*, the scribe apparently received 'Sawles Ward'. He constructed a much briefer quire (ix, an eight) which would hold it. But then he acquired, or decided (changing his plan) to include further materials initially from what appears the same 'Katherine Group' exemplar as had provided the preceding text. The production appears to have been planned to be continued in eights, as evidenced in quire x. But at some point – it might have been as late as his work on fol. 126 (the fourth leaf of quire xi) – the scribe received item 4, in this case from a completely foreign source, and produced the expansive quire xi (another twelve) to fully contain this new piece. (Had he been planning a series of eights, he would have had to have made this decision in time to have inserted fols. 127–30, now the two central bifolia of quire xi, so as to produce the now observed continuous copying.) And a further decision (or arrival of new copy) extended the manuscript to its present proportions. In essence, the scribe appears to have 'concluded' the book four or five times, only the last such decision answering to the present dimensions of the manuscript.

Book histories like these might lead one to query Dobson's view of 'Wigmore texts' as a concerted local canon, the designed product of an 'AB community'.[18] After all, merely considering the 'Katherine Group', one is struck by the diversity of subject matters and prose styles, as well as that of imagined inscribed audiences, displayed among the five texts. While the texts do cohere in manuscripts such as Royal 17 A.xxvii (mentioned above) and Bodleian Library, MS Bodley 34, these collections appear a special, and not the usual, case.[19] But codicological evidence, like that provided by Lambeth

[18] As would the fact that, although the house owned the unique copy of *Ancrene Wisse*, Cambridge, Corpus Christi College, MS 402, it only received it as a donation (requested by the precentor of the house, that officer responsible for the library) from a south Shropshire family *c.* 1300. See *The English Text of the Ancrene Riwle: Ancrene Wisse*, ed. J. R. R. Tolkien, EETS 249 (1962) frontispiece and pp. xvii–iii.

[19] In part, the theory of a coherent group has been bolstered by ascribing priority and antiquity to Bodley 34, rather than the Royal MS, certainly dispersed copying and not from Wigmore. Moreover, the texts appear in Royal in a different order and dispersed among 'booklets' copied by three scribes. In fact, the Royal MS is

Palace, MS 487, might well imply a much less centralized and organized group of texts, available only fitfully and sporadically to book producers and the readers they served.

certainly older, perhaps by as much as a quarter century, and Bodley 34 is contemporary with books like Nero and Titus.

6

Pastoral Texts and Traditions:
The Anonymous *Speculum Iuniorum* (*c.* 1250)

Joseph Goering

The anonymous *summa* entitled *Speculum iuniorum* deserves pride of place among the masterpieces of Latin pastoral literature written for the education of priests and pastors of souls in England during the thirteenth and four-teenth centuries. This ambitious work, written around 1250 possibly by a Dominican friar, and extending to more than 100 folios in many of the twelve known manuscript copies,[1] is a unique amalgam of the latest teachings of the schools and the practical literature of pastoral care. It provides us, among other things, with a clear view of the syllabus of studies in theology and law that was thought appropriate for a shepherd of souls in the middle years of the thirteenth century and well beyond.

The author of the *Speculum* remains stubbornly anonymous, despite Leonard Boyle's ingenious attempt, published in 1967, to identify him as an otherwise unknown 'Master Galienus'.[2] In a PhD dissertation written under Fr Boyle's supervision I argued that this identification could not be maintained.[3] This is not the place to rehearse the details of the argu-

---

[1] The known manuscript copies are: London, British Library, MS Add. 62130 (formerly Fountains Abbey, Vyner MS 6108), fols. 190r–253v (text incomplete at end); London, Lambeth Palace Library, MS 485, fols. 121r–226r; Cambridge, Gonville and Caius, MS 52/29, fols. 1r–43r; Cambridge, St John's College, MS 113, fols. 1r–132r; Cambridge, University Library, MS Ff.iv.45, fols. 30r–127r; Oxford, Bodleian Library, MS Bodley 655, fols. 1r–168v; Oxford, Bodleian Library, MS Bodley 767, fols. 8r–124v; Oxford, Bodleian Library, MS Laud lat. misc. 166, fols. 9r–141r; Oxford, Bodleian Library, MS Rawlinson A. 367, fols. 84r–214v (MS imperfect at end); Oxford, Bodleian Library, MS Wood Empt. 22, fols. 2r–195r (text incomplete: missing the beginning of Book Two); Oxford, Corpus Christi College, MS 360, fols. 79r–99v (incomplete copy of Book Two, de sacramentis); Worcester, Cathedral Library, MS F. 38, fols. 216v–270r. Quotations below will be given from MS Bodley 655 of the Bodleian Libaray, Oxford, unless otherwise indicated.

[2] L. E. Boyle, 'Three English Pastoral *Summae* and a "Magister Galienus"', *Studia Gratiana* 11 (1967), 133–44 (pp. 141–4).

[3] J. Goering, 'The Popularization of Scholastic Ideas in Thirteenth Century England and an Anonymous *Speculum iuniorum*' (unpublished PhD dissertation, University of Toronto, 1977), pp. 255–6 (c. 4 n. 79).

ments.[4] Suffice it to say that Fr Boyle eventually gave his *imprimatur* to my argument. Whether he added his wholehearted *placet* remains to be learned in another place.

But, if the text of the *Speculum* remains anonymous, nevertheless a little light can be shed on the place, time and context of its composition. All of the extant manuscript copies (see above note 1) are preserved in English libraries and are apparently of English provenance. The author shows himself to be quite familiar with the series of English pastoral manuals written in the early thirteenth century, including Robert of Flamborough's *Liber penitentialis* (*c.* 1213), Thomas of Chobham's *Summa cum miserationes* (*c.* 1215), Richard of Wetheringsett's *Qui bene presunt* (*c.* 1220) and Robert Grosseteste's *Templum Dei* (*c.* 1225). This evidence would suggest that the author is an Englishman, and that his text circulated largely, if not exclusively, in England.

The author was also, almost certainly, a student in the schools. He quotes extensively and often explicitly from the Parisian theological masters of the first half of the thirteenth century, William of Auxerre, Philip the Chancellor, Alexander of Hales (OFM), John of la Rochelle (OFM), and from the early writings of Albert the Great (OP). He also cites the two earliest Oxford Dominican masters, Robert Bacon (OP) and Richard Fishacre (OP), both of whom died in 1248. In addition to these, he presents extensive extracts from the *Summa de paenitentia* and *de matrimonio* of Raymond of Penyafort (OP) and the *Summa de vitiis* and *de virtutibus* of William Peraldus (OP), and he offers some refinements to Raymond of Penyafort's teachings by way of excerpts from the *Summa super titulis decretalium* of Godfrey of Trani. All of these texts were composed before 1250.[5] Reference is made, in addition, to a 'new decretal' (*Vult etiam nova decretalis, de sent. ex. Cum medicinalis*), which was issued by Pope Innocent IV at the general council held at Lyon in 1245, and sent by him to the universities on 25 August 1245.[6] This reference provides a firm *terminus post quem* for the composition of the *Speculum*. The absence of quotations from such mid-century English theologians as Richard Rufus

---

4 In brief, Fr Boyle's argument hinges on a manuscript copy of another pastoral summa, the *Signaculum apostolatus mei*, that reads: 'as master Gal<ienus> says in his summa' ('Sicut recitat magister Gal<ienus> in summa sua'), and then goes on, so Fr Boyle argued, to 'fill out' this reference with a passage from the *Speculum iuniorum*. I was able to show that there is no connection, either syntactically or substantially, between the opinion ascribed to Master Galienus in the *Signaculum apostolatus mei* and the passage quoted from the *Speculum iuniorum* that follows.

5 The most recent text quoted by the *Summa iuniorum* is probably from the *Summa de virtutibus* of William Peraldus, which has been dated to 1248 or 1249; see A. Dondaine, 'Guillaume Peyraut. Vie et oeuvres', *Archivum Fratrum Praedicatorum* 18 (1948), 171, 186–7.

6 MS Bodley 655, fol. 40r. See S. Kuttner, 'Die Konstitutionen des ersten allgemeinen Konzils von Lyon', *Studia et documenta historiae et iuris* 6 (1940), 70–131; rept. in idem, *Medieval Councils, Decretals and Collections of Canon Law* (Ashgate, 1992).

(OFM) and Thomas of York (OFM), or from Bonaventure (OFM), Thomas Aquinas (OP), or the Franciscan *Summa fratris Alexandri* on the continent, also strengthen the case for a date of *c.* 1250 for the composition of the *Speculum*.

Finally, it seems likely, on balance, that the author was a Dominican friar. This is suggested, first and foremost, by the repeated references to the Dominicans as 'brother' (*frater*): 'frater Ricardus de Fyssacre', 'frater Rob. Bacun', 'frater Reymundus [de Penyafort]', etc., a term that is not used of the Franciscan friars Alexander of Hales and John of la Rochelle, for example. His quotations from the earliest Dominican masters at Oxford also lend weight to the hypothesis, especially since one of them, Robert Bacon, is rarely quoted in the extant scholastic literature. Finally, the term 'juniors' (*iuniores*) is used in the statutes of the Dominican order to designate young students just beginning their theological education.[7]

But if the author was an English Dominican friar writing around the year 1250, how should we understand the mutual ignorance of the two great mid-century English Dominican *summae*, this anonymous *Speculum iuniorum* and the homonymous *Summa iuniorum* (or *Summa ad instructionem iuniorum*), written about the same time by Simon of Hinton, the provincial prior of the English Dominicans from 1254 to 1261?[8] As far as I have been able to determine, neither *summa* shows any knowledge of the other. Our *Speculum iuniorum* does, indeed, quote a passage on prayer and ascribe it to Simon of Hinton (*in Morum* (!) *fratris S. de Hemptone*), but this passage is not to be found in Simon's *Summa iuniorum*.[9] So it would seem that our author is familiar with 'brother Simon of Hinton', but not with his *Summa ad*

---

7   'Item, quod fratribus iunioribus, aptis ad studium, parcatur a discursibus et aliis occupacionibus', *Acta capitulorum generalium ordinis Praedicatorum*, I, *Monumenta ordinis fratrum Praedicatorum, Historica*, ed. B. M. Reichert (Rome, 1898), p. 99. See also M. M. Mulchahey, *'First the Bow is Bent in Study …': Dominican Education before 1350* (Toronto, 1998), 204–18.

8   On Simon and his eventful career in the Dominican Order, see: S. Tugwell, 'Hinton, Simon of (fl. *c.* 1248–1262)', *ODNB*. A useful, but late, and interpolated edition of the *Summa* is printed in *Joannis Gersonii doctoris theologi et cancellarii Parisiensis Opera Omnia* (Antwerp, 1706), 1: 233–422; a critical edition, based on her Toronto PhD dissertation, is in preparation by S. Carroll-Clark. On the *summa* see A. Dondaine, 'La somme de Simon de Hinton', *Recherches théologique ancienne et médiévale* 9 (1937), 5–22, 205–18. Most recently see R. Newhauser and I. P. Bejczy, 'Two Newly Discovered Abbreviations of Simon of Hinton's *Summa Iuniorum*, Concentrating on the Virtues and Vices', *Archivum Fratrum Praedicatorum* 75 (2005), 95-144.

9   The attribution to Simon is not found in the copy of the *Speculum* in Bodley MS 655, but see, for example, Lambeth Palace MS 485, fol. 185v; MS Bodley 767, fol. 98r; and MS Laud lat. misc. 166, fol. 99r, etc. All of the manuscripts of the *Speculum* that mention Simon of Hinton agree in ascribing the work obscurely 'in Morum'; it is uncertain to what work this might refer. The passage attributed to Simon begins: 'Qualiter debet orare, sive qualis debet esse oratio. Et quia oratio est actus orantis, quasdam conditiones debet habere quo ad actum orandi, quasdam, quo ad orantem. Quo ad actum orandi debet esse breviloqua, submissa, integra, simplex,

instructionem iuniorum. Simon, for his part, seems not to have used any part of the *Speculum iuniorum* in his own *Summa iuniorum*. As neither of these two *summae* has been precisely dated, the safest hypothesis may be that they are exactly contemporaneous, and that the reason the one is unknown to the other is that they were both being composed at the same time, that is, some time around the year 1250. We know, in any case, that both *summae* were being read side by side soon after their composition, because they were used extensively by an anonymous English author to compose a third treatise, the *Signaculum apostolatus mei*, written probably between1260 and 1270.[10]

Whereas Simon of Hinton's *Summa iuniorum* is organized in a straightforward way, treating first the articles of faith, then the Lord's Prayer, the sacraments, the virtues, the gifts of the Holy Spirit and the vices, the *Speculum iuniorum* covers the same ground (and more), but it does so in an original and unusual fashion. A prologue, surviving in only one manuscript copy of the *Speculum iuniorum*, describes the author's intention:

> Here begins the *Speculum iuniorum*, extracted from diverse books of the fathers and the philosophers as well as from the writings and *summulae* of the masters. It is given this name because young students can see in it clearly, as in a mirror, the truth of many things and then, if necessary, seek from more advanced students and from the elders an exposition or confirmation of that truth.
>
> This 'mirror' is divided into five books. In the first is treated the evil of guilt and of punishment; in the second, the good in general and the seven sacraments of the Church; in Book Three, the virtues, the gifts of the Holy Spirit and the beatitudes; in Book Four, the soul and its powers; and the angels and God in Book Five.[11]

The text of the *Speculum*, as it comes down to us, contains only Books One and Two as described in this prologue. The other three books were clearly planned; there are internal references to them in Books One and Two,[12] but

---

matura, communis, et instans.' This passage may eventually be identified in one of Simon's many other writings; see Sharpe, *Handlist*, pp. 614–16 (no. 1637).

10   See Boyle, 'Three English Pastoral *Summae*', pp. 141–4.

11   'Incipit Speculum iuniorum de diuersis libris sanctorum et philosophorum necnon et scriptis et summulis magistrorum extractum, quod ideo hoc nomen sortitum est quia in eo tamquam in speculo possunt iuniores super multarum ueritatem luculenter conspicere, et si opus fuerit, conspecte ueritatis expositionem siue confirmacionem a prouectioribus et senioribus requirere.

'Distinguitur autem hoc speculum in quinque libros. In primo agitur de malo culpe et pene. In secundo de bono in genere et de septem sacramentis ecclesie. In tercio de uirtutibus, donis Spiritus Sancti, et beatitudinibus. In quarto de anima et eius potenciis, in quinto de angelis et Deo.' Worcester MS F.38, fol. 216v.

12   For example, in Book Two, the author points to a future discussion of the virtues, not found in the text as it now exists, and intended, according to the prologue, for Book Three ('Antequam dicatur de uirtutibus per quas fit bonum, prius dicendum

the subsequent books seem never to have been written. None of the extant manuscript copies shows any signs of originally having contained more than two books, or any awareness that there were more to be copied. Even the Worcester manuscript containing the prologue concludes Book Two with the words: *Explicit liber qui dicitur Speculum iuniorum*. What remains, however, is anything but a truncated *summa*. It was seen in its own day as a complete work, and even without the planned Books Three to Five, it has a self-sufficiency and an order which mark it out as an important if unusual *summa*.

The *Speculum* is organized according to the principles of the scholastic *divisio textus* – the division and subdivision of the text to be commented upon.[13] In this case, however, the author takes as his 'text' not a written source such as the Bible or the works of Aristotle, but rather the world itself and all things in it. The first and broadest division of the materials is the one into good and evil, *bonum* and *malum*. The first book of the *Speculum* treats of evil, and the second treats the good. The additional three books announced in the prologue would not have altered this basic structure, but would have expanded further on the *bonum*. This primary division or *distinctio* is only the tip of the iceberg. The entire text of the *Speculum* is constructed, both in its conceptual organization and in its schematic layout on the page, as a grand structure of distinctions and subdistinctions, as will be seen in the discussion below. I know of no other text that applies the method so systematically and so thoughtfully to such a vast range of materials. Also unusual is the large number of contemporary and near-contemporary authors whose works are excerpted and melded together here into a coherent and sophisticated exercise of theological instruction. Remarkable, too, is the diversity of these sources, including treatises of canon law as well as theology and philosophy, and popular *summae* as well as the more technical scholastic writings. Such diverse texts seldom rub shoulders in a single medieval work, and, even more remarkably, as we shall see, our author acknowledges his contemporaries explicitly, frequently naming the authors and works on which he relies.

The *Speculum* opens with a quotation ascribed to Book Two of Anselm's *Cur Deus homo*: 'Rationalem creaturam a Deo factam esse ...'

---

est de sacramentis', Oxford MS Bodley 655, fol. 75). So, too, there is a reference in Book Two to the angels, 'about which more will be said below' ('In ecclesia triumphante in patria est ordo in spiritibus angelicis ... de quibus dicetur infra', ibid. fol. 114v). The angelic orders are not mentioned again in Book Two; according to the Prologue, a discussion of the angels was planned for the fifth book.

13 For an elegant discussion of the method, see J. F. Boyle, 'The Theological Character of the Scholastic "Division of the Text" with Particular Reference to the Commentaries of Saint Thomas Aquinas', in *With Reverence for the Word: Medieval Scriptural Exegesis in Judaism, Christianity, and Islam*, ed. J. D. McAuliffe, B. D. Walfish and J. Goering (Oxford, 2003), 276–83.

'The rational creature was made by God, without doubt, to be happy in enjoying God. And it was made rational so that it might discern the difference between good and evil, and between the greater and lesser evil and between the greater and lesser good. ... Similarly it can be shown that the creature received this power of discernment that it might despise and avoid evil, the greater the evil the more to avoid it, and to love and choose the good, loving the highest good most highly.' These are the words of Anselm in the beginning of the second book, *Why God became Man*.[14]

Having thus captured the attention and the interest of his reader, who is to be counted among the rational creatures and thus capable of distinguishing good from evil and the various degrees of both, the author proceeds to divide the entirety of the *Speculum* into the two parts distinguished by Anselm, *De malo* and *De bono*.

Book One (On Evil) begins with some general considerations of the nature of evil in itself, citing first a series of definitions from Augustine and (Pseudo-) Dionysius, and complementing these with long excerpts from William of Auxerre's *Summa aurea* ('secundum Altissiodorensem'), Richard Fishacre's commentary on Lombard's *Sentences* ('Extractum de Fissacre'), and Peter Lombard's *Sentences* ('Hec probantur ii. Sententiis'), concerning the origin and the place of evil in the world. The remainder of Book One is built around a series of precise distinctions outlining the various types or divisions of evil. The fundamental distinction, we learn, is between evil that is done (*malum culpe*) and evil that is suffered (*malum pene*).

Evil that we do (*culpa*) is first presented in terms of eight traditional divisions of sins: (1) Original sin and actual, (2) mortal sin and venial, (3) the seven deadly sins, (4) sins of thought, word and deed, (5) sins of commission and omission, (6) sins of one's own perpetration and sins of participation with others, (7) sins of weakness (*in Patrem*), ignorance (*in Filium*) and malice (*in Spiritum sanctum*) and (8) sins against God, neighbour and self. These types of sins are explicated by means of quotations from various ancient authorities, drawn largely from the two great twelfth-century textbooks of the schools, Gratian's *Decretum* and Peter Lombard's *Sentences*. But the bulk of the treatment is given over to the discussions taken from the modern masters. Many thirteenth-century masters are acknowledged

---

14 '(Incipit liber primus Speculi iuniorum, De malo culpe et pene). Rationalem creaturam a Deo factam esse ut Deo fruendo beata esset dubitari non debet. Ideo namque rationalis est ut discernat inter bonum et malum, et inter maius malum et minus malum, et inter maius bonum et minus bonum. Alioquin frustra facta esset rationalis. Set Deus non fecit eam frustra rationalem, quare ad hoc eam factam esse rationalem dubium non est. Simili ratione probatur quod ad hoc accepit potestatem discernendi ut odisset et vitaret malum, et maius malum magis vitaret, ac amaret et eligeret bonum, et maius bonum magis amaret, et summum bonum summe amaret. Hec sunt uerba Anselmi in libro ii., Cur Deus homo.' (MS Bodley 655, fol. 6r)

explicitly or implicitly. For example: Thomas of Chobham ('in summa Cum miserationes'), William Peraldus ('in Summa vitiorum'), Robert Grosseteste ('R. Lincolniensis in Templo'), Richard of Wetheringsett ('Ricardus in summa Qui bene presunt'), William of Auxerre's *Summa aurea* ('Altissiodorensis'), Raymond of Penyafort's *Summa de paenitentia* ('Reymundus'), Richard Fishacre's *In libros sententiarum* ('Fissacre') along with numerous tantalizing and still unidentified passages taken apparently from contemporaries in the schools, and designated broadly as 'in some commentaries' [in quibusdam postillis] or simply as 'magisterial' [magistralis].

The discussion of sins is concluded by advice concerning how one type of evil should be compared with another in order better to avoid the evils which are greater. A discussion of the greatest sins most to be avoided, i.e. simony, usury, heresy, schism, apostasy, divination (*sortilegium*) and murder, concludes this part of Book One. The author leans heavily here on authorities in canon law such as Raymond of Penyafort, Godfrey of Trani's *Summa super titulis decretalium* ('Goffredus') and Robert of Flamborough's *Liber poenitentialis* ('casus … extracta sunt de penitentiali magistri Roberti de Flaveny qui incipit sic: Res grandis, etc.')

Evil that we suffer (*malum pene*) is the topic of the rest of Book One. Here the author introduces the reader to a wide range of very useful distinctions concerning punishment and suffering. He begins with several definitions of 'pain' ascribed to 'Frater Rob. Bacun'. Although the source of these has not yet been identified, this is a rare and precious reference to the teaching activities of Robert Bacon, the Dominican lector at Oxford who died in 1248.[15] Bacon's definitions are followed by the distinction of eternal and temporal pain. The former comprises the pains or punishments of the damned in hell, the details of which are important for preaching, and are drawn largely from Richard Wetheringsett's *summa* ('in summa Qui bene presunt') and from William Peraldus, *Summa de virtutibus* ('extracta de Summa uirtutum'). 'Temporal pain' is the subject of the rest of Book One. The time-limited punishments in purgatory are discussed briefly with an excerpt from Richard Fishacre ('Fissacre'). These are distinguished from this-worldly pains, which are either natural (i.e. physical and mental suffering) or inflicted (i.e. punishments). Of the punishments, some are unjust and some are justly inflicted. These latter punishments, both civil and ecclesiastical, are discussed and distinguished at length on the basis of the legal expertise found in Raymond of Penyafort's *Summa de paenitentia* ('hoc totum de Reymundo', etc.) and in Godfrey of Trani's *Summa super titulis* ('hec omnia de Gofrido', etc.). Some additional material is taken from Grosseteste's *Templum*, and from an as yet unidentified jurist ('opinio cuiusdam magni iurisperiti').

---

[15] On Robert Bacon, OP, see J. Dunbabin, 'Bacon, Robert (d. 1248)', *ODNB* online, accessed 16 July 2008.

Book One extends to some 160 pages of typescript. Book Two, *De bono*, is more than twice as long, at 340 pages, and at that it encompasses only the first of four books originally planned to treat of the Good. Book Two opens with a series of definitions of the Good drawn from Philip the Chancellor's *Summa de bono* ('a summa Cancellarii'), and, without acknowledgement, from Albert the Great's *Summa de bono*. The author then introduces his readers to various divisions of the Good. First he distinguishes the goodness of things [*bonitas rei*] from the goodness of deeds [*bonitas operis*] and then further subdivides each. For example, the goodness of things can be either innate, acquired or infused; the first is the inborn good of nature, the second is gained through the acquisition of good habits and especially the cardinal or 'political' virtues, and the third comes from freely given grace and especially from the theological virtues. The goodness of deeds is similarly subdivided (goodness in essence, in general, in circumstances and in intention), each leading to further sets of subdistinctions that seek not so much to provide answers to difficult questions, as to present the student with a well-rounded picture of the complicated issues surrounding moral behaviour and human action.

A second major division treats of the subject in which the good is found, namely in God and in creatures. The good in God is uncreated, unchangeable, and possessed in its essence, whereas the good in creatures is created, changeable and possessed only by participation. Each of these goods is further subdivided, introducing the beginning student elegantly and effortlessly to the language and the conceptual tools of the theologian and the canonist.

The third major division of the Good concerns the end toward which it leads. Here the author follows Peter Lombard (and Augustine) in distinguishing goods to be used, goods to be enjoyed and goods to be both used and enjoyed. The goods to be used are further subdivided according to the three kinds of life that they serve, namely, the life of nature, the life of grace, and the life of glory. Each of these topics – nature, grace and glory – then receives long and detailed discussion and distinction drawn from the latest teachings of the schools, including the contemporary masters ('magistralis'), and such named authorities as William of Auxerre ('Antisiodorensem'), Philip the Chancellor ('extracta de summa Cancellarii'), Alexander of Hales's *Glossa in Sententiis* ('Hales'), Richard Fishacre ('Frater Ricardus de Fyssacre') and (without acknowledgement) John of la Rochelle's *Tractatus de divisione multiplici potentiarum animae*. One definition of grace, 'Gracia est liberalitas dantis sine meritis accipientis', is ascribed to an otherwise unknown Gilbertus Scotus ('Hec diffinitio est Gileberti Scoti'). The discussion of the goods of glory [*bona glorie*] are particularly indebted to the Ps. Anselm's *De similitudinibus* ('Anselmus'), the *Summa de virtutibus* of William Peraldus ('De summa virtutum'), the *summa Qui bene presunt* ('in summa Qui bene presunt'), and to Robert Grosseteste's questions *De dotibus* ('In quibusdam questionibus Lincolniensis').

The same technique of teaching by distinction and subdistinction is used in the discussion of the Good represented by the Church's seven sacraments. This discussion comprises the final two-thirds of Book Two. A detailed description of the contents of this last part would extend beyond the limits of this essay. Instead, a brief presentation of the sacrament of penance may convey something of the author's method. It will have the added benefit of providing a small footnote to one of Bella Millett's particular interests – the conditions of confession.[16]

The author's division of the text, indicated by rubrics and connecting lines in the manuscripts, can be represented thus:

De penitentia
A   Quid sit
    1   Definitiones
    2   Exterior (sacramentum)
    3   Interior (virtus vel gratia)
B   Quot sunt eius species
    1   Sacramentum tantum, res et sacramentum, res tantum
    2   Sollemnis, publica, privata
C   Quot et que sunt necessaria ad veram penitentiam
    1   Penitens
    2   Sacerdos
    3   Contritio
        a   Quid sit
        b   Que sunt cause inductive
        c   Qualis debet esse
        d   De effectu
    4   Confessio
        a   Quid sit
        b   Quare facienda (ad quid valet)
        c   Cui facienda
        d   Qualis debet esse
        e   Qualiter sacerdos debet procedere audiendo
        f   Que pena revelanti confessionem
    5   Satisfactio
        a   Quid sit
        b   Qualis debet esse
        c   In quibus consistit
        d   Qualiter sacerdos debet imponere
        e   De falsa penitentia siue satisfactione
        f   De penitentia infirmorum
D   De impedimentis penitentie

[16]   See B. Millett, '*Ancrene Wisse* and the Conditions of Confession', *English Studies* 80 (1999), pp. 193–215.

The bulk of the treatment of these topics is drawn, implicitly and often explicitly, from Raymond of Penyafort's *Summa de paenitentia*, Godfrey of Trani's *Summa super titulis*, Robert Grosseteste's *Templum* and Richard Fishacre's commentary on Lombard's *Sentences*. The discussion of the 'conditions of confession' ['qualis debet esse confessio'] begins with a list of thirteen characteristics of a true and fruitful confession:

> Confession should be bitter, prompt, complete, unvarnished, voluntary, faithful, personal, accusatory, true, discrete, pure, deliberate and frequent.

> [Confessio debet esse: Amara, festina, integra, nuda, voluntaria, fidelis, propria, accusatoria, vera, discreta, pura, morosa, et frequens.]

These conditions are extracted *seriatim* from Raymond of Penyafort's long discussion of them in his *Summa de paenitentia*.[17] The first condition, 'bitterness' [*amaritudo*] is further distinguished into the five signs by which the confessor will recognize it: embarrassment or shame [*erubescencia* or *verecundia*], courage in overcoming shame [*fortitudo vincens pudorem*], tears [*lacrimae*], humility [*humilitas*] and prompt obedience [*promptitudo obedientie*]. These signs are illustrated with scriptural and patristic authorities and examples, all drawn from Raymond of Penyafort and Richard Fishacre.[18]

Our author goes on to explicate the condition 'timely' [*festina*] in the same manner. He includes long excerpts from Fishacre, disputing whether one can delay confession until Lent, for example, or, rather, is bound to confess as soon as one is conscious of committing a sin. The third condition of a true confession, 'comprehensive' [*integra*] is also discussed by means of excerpts from Raymond and Richard, with the addition of two verses, drawn from Wetheringsett's *Summa Qui bene presunt*, memorializing nine 'circumstances' [*circumstantiis*] which exacerbate or mitigate the seriousness of a particular sin:

> [Holy] orders, knowledge, [sacred] time and place, aggravate the sin, As does one's condition, the number of sins, the cause, and delay in confession.[19]

The author then returns to Raymond's original list of thirteen conditions of a true and fruitful confession, illustrating each of the remaining conditions briefly with extracts drawn from Raymond himself and from Richard Fishacre.

---

17 Raymond of Penyafort, *Summa* 3.34.23–30, cols. 817–28.

18 Ibid., 3.34.23, cols. 817–18; Richard Fishacre, *in 4 Sent. d. 17* (Oxford, Oriel College MS 43, fol. 404r).

19 'Agrauat ordo, locus peccata, sciencia, tempus / Etas, condicio, numerus, copia, causa, mora' (MS Bodley 655, fol. 97r). See G. Dinkova-Bruun, 'Notes on Poetic Composition in the Theological Schools *ca.* 1200 and the Latin Poetic Anthology from MS Harley 956: A Critical Edition', *Sacris erudiri* 43 (2004), 299–391 (p. 339).

He concludes the discussion of the last condition, 'frequent' [*frequens*] with a brief excerpt from the *Qui bene presunt*, which recommends the advice of William de Montibus that one should sometimes confess again things previously confessed, especially at the end of one's life, or when confessing to a new priest, or when the sin is particularly embarrassing.[20]

In this way the author of the *Speculum iuniorum* covers the rest of the topics under the sacrament of penance, as well as the other six sacraments discussed in Book Two, namely baptism, confirmation, Eucharist, extreme unction, holy orders and marriage. In doing so, he introduces the beginning student to the relevant distinctions, the terminology and the methods that were in use in the schools to discuss the practical needs of the *cura animarum*. He also leaves for us a precious annotated guide to the sources, the authorities and the arguments of this important period in the history of the schools.

Much more could be written about this fascinating and original *Speculum*, for example, about the physical disposition of the entire text into *schemata* and *distinctiones*, or about the usefulness of the author's explicit citations for clarifying some of the mysteries that still surround many mid-thirteenth century scholastic authors and texts. For now, however, it will suffice to have removed a little of the dust covering this neglected 'Mirror for Beginners'. Once it has been properly polished, and edited, it can take its rightful place among the major achievements of the pastoral writings of thirteenth- and fourteenth-century England.[21]

---

[20] 'Consilium magistri Willelmi de Montibus fuit omnia etiam prius confessa iterare post recidivacionem, specialiter cum fiat confessio novo sacerdoti, et etiam semel in anno, et precipue in mortis articulo, et maxime ea peccata que magis pudet confiteri, cum pudor in confessione sit magna pars satisfactionis' (MS Bodley 655, fol. 98r). The *Qui bene presunt* reads: 'Fuit etiam consilium cancellarii Lincolnie in recidiuatione, specialiter si facta fuerit confessio nouo sacerdoti, et eciam semel in anno, et precipue in mortis periculo, omnia prius confessa iterare, et maxime ea que pudet confiteri, dum pudor in confessione sit maxima pars satisfactionis' (Cambridge, University Library, MS 3471, fol. 149v).

[21] The present author is preparing a critical edition of the text.

7

Reading Edmund of Abingdon's *Speculum* as Pastoral Literature*

Cate Gunn

Edmund of Abingdon's[1] *Speculum religiosorum*, composed originally for a religious audience, is an examination of what it means to live perfectly. His own career acquainted Edmund with a number of different forms of religious life: although he was associated with monastic houses – he spent time not only at the Augustinian house of Merton but also the Cistercian house of Pontigny – he was a secular priest. C. H. Lawrence suggests that Edmund wrote the *Speculum* around 1213–14 when he was staying at Merton Priory,[2] before he incepted in theology at Oxford,[3] and some years before he became archbishop of Canterbury in 1234. It combines catechetical material with a guide to contemplation, and although written originally in Latin gained widespread popularity through translation into French as the *Mirour de Seinte Eglyse*, and is later found in Middle English as the *Mirror of Holy Church* alongside works by Richard Rolle.

There is little in the *Speculum* that is original: Edmund used material from Christian authorities, such as the Church Fathers Augustine and Gregory, and the more recent mystical writers Bernard of Clairvaux and Hugh of St Victor, to compose his spiritual guide. The *Speculum* is concerned with the

---

* Co-operating with other contributors in the production of this volume has given me the opportunity to ask for help from eminent scholars on medieval pastoral literature; I am particularly grateful to Jocelyn Wogan-Browne, Ralph Hanna and Joseph Goering for the assistance they have generously given me in the writing of this paper. I am also grateful to Catherine Innes-Parker for her advice, and to Nicholas Watson for allowing me to read his paper in advance. My thanks to Dr P. J. Fitzpatrick for reading this paper and for his encouragement ever since I was his student at Durham.

1 Although there is still a debate over the name Edmund Rich, I am following current academic practice in referring to the author of the *Speculum* as Edmund of Abingdon.
2 C. H. Lawrence, *The Life of St Edmund by Matthew Paris* (Oxford, 1996), pp. 26–8.
3 That is, he began teaching theology, having lectured in the arts earlier. James McEvoy gives a brief account of Edmund's career at Oxford when he discusses the early development of the university in *Robert Grosseteste* (Oxford, 2000), pp. 13–14.

ascent to contemplation but its interest is not limited to those in a dedicated religious life; the catechetical material was useful for those in charge of lay people and the work as a whole can be considered a work of *pastoralia*. There are two significant Latin versions, both present in a number of manuscripts:[4] as well as the original *Speculum religiosorum*, a later version, *Speculum ecclesie*, is a translation back into Latin from the Anglo-Norman *Mirour de Seinte Eglyse*.[5] The differences between these two versions suggest something about the wide appeal of the work which could address both professed religious and more general readers.

There is a temptation to accord *Speculum religiosorum* priority as the original version authored by Edmund, but the other versions have equally valid places in medieval spirituality and are important for our understanding of the development of that spirituality. Bella Millett, in the introduction to her recent edition of *Ancrene Wisse*, calls into question the binary opposition of 'author' and 'scribe' which is constructed on an assumption of the superiority of the original text:

> In a tradition which sees textual transmission primarily as a degenerative process, the progressive destruction of the form and sense of the author's original by repeated copying, this binary opposition can become a Manichaean dualism, in which the scribes are identified with the forces of darkness: they are responsible for the 'corruption' of their text by 'scribal error' (a term sometimes applied by editors to all non-authorial variants), and, if they draw on more than one exemplar, for its 'contamination'.[6]

While the editors of Edmund's *Speculum* are not so explicit in their value judgements, there is an implicit assumption that the preferred edition is one as close as possible to Edmund's original; this is certainly the ideal to which

---

4 The original thirteenth-century text is no longer extant; Helen Forshaw uses the late fourteenth/early fifteenth century text in Oxford, Bodleian MS Hatton 26, which she believes to be a close copy of the original, as the basis of her edition of *Speculum religiosorum*. She presents it in parallel with the text of *Speculum ecclesie* principally from BL, Royal MS 7 A. 1: Edmund, *Speculum*; the manuscripts containing the texts are described pp. 1–14. References to this edition will be inserted in the text, preceded by *SR* [for *Speculum religiosorum*] or *SE* [for *Speculum ecclesie*].

5 The translation from the *Merure* into Latin probably took place in the second half of the fourteenth century, Introduction to Edmund, *Speculum*, p. 16. Helen Forshaw shows how the *Speculum ecclesie* versions are dependent on the Anglo-Norman *Mirour*, 'New Light on the *Speculum Ecclesie* of St Edmund of Abingdon', *Archives d'histoire doctrinale et littéraire du Moyen Age* (1972 for 1971), 7–33. Alan Wilshere also argues that the Latin text is the original, rather than the French as was once thought, based on the scholastic vocabulary of the text in Hatton 26, A. Wilshere, 'The Latin Primacy of St Edmund's "Mirror of Holy Church"', *MLR* 71 (1976), 500–12.

6 *Ancrene Wisse*, ed. Millett, Textual Introduction, I, xlvii.

the translator David Theroux aspires.[7] In their drive to establish a 'correct' edition neither Helen Forshaw nor A. D. Wilshere, who has edited two forms of the Anglo-Norman *Mirour*, show any interest in the *mouvance* of the textual tradition. Indeed, Wilshere's explicit concern is with excavating 'what exactly' Edmund wrote, arguing that 'both Latin and French versions are necessary if we are to disinter, so far as is possible … the primal form of the treatise as it came from the hands of St Edmund'.[8] However, *Speculum religiosorum*, like *Ancrene Wisse*, underwent adaptation and translation leading to non-authorial variations which illustrate the dissemination of pastoral literature and its later vernacularization.[9]

Although it was originally written in the early thirteenth century, there is no extant manuscript of Edmund's original *Speculum religiosorum* dating from before the late fourteenth century; however, the manuscript tradition, such as it is, can provide evidence for the work's reception and uses. Forshaw does not seek to preserve the dynamism of the textual tradition; nevertheless, by presenting two states of the work in parallel, her edition of the *Speculum* does allow us to trace that tradition. Forshaw argues that the late fourteenth or early fifteenth-century text found in Oxford Bodleian MS Hatton 26 is probably a direct copy of a thirteenth-century source; this text is bound with thirteenth-century material and Forshaw accepts 'Dr. Hunt's suggestion that all the evidence implies that the second scribe was replacing the badly worn gatherings of the original volume'.[10] Certainly, a later hand (Ralph Hanna suggests around 1400) continues the thirteenth-century copy of one of the texts, *Liber scintillarum*, without a break in the text,[11] which would suggest the replacement of damaged gatherings. However, it is possible

---

7   Theroux translates 'Helen Forshaw's reconstructed text, *Speculum religiosorum*, as closest to the original version of the *Mirror*', D. J. Theroux, *Saint Edmund of Abingdon's Mirror of Religious, Part I – Introduction*, www.sse.org/pdf / StEdmundMirrorPartI.pdf, © David J. Theroux, SSE, 1990, p. 15; the translation is found at *Part II – A Translation* www.sse.org/pdf/StEdmundMirrorPartII.pdf. My translations are indebted to, but not identical with, those of Theroux.

8   Edmund, *Mirour*, p. i.

9   A belief that non-authorial variations are valid forms of the *Ancrene Wisse* was the motivation for the edition that Millett has produced, arguing that 'an edition for general scholarly use cannot limit itself to a corrected text of A'. Millett's editorial approach takes into account the 'dynamic' textual tradition of the work, 'and although it attempts, wherever possible, to distinguish between the contribution of the original author and that of his successors to the textual tradition of *Ancrene Wisse*, it does not treat the former as the only significant part of its textual history'; Millett, *Ancrene Wisse*, Textual Introduction, I, lx–lxi. This is a point developed by Watson in his paper in this volume; indeed, he argues that the inclusivity of the original text suggests it *'aspires* to the vernacular'.

10   Forshaw, Introduction to Edmund, *Speculum*, p. 2.

11   Oxford, Bodleian MS Hatton 26, fol. 146, see F. Madan, H. H. E. Craster and N. Denholm-Young, *A Summary Catalogue of Western Manuscripts in the Bodleian Library at Oxford*, II, Pt. 2 (Oxford, 1937), entry 4061. I am grateful to Ralph Hanna

that a different early fifteenth-century hand continues with the collection of texts, which includes not only *Speculum religiosorum* (fol. 183v–fol. 204 – the last text in this section) but also the *Emendatio vitae* of Richard Rolle (called here *De conversione peccatoris* and immediately preceding the *Speculum*) and the *Horologium sapientiae* of Henry Suso, neither of which could have been in a thirteenth-century original. There is a final thirteenth-century section, containing various pieces on the vices, but the first of these begins in mid-chapter (the first full chapter, titled *De susurratione*, starts part way down the first column of fol. 205r), so there is no evidence that any real attempt was made to reconstruct the thirteenth-century book, and indeed there is no reason to assume that the works now bound together in MS Hatton 26 had a common source. The texts from the early fifteenth century section, between fol. 146 and fol. 204, may have been copied at the Augustinian house of Stafford; an inscription at the end of *Speculum religiosorum*, at fol. 204v, states 'Iste libere constat de domo sancti thome martiris iuxta Staffordiam', but this is in a later hand than the rest of this section.

The text of *Speculum religiosorum* found here may well have been copied from an early thirteenth century original, but the manuscript evidence does not prove this; what it does show is its acceptance amongst Latin pastoral material in an Augustinian library in the fifteenth century. The house at which Edmund may have composed *Speculum religiosorum*, Merton,[12] was also Augustinian. *Speculum religiosorum* was written for members of a religious community, maybe new converts or novices,[13] yet it was also clearly relevant to the wider Augustinian community and their concerns.

Speculum religiosorum is ultimately concerned with the contemplation of God; there are, however, three ways of approaching this: through creatures, through the scriptures and finally contemplating God in his own nature (*SR* §18, p. 44). The second step, the contemplation of God in the scriptures, consists of the kind of catechetical material one needs to know in order to live a good and faithful life. These pastoral and catechetical elements, which include the seven mortal sins, the seven virtues, the seven gifts of the Holy Spirit, the articles of faith and the sacraments, would guide readers in their own lives and vocations but may also have aided them in their pastoral

---

for his help in interpreting the evidence of the writing and compiling of this manuscript, inconclusive as it is.

[12] The library at Merton would probably have been able to supply Edmund with the necessary books for the composition of the *Speculum*, according to a later list of books held, *Registrum Anglie de Libris Doctorum et Auctorum*, Corpus of British Library Catalogues, 2, ed. R. H. and M. A. Rouse, Latin text est. by R. A. B. Mynors (London, 1991), p. 252.

[13] Watson points this out in an early draft of his paper, referring to a passage close to the beginning of *Speculum religiosorum*: 'Cum ergo consilio Domini religionem ingrediens adhesisti', *SR* §2, p. 32.

duties. While we cannot assume that all Augustinian canons had a pastoral vocation, certainly some did have duties of care towards lay parishioners.

The manuscript tradition of the later *Speculum ecclesie* also has an Augustinian association, since the best copy belonged to an Augustinian house, St Mary Overie in Southwark. This manuscript, now BL MS Royal 7 A 1, like MS Hatton 26, was written around 1400 and, though in more than one hand, is a single, continuous collection of works of high-medieval spirituality, including works reputed to be by Bonaventure, and prayers and meditations by Anselm.[14] The nature of the readers (or audience) of the two Latin versions of the *Speculum* – Augustinian or otherwise – suggests at least part of the nature of the *mouvance* of Edmund's text. Any discussion of the readership of Edmund's work needs to consider the readers to whom the text is primarily addressed, and how far the adaptation of the text suggests a changing audience.

Both *Speculum religiosorum* and *Speculum ecclesie* open with an address to the audience: a quotation from the first epistle to the Corinthians, Videte vocacionem vestram ['Consider your vocation', I Cor. 1. 26]. *Speculum religiosorum* suggests that this 'applies particularly to religious' ['Verbum hoc Apostoli precipue competit religiosis']. In *Speculum ecclesie* these words are 'relevant to us religious men', ['Ista verba Apostoli pertinent ad nos homines religiosos'] (*SR* §1, p. 32; *SE* §1, p. 33). Edmund is clearly using the term *religiosi* to mean men leading a dedicated life of religion; the use of the noun to mean someone belonging to a Christian religious order dates back to the eighth century.[15] It did not necessarily mean a monk, however; Raymond of Penyafort uses the term in the thirteenth century to suggest a variety of forms of religious life: 'plures monachi, vel regulares, vel alii religiosi'.[16] In *Speculum religiosorum*, the term could mean canons as well as monks.

Does using *religiosi* to qualify the noun *homines*, especially with reference to the readers of *Speculum ecclesie*, suggest that these men are to be understood differently – more generally as men of religion – than the original monastic readers? In the twelfth century the use of the adjective *religiosus* was not confined to those who had taken religious vows. For example, in the *Ecclesiastical History* of Orderic Vitalis, *religiosus* is most often used to indicate 'men of religion' in the sense of monks or regular canons, but it was also used of married women, parents and noble men to mean 'pious';[17] and the term

---

14 See G. F. Warner and J. P. Gilson, *Catalogue of Western Manuscripts in the Old Royal and King's Collections*, I (London, 1921).

15 The first example for the definition of *religiosus* as 'in conventual religious order' in the forthcoming volume of the *Dictionary of Medieval Latin from British Sources* (ed. R. E. Latham et al. for the British Academy) is from Alcuin. I am grateful for a preview of this entry prior to its publication.

16 Raymond of Penyafort, *Summe de poenitentia et matrimonio* Liber 1 (Rome, 1603; rep. Farnborough), p. 14.

17 E.g. 'Generosam et religiosam nomine Ittam habuit uxorem', *The Ecclesiastical*

is used in the mid-twelfth century *Foundation of Waltham Abbey* to describe a wife.[18] The term could still mean 'pious' when Thomas Eccleston wrote his *Tractatus* in the mid-thirteenth century.[19] However, the adjectival form in *Speculum ecclesie* is probably due to its translation from the French 'gent [or genz] de religion' which is found in both versions of the Anglo-Norman *Mirour de Seinte Eglyse*, in the edition by A. D. Wilshere.[20] The *Anglo-Norman Dictionary* edited by William Rothwell suggests only *monk* or the noun *religious* as translations of the phrase *gent(z) de religiun*,[21] but a thirteenth-century French version of *Ancrene Wisse* suggests a wider meaning: the potential readers for this *Vie de gent de religion* include 'monie, ou chanoine, ou frere blanc ou bis ou noir, ou nonein, ou recluse, ou en autre manere de religion, vus homme ou vus femme' ['monk or canon or white friar or grey or black, or nun, or recluse, or in any other form of religion whether man or woman'].[22] That is, the 'gent de religion' is someone living a dedicated religious life, but the term is not limited to a specific order.

The first chapter of *Speculum religiosorum* continues with a quotation: 'Religionem intrare summe perfectionis est' ['To enter into religion is the height of perfection'] (*SR* §1, p. 32). David Theroux translates 'Religionem intrare' as

History of Orderic Vitalis, ed. M. Chibnall, II (Bk 4) (Oxford, 1969), 206.15; *religiosus* is also used as an adjective to qualify *monachus* at 108.9, suggesting that the two terms were not synonymous (ibid.). The Index verborum is in vol. I (1980).

18 'Uxor autem ejus, Glitha nomine, … mulier religiosa et sanctis exercitiis dedita', *The Foundation of Waltham Abbey (De Inventione Sanctae Crucis …),* ed. W. Stubbs (Oxford, 1861), cap. 12.

19 'Huic revelavit Dominus [dolum] cuiusdam mulieris religiosae', Thomas Eccleston, *Tractatus de adventu Fratrum Minorum in Angliam,* ed. A. G. Little (Manchester, 1951), p. 15. Leo Sherley-Price translates this phrase as 'a certain pious woman', *The Coming of the Franciscans* (London, 1964), p. 11.

20 Edmund, *Mirour,* pp. 4 and 5 (see also pp. 44 and 45). Wilshere divides the twenty-three manuscripts of complete or partial texts of the *Mirour de Seinte Eglyse* known to him into two broad versions (*families* may be a more appropriate term) which he names 'A. The unrevised "religious" version' and 'B. The revised "lay" version', *Mirour,* p. vi. Texts of both date from the thirteenth and fourteenth centuries.

21 *Anglo-Norman Dictionary* ed. William Rothwell et al., for MHRA and ANTS (London, 1992); the *Dictionnaire historique de la langue française,* ed. A. Rey (Paris, 1992) does not give the phrase 'gens de religion' but of the adjective *religieux* it does suggest that the term became less likely to be applied solely to a member of a religious order: 'Le mot suit le développement sémantique de *religion*: emprunté en parlant d'une personne qui vit en vertu de sa foi, selon les règles de sa religion (v. 1112), il a pris une valeur subjective: "animé par une foi sincère" (v. 1278).'

22 Millett, *Ancrene Wisse,* Textual Introduction', I, xxiii, referring to W. H. Trethewey (ed.), *The French Text of the Ancrene Riwle,* EETS OS 240 (1958), 267/4–6; I am grateful to Bella Millett for suggesting this reference and adding, 'Since this is distinguished from other sections addressed to a more general audience, I think we can assume that "religion" here is used to refer to a way of life rather than piety in general', personal correspondence, 25.10. 2007.

'To enter a religious community'[23] but, interestingly, the sermon attributed to Eusebius that is quoted says, 'Venire quidem ad eremum, summa perfectio est'.[24] *Eremus*, originally meaning desert or wasteland, is the root from which we get *eremitical* and *hermit*, suggesting a life withdrawn from the world; it does not imply community. The next section begins, 'Unde religioso summe necessarium est vivere perfecte' ['And so for the religious the greatest necessity is to live perfectly'] (*SR* §2, p. 32). The *Speculum ecclesie* version varies significantly: 'Et ideo, tu qui vivis in religione seu congregacione, sequere viam perfectionis' ['And therefore, you who live in religion or congregation, follow the way of perfection'] (*SE* §2, p. 33),[25] suggesting that being 'in religione' was not necessarily the equivalent of being a member of a religious community. We are faced, not only with the difficulties of modern translation, but also with a flexibility over terms in the Middle Ages; and, indeed, there was a fluidity in forms of religious life ranging from the strictly enclosed, through semi-religious forms of living to devout laity.

The question of audience is further complicated by a reference to 'laicus' in *Speculum religiosorum*. Although the original text was primarily addressed to a literate, coenobitic readership, the beginning of the 'didactic tract'[26] on how God is to be contemplated in the scriptures raises the question of how someone who cannot read Latin, 'laicus vel illiteratus', can access this material. The answer is that what can be written can also be preached and expounded: the illiterate should listen to sermons (*SR* §25, pp. 46–8). Forshaw argues that 'laicus' refers to *conversi*;[27] but the use of this term also opens up the possibility of a non-religious audience of 'listeners'.

Such an audience is explicitly addressed by *Speculum ecclesie*, where the person who is illiterate is not mentioned in the third person, but addressed directly: 'Queres a me: "Quomodo unquam perveniam ad contemplacionem Dei in sacra scriptura?" Iam dulciter michi attendas' ['You ask me: "How will I ever arrive at the contemplation of God in holy scripture?" Now listen to me receptively'] (*SR* §25, p. 49).[28] The advice about who to listen to is less specific here and does not assume a religious community; you should listen, not to the 'doctors of the church and preachers' ['doctores ecclesie predicatores'] as in *Speculum religiosorum* (*SR* §25, p. 48), but to 'every good thing which is

---

23 Edmund, *Speculum*, p. 32; trans. Theroux, II, 190.
24 Quoted by Forshaw, Edmund, *Speculum*, n. 8–9, p. 32; from Eusebius 'Gallicanus', *Collectio Homiliarum*, ed. F. Glorie, Hom. ix, CCSL, 101 A (1971), p. 522.
25 The same distinction is found between the A and B forms of *Mirour de Seinte Eglyse*: only B contains a reference to *congregacion*, §1, p. 7.
26 H. Forshaw, 'St Edmund's *Speculum*: A Classic of Victorine Spirituality', *Archives d'histoire doctrinale et littéraire du Moyen Age* 39 (1973 for 1972), 7–40 (p. 15).
27 Ibid., n. 43, p. 18.
28 It is not easy to find a good translation for *dulciter*; it is clearly translated from the French *doucement* which is found in both versions of the *Mirour*, ed. Wilshere, §7, pp. 22 and 23.

said to you by the wise' ['omne bonum quod a sapientibus tibi dicitur'] (*SE* §25, p. 49). In both cases, the reader or listener is advised to pay attention to whatever will aid them to live well, avoid sin and attain virtue.

This advice is not limited to the religious life, but is the sort of advice that became popular in vernacular pastoral literature aimed either directly at lay people, or at those charged with their spiritual care, over the course of the thirteenth and fourteenth centuries; the material listed – in both versions – is that which priests should ensure their parishioners knew, such as the seven mortal sins, the seven virtues, Ten Commandments, articles of faith and sacraments.[29] It is in this catechetical material, in the section on the six – or seven – works of mercy that we again come across a shift in terminology between the two versions that suggests a broadening audience. In *Speculum religiosorum*, after the listing of the six works, there is an argument concerning their performance:

> Sed nunc dicit claustralis: 'Ego quidem non possum facere opera misericordie, quoniam hic sub aliena potestate me sponte supposui.'
>
> (*SR* §72, p. 70)

> [But then a *claustralis* says: 'But I am not able to perform works of mercy because I have subjected myself voluntarily here under another's authority.']

David Theroux translates *claustralis* as 'monk'.[30] The *Speculum ecclesie* version is rather different: here the objection comes from someone addressed in the second person, who replies, 'I who am in religion' am not able to perform the works of mercy, not because I am under another's authority, but because I do not have the means to do so.[31] Lawrence suggests that the lack of means is proof of monastic status,[32] but the speaker claims neither to be *claustralis* nor to be under authority; we seem again to have a less strict idea of what it means to be 'in religione'. It is possible that the performance of works of mercy was to be understood allegorically, as the injunction to help widows

---

[29] One could compare the catechetical material in the *Speculum* with the near-contemporary *Summa confessorum* of Thomas of Chobham, or the synodal statutes drawn up by Richard Poore for the diocese of Salisbury in 1219, *Councils and Synods with Other Documents Relating to the English Church*, II *1205–1313*, ed. F. M. Powicke and C. R. Cheney, Pt. 2, *1265–1313* (Oxford, 1964), pp. 57–65.

[30] Theroux, *St Edmund's Mirror of Religious*, II, p. 223; Du Cange associates *claustralis* with enclosed monks, www.uni-mannheim.de/mateo/camenaref/ducange/bd1/jpg/s1119.html.

[31] 'Ego, qui dum in religione, non habeo potestatem dandi cibum, necque potum, vestimentum, nec hospicium, quia non habeo ex quo possum illud facere.' He also claims not to be able to visit the imprisoned, comfort the sick or bury the dead because 'sum in alterius voluntate constitutus', *SE* §72, p. 71. These could even be the words of an anchorite, who could be considered 'in religion' but not in a regular order.

[32] Lawrence, *Life of St Edmund*, p. 28.

and orphans is explained for the anchoresses who read *Ancrene Wisse*;[33] what matters is that one acts with compassion in one's heart. Towards the end of the chapter on the works of mercy, Edmund claims that the poor, those who neither have nor desire riches, are truly religious: 'ut sunt sancti viri vere religiosi' (*SR* §74, p. 72). *Religiosi* here seems to be a noun ['such holy men are truly religious'], but its role in the corresponding sentence in *Speculum ecclesie* is not clear: 'Isti sunt sancti homines religiosi' (*SE* §74, p. 73). In both these cases, however, the true religious is one who lives in poverty, rather than one who belongs to a particular order.

The indications are that *Speculum ecclesie* was written for a different (and expanded) audience from the readership of *Speculum religiosorum*; while the earlier text is clearly addressed to professed religious, the later one seems more inclusive, addressing those who wish to follow the religious life in other forms. It may also be significant that one text of the *Mirour de Seinte Eglyse*, which appears to be intermediate between the two forms of the Latin *Speculum*, was titled 'Sermon a dames religioses';[34] these women were probably nuns, but a growing body of vernacular devotional and pastoral literature was being made available for devout women wishing to follow a religious vocation in alternative forms.[35]

The differences in content between the two texts of the *Speculum* suggest as much about the varying audiences as the direct indications of intended readership so far considered. Such differences are most apparent in the treatment of catechetical material and the meditations of the life of Christ. The works of mercy, for example, differ significantly in the two texts: the original *Speculum religiosorum* contained the six works of mercy as found in St Matthew's gospel, feeding the hungry, giving drink to the thirsty, clothing the naked, taking in strangers, visiting the sick and comforting those in prison [Matt. 26. 35–6]. Both French versions also give six, numbered, works of mercy and like *Speculum religiosorum*, they conclude, contrary to the order found in Matthew, with comforting the sick.[36]

The listing of six works of mercy was standard until the end of the twelfth century when we start to find the inclusion of a seventh work, burying the

---

33   *Ancrene Wisse*, ed. Millett, Preface, 110–13, I, 4: the widows are those who have lost their spouse, Christ, through sin while the orphans have similarly lost their father, God; the duty of care towards them is of comfort and prayer. Gregory the Great also offers an allegorical interpretation, *Moralia in Job*, Liber 19, 20, ed. M. Adriaen, CCSL 143A (Turnhout, 1979), pp. 981–2. Cf. Raymond of Penyaforte, *Summe de poenitentia* Liber 3, p. 274.

34   This is a member of the 'A' family of texts found in St John's College Oxford MS 190 and dating from the late thirteenth century; *Mirour* ed. Wilshere, pp. vi–vii, 4.

35   I pursue this argument more fully in Gunn, *AW From Pastoral Literature*, esp. chap. 12, 'Reading *Ancrene Wisse* as Vernacular Spirituality'.

36   *Mirour* ed. Wishere, pp. 42 and 43.

dead, from the book of Tobit;[37] *Speculum ecclesie* includes the seventh work of mercy in chapter 16, 'De septem operibus misericordie'.[38] Numbered lists,[39] such as the works of mercy and other lists in the catechetical section of the *Speculum*, became popular with more widespread preaching since they were convenient and memorable. The ninth chapter of the Lambeth Council of 1281, usually known by its opening phrase, 'Ignorantia sacerdotum', includes the seven works of mercy among the items priests should preach to their congregations.[40] The works of mercy were now firmly part of the pastoral care of lay people.

It was also required that lay people know the creed and one of the most apparent differences between the two texts of the *Speculum* is in their treatment of the articles of faith.[41] In *Speculum religiosorum* the twelve articles comprise five articles of faith, based on the creed, and the seven sacraments: baptism, confirmation, penitence, communion, ordination, matrimony and extreme unction. These twelve articles follow the three theological virtues, faith, hope and charity: there is a logical development allowing clear and concise exposition of the basic elements of Christianity. However, we do not get any explanation of what a sacrament is or how the sacraments fit into the divine economy. Instead the twelve articles of faith are listed simply in a chapter entitled 'De duodecim fidei et septem sacramentis', the seven sacraments being the articles of faith numbered six to twelve. Theroux points out that the first three articles are much more simply stated in the French A text; following Wilshere's argument in his introduction to the *Mirour*, especially with regard to passages in the didactic or catechetical chapters,[42] Theroux believes that the French A text is at times a more reliable indication of the original text by Edmund. This would make the first three articles of faith as short and concise as the other articles.[43] In other words, Edmund of Abingdon was providing only a brief reminder of the articles of faith and the sacraments to readers who were well acquainted with them.

---

[37] In the late twelfth century, Peter the Chanter mentioned 'septem opera misericordiae' in his *Verbum Abbreviatum*, cap. 79 in *PL* 205, 0236; cf. cap. 132 at *PL* 205, 0326.

[38] The text of *Speculum religiosorum* in BL MS Harley 5441 titles this chapter 'De septem operibus misericordie' but lists only six works.

[39] *Chiffre* in French, see 'Miséricorde (œuvres de)' in *Dictionnaire de Spiritualité*, X (Paris: Beauchesne, 1980), col. 1341. *SR* states there are 'sex opera misericordie' and lists them; *SE* numbers the seven works: 'Primum est cibare esurientes; secundum est [… etc.]' pp. 68–9.

[40] *Councils and Synods*, pp. 900–4.

[41] Edmund, *Speculum*, pp. 62–9.

[42] 'The simplest hypothesis to account for this tangle of evidence is that, at a stage now lost, a scribe copying the original Latin I added certain material. ... There can be no question that the Hatton 26 recension contains the virtually complete Latin text as it came from the hands of St Edmund; but into that text has been inserted, at some much later date, additional matter.' Wilshere, Introduction to *Mirour*, p. xvi.

[43] Theroux, trans., *Mirror of Religious* II, 218, n. 22.

The inclusion of the sacraments within a list of the articles of faith is unusual but not unique.[44] The articles of faith are first found in twelfth-century theological writings; one of the earliest references to them as a numbered list (in this case, seven) is in the Parisian text, *Summa de poenitentia iniungendi* from around 1200.[45] They are soon found in texts by English authors, and with what became the common number of twelve. In William de Montibus's *Numerale* the twelfth article 'is devoted to faith in the Church's seven sacraments'.[46] In Robert Grosseteste's *Templum Dei* we find the 'unusual enumeration' of the articles present also in Edmund's *Speculum*; Joseph Goering points out that Grosseteste's enumeration – five articles of faith derived from the creed and seven concerning the sacraments – became very popular: 'It is repeated by Edmund of Abingdon, Archbishop of Canterbury, by Walter of Cantilupe, Bishop of Worcester, and later, by Peter Quinel, Bishop of Exeter (1287).'[47] This suggests that Edmund's formulation is dependent on Grosseteste's, but if the dating of *Speculum religiosorum* to 1213–14 is correct it predates the *Templum Dei* by at least five years.[48] It is possible that both works had a common source; it is not clear whether Edmund and Grosseteste were at Oxford at the same time, though James McEvoy, who refers to them as colleagues, points out that Grosseteste was appointed to the commission to enquire into Edmund's sanctity because of his personal acquaintance.[49] There are not sufficient similarities in wording to suggest direct borrowing, and whereas Edmund was writing his *Speculum* for the members of a religious community, the *Templum Dei* was explicitly written for the instruction of priests.[50] While the *Templum Dei* may not have been accessible – intellectually or financially – to many parish priests in the thirteenth century, many schools

---

44 It is not found in the *De sacramentis* of Hugh of St Victor, a source for some of Edmund's *Speculum*, nor in the very full thirteenth-century *Summa aurea magistri Guillelmi Altissiodorensis* [of William of Auxerre], ed. J. Ribaillier, 5 vols. (Spicilegium Bonaventurianum 16–20) (Paris, 1980–87); the sacraments are discussed in Liber 4, Spic. Bon. 19 (1985).

45 J. Goering, 'Christ in Dominican Catechesis: The Articles of Faith' in *Christ Among the Medieval Dominicans: Representations of Christ in the Texts and Images of the Order of Preachers*, ed. K. Emery Jr and J. Wawrykow, Notre Dame Conferences in Medieval Studies 7 (Notre Dame, 1998), pp. 127–38 (p. 129); I am very grateful to Joseph Goering for this and other references to the articles of faith, and to Jonathan Hall for pointing me in the right direction.

46 Ibid., p. 129.

47 Ibid.

48 A date of composition between 1220 and 1230 is suggested, Goering and Mantello, Introduction to Grosseteste, *Templum Dei*, pp. 4–5. It is, of course, possible that the *Speculum* was written later, as a response to the Fourth Lateran Council, but the text contains no explicit references to the Council to support this possibility.

49 McEvoy, *Grosseteste*, p. 14.

50 Goering and Mantello, Introduction to Grosseteste, *Templum Dei*, p. 6; this is also the case for subsequent treatises, such as that which Cantilupe appended to the Worcester constitutions, see J. Goering and D. S. Taylor, 'The *Summulae* of Bishops

of theology were flourishing in England at the time and, like the 'laicus vel illiteratus' Edmund refers to (*SR* §25, p. 46), clergy who were not scholars could nevertheless be educated through hearing sermons.

The catechetical material in *Speculum religiosorum* is outlined briefly as though to remind those entering into – or continuing in – the religious life of the elements of their faith, but in *Speculum ecclesie* the material on the articles of faith and the sacraments is expanded into two chapters: 'De duodecim articulis fidei', which covers the first five articles of faith in some detail, and 'De septem sacramentis ecclesie' which describes the seven sacraments much more fully than in *Speculum religiosorum*. Similarly, the A text of the *Mirour* lists twelve articles of faith, the last seven of which are the seven sacraments, while the B text provides much more detail to the first five articles and then starts a separately numbered list for the seven sacraments, again more fully described.[51]

Lawrence points out that the instructions on baptism in *Speculum ecclesie* are 'clearly intended for parish clergy'; similarly, he points out that the 'practical suggestions' included in the section on the third commandment – 'Keep holy the Sabbath' – were 'obviously not directed at a religious community'. *Speculum ecclesie* instructs the reader to 'go to church and devoutly say Lauds or hear it quietly' ['debes ire ad ecclesiam, et devote matutinas dicere vel sine garula dulciter audire'] (*SE* §44, p. 57); this 'might be applicable to a parish chaplain'.[52] The changes and additions to the original form of the *Speculum* for different readerships over the course of the fourteenth century may have been directed at the pastoral concerns of clerics in charge of lay congregations.

Another indication of the differing purposes and audiences of *Speculum religiosorum* and *Speculum ecclesie* is their treatment of the meditations on the life of Christ. Following the *Speculum*'s treatment of the contemplation of God in the scriptures, the meditations on the life of Christ form part of the progress towards the contemplation of God in himself: they provide a means to contemplate God in his humanity. Each pair of meditations (one from the account of the Passion and one from some other mystery of Christ's life) is linked with one of the canonical hours; this would seem to associate these meditations closely with a monastic life, but it is possible that such a pattern of meditations could be pursued in a lay or semi-religious life.

The readers of *Speculum religiosorum* are told that the meditations have been divided up between the seven hours of the day and night in which praises to God are sung in church ['per septem horas diei et noctis distinxi, in quibut solent laudes Deo in ecclesia decantari'] (*SR* §92, p. 82). In *Speculum*

Walter de Cantilupe (1240) and Peter Quinel (1287)', *Speculum* 67 (1992), 576–94 (p. 577).

[51] *Mirour* ed. Wilshere, pp. 34–41.

[52] Lawrence, *Life of Edmund*, p. 29, the translation is by Lawrence.

ecclesie, however, they are divided among the seven hours of the day – there is no mention of night offices – which 'you sing in a monastery or church'['quas cantas in monasterio vel ecclesia'] (*SE* §92, p. 83); this suggests the possibility of hours sung in a non-monastic church. While in *Speculum religiosorum* the word 'hora' is always included, this is not the case in *Speculum ecclesie*; for example, the meditation on the incarnation of Christ and his crucifixion that is set 'ante horam sextam' in *Speculum Religiosorum* is to be done 'ante meridiem' in *Speculum ecclesie*. As well, a verse in English is inserted into this meditation, which suggests the lay, vernacular appropriation of these meditations.[53] Such changes fit into the pattern of increasing extra-monastic devotion, to which the development of Books of Hours and the popularity of *Ancrene Wisse* also bear witness.[54]

The most significant difference between the two versions of the *Speculum* may be the subtle change in tone: thinking about the place and time in which Christ was born ['loco et hora in quibus Christus natus est'] (*SR* §93, p. 82) in *Speculum religiosorum*, becomes thinking on the time, place and hour in which our sweet Lord Jesus Christ was born ['tempus, locum et horam in quibus natus fuit Dominus noster Iesus Christus dulcis'] (*SE* §93, pp. 84–5) in *Speculum ecclesie*. The grammatical form seems to be due to the transition through Anglo-Norman; more important, the language is in keeping with the more affective meditations on the life of Christ that became popular in the later Middle Ages. Further evidence of the association of *Speculum ecclesie* with affective devotion is suggested by the manuscript owned by the Augustinian priory of St Mary Overie, which also includes the *Meditations on the Life of Christ* and the *Stimulus amoris*, both attributed to Bonaventure and typical of later medieval devotional writing. Lengthy meditations, often translated into the vernacular and including much material not in the Gospel accounts, invited the meditator to participate in and enter into the lives of Jesus, Mary and the disciples. Such an approach is found in Aelred's 'Threefold Meditation' which forms part of his *Rule of Life for a Recluse*:

> First enter the room of blessed Mary and with her read the books which prophesy the virginal birth and the coming of Christ. Wait there for the arrival of the angel …[55]

---

53 'Now gothe þe son undir wodde, / Me rewey Mary þy faire rodde. / now gothe þe son undir þe tree, / Me rewei Marie þi son and þee', *SE* §103, p. 93.

54 Cf. Bella Millett, '*Ancrene Wisse* and the Book of Hours' in *Writing Religious Women*, pp. 21–40 (p. 31).

55 'Ac primum cum beata Maria, ingressa cubiculum, libros quibus virginis partus et Christi prophetatur aduentus euolue. Ibi aduentum angeli praestolare ut uideas intrantem', Aelred, *De Institutione*, pp. 662–3; trans. Macpherson, 'Rule of Life', p. 80.

Aelred's meditations are vigorously developed in fourteenth- and fifteenth-century Middle English versions.

The meditations in *Speculum religiosorum* are restrained; Helen Forshaw, writing as Mary Philomena SHCJ, points out that this restraint and simplicity is preserved in later versions of the *Speculum*, with the exception of one of the Middle English versions, and the interpolation of extra material ('reminiscent of the Franciscan *Meditationes Vitae Christi*') in two Latin texts of *Speculum ecclesie*. Forshaw expresses disapproval of the attempts to 'make more vivid and present to the mind's eye the events of Christ's life and to rouse suitable emotions in the reader',[56] but the fact that Edmund's material could be adapted in this manner to rouse emotions shows how this generative text continued to be of value in changing circumstances and to different readers.

It is clear that *Speculum ecclesie* was addressed to a broader audience than was the original *Speculum religiosorum*, while the vernacularization of the *Speculum* as the French *Mirour* and the later Middle English *Mirror of Holy Church* reflects a continuing adaptation to changing audiences. Indeed, the developmental history of Edmund's text from *Speculum* to *Mirror* is a microcosm of the development of pastoral literature in the Middle Ages, and the adaptability of the text – as witnessed by the various extant editions and translations – are a great part of its interest. As Wilshere claims, 'Evidently the *Speculum Ecclesie* answered an extensive contemporary need.'[57] This suggests the growing popularity of the Latin text, which was copied and translated back into Latin in the fourteenth and fifteenth centuries.[58] Most of the surviving copies of Edmund's works, however, are in fact the French *Mirour*: there are twenty-eight Anglo-Norman manuscripts listed in *Anglo-Norman Literature: A Guide to Texts and Manuscripts*,[59] most dated between 1250 and 1350, suggesting that its applicability to lay (or at least non-Latinate) audiences was the source of much of its popularity. It was translated into English and copied many times in the fifteenth century; the two main Middle English versions are represented by texts in the Thornton manuscript, Lincoln Cathedral Library, A. 1.17 and the Vernon manuscript, Bodleian, MS Eng. poet a. 1.[60] There are also many extracts and fragments.[61] In the paper following, Nicholas Watson examines the teaching of the *Speculum* focusing on the Middle English translation, and tracing its role in the reform move-

---

[56] Mary Philomena, 'St Edmund of Abingdon's Meditations before the Canonical Hours', *Ephemerides Liturgicae* 78 (1964), 33–57 (pp. 56 and 57).
[57] Wilshere, Introduction to *Mirour*, p. iv.
[58] The earliest Latin versions are in late fourteenth and early fifteenth century manuscripts; the twenty-four Latin texts Forshaw lists are mostly in fifteenth-century hands, Edmund, *Speculum*, ed. Forshaw, pp. 1–14.
[59] Dean and Boulton, *Anglo-Norman Literature*, pp. 343–4.
[60] Horstmann, *Yorkshire Writers*, p. 219 and 240.
[61] V. M. Lagorio and M. G. Sargent in Hartung, *Manual*, pp. 3460–1.

ments of the fourteenth century. This transition from Latin to the vernacular suggests a broadening of the audience and both reflects and partly constitutes the growth in lay piety and the development of vernacular spirituality in the late Middle Ages.

8

Middle English Versions and Audiences of Edmund of Abingdon's *Speculum Religiosorum*

Nicholas Watson

Unlike its nearest early thirteenth century insular counterpart, *Ancrene Wisse*, which was rendered into Anglo-Norman within thirty years of its final revision and Latin within fifty, Edmund of Abingdon's *Speculum religiosorum* circulated in only two of England's three languages for well over a century. Despite its composition by one of England's most celebrated saint-bishops, translation into Anglo-Norman (usually as *Mirour de seinte eglyse*) and retranslation several times into Latin (often under a title such as *Speculum ecclesie*), the first Middle English versions of the work date from the late fourteenth century. Where *Ancrene Wisse* played a fundamental role in the development of Middle English prose, the eight or so translations now known collectively as *The Mirror of Holy Church*, which survive in thirteen manuscripts and two early printed editions, were made too late to be of much significance to the history of Middle English stylistics or philology.[1]

Work on the *Speculum* and its translations in general lags behind *Ancrene Wisse* scholarship, egregiously so with respect to its Middle English versions. Helen Forshaw's edition of the Latin original and one later Latin retranslation was published in 1973, Alan Wilshere's edition of the two redactions of the *Mirour* nine years later: twin culminations of a scholarly project that established the current consensus on this exceptionally mobile work's early history.[2] Yet little further work on any version has been done since the early 1980s and this has left research into the Middle English versions in particular in a primitive state. Despite the presence of independent prose translations of the work in three celebrated manuscripts – Vernon, Simeon and Thornton – and the availability, for over a century, of transcriptions by Carl Horstmann

---

[1] H. P. Forshaw, 'New Light on the *Speculum Ecclesie* of Saint Edmund of Abingdon', *Archives d'histoire doctrinale et littéraire du Moyen Age* 38 (1973), 7–33; A. Wilshere, 'The Latin Primacy of St Edmund's "Mirror of Holy Church"', *MLR* 71 (1976), 500–12. Middle English versions are tentatively listed in V. M. Lagorio and M. G. Sargent, 'English Mystical Writings', Chapter 32 of Hartung, *Manual*, 3049–137 and 3405–71 (pp. 3460–1).

[2] Edmund, *Speculum*; Edmund, *Mirour*.

of the first and third of these, as well as of Vernon's two verse versions, there is still no published critical edition of any version of the *Mirror* and no comparative critical study.[3] At present, we do not even know exactly how many translations there were and which Latin or Anglo-Norman version they translated.[4] It is not that the *Mirror* is not well known. Rather, the very ubiquity of this spiritual classic has caused it to be taken for granted.

Yet an analysis of the *Mirror* in relation to the *Speculum* tradition as a whole has much to teach us both about the development of insular vernacular religious thought in general and about the importance of early thirteenth century theological and pastoral categories to late medieval writers and readers in particular. Written at a time of ferment, when the evangelistic possibilities of pastoral theology, and of the vernacular, were attracting much attention, the three central works of the early thirteenth century vernacular religious canon – the *Speculum* (courtesy of its early Anglo-Norman translation), *Ancrene Wisse* and Robert Grosseteste's *Chastel d'amour* – all provided later writers with conceptual challenges: particularly around their notions of spiritual perfection and their demanding but seemingly inconsistent assumptions as to the spiritual status of their intended readers. To follow any of these texts through the twists and turns of its history offers insights both into these challenges and into the broader changes and continuities between the pastoral innovation of the early thirteenth century and its working out in the centuries that followed. The present essay, a sketch for a more detailed (though still far from comprehensive) study in progress,[5] works towards a brief examination of a few of the Middle English *Mirror* texts as expressions of the apparently conflicting audiences and spiritual assumptions implied by Edmund's original Latin work.

---

3   Horstmann, *Yorkshire Writers*, I, 219–40 (Thornton, i.e. Lincoln, Cathedral Chapter Library MS A.1.17), 240–61 (Vernon, i.e. Oxford, Bodleian Library, MS Eng. Poet. A.1); *Minor Poems of the Vernon Manuscript*, EETS, OS 98 (London, 1892), pp. 221–51 and 268–97. There is an edition of the 'interpolated' version of the *Mirror* in Cambridge, University Library MS I.i.40 in H. W. Robbins, 'An English Version of St Edmund's *Speculum* Ascribed to Richard Rolle', *PMLA* 40 (1925), 240–51.

4   Lagorio and Sargent, 'English Mystical Writings', in Hartung, *Manual*, do little to clarify the situation, about which they indeed admit uncertainty (p. 3116). Their discussion draws mainly on C. R. Goymer, 'A Parallel-Text Edition of the Middle English Prose Versions of *The Mirror of St Edmund* Based on the Known Complete Manuscripts' (unpublished MA dissertation, University of London, 1961–2), which in turn draws on H. W. Robbins, *Le Merure de Seinte Eglise by Saint Edmund of Pontigny* (Lewisburg PA, 1925), foundational studies many of whose conclusions are now obsolete.

5   *Speculum religiosorum* and its descendants are key texts in my *Balaam's Ass: Vernacular Theology and Religious Secularization in Later Medieval England* (in progress).

THE AUDIENCES OF *SPECULUM RELIGIOSORUM*

Wilshere argues that Edmund wrote the *Speculum* at the house of the Augustinian canons at Merton, Surrey, in 1213–14. Wilshere bases his case on the dual availability, during this one year of Edmund's life, of leisure and books, claiming that, while the *Speculum* is a work of learning, its tone is too distant both from the arguments of the schools and the priorities of his later career to have been written at any other time, including the months he spent at the Cistercian house of Pontigny, where he was buried in 1240, six years after his consecration as archbishop of Canterbury.[6]

Although this dating is tenuous, Forshaw's studies of the sources of *Speculum* show that its contemplative theology is indeed partly Augustinian in origin. Materials apparently derived from Hugh of St Victor's *De arca morali* and *De arrha animae* provide the work with its framework: a systematic ascent from knowledge of the self to knowledge of God, via inculcation of self-disgust and spiritual gratitude, followed by contemplation of the creation, the scriptures and Christ in his human, and finally divine, natures. Within this framework, pastoral theology gives it much of its detailed content in the form of a long discussion, ostensibly of the meaning of the scriptures, in practice of catechetical matters like the Deadly Sins, the articles of faith and the Works of Mercy, some of which topics were also beginning to appear in the new 'syllabuses' of truths all Christians should know published in synodal statutes during Edmund's lifetime.[7] Apart from a long exposition of the *Pater Noster*, which developed a career of its own, Edmund's discussion of these items is notably laconic, paying more attention to the purpose of catechetical items and their inter-relationships than to exposition of the items themselves. Structure, here, is as important as content.[8]

This kind of pastoral material, which brings contemplative theology down to earth through the tabulation of the ethical priorities that govern the religious life, was becoming widespread in the early thirteenth century, but is compatible with the priorities and interests of a pastoral order like the

---

[6] *Mirour*, ed. Wilshere, pp. xviii–xix, drawing on C. H. Lawrence, *St Edmund of Abingdon: A Study of Hagiography and History* (Oxford, 1960), pp. 121–2. Earlier scholars assumed the work was written in Anglo-Norman at Pontigny in 1240: see, e.g., M. D. Legge, 'St Edmund's *Merure de Seinte Eglise*', *MLR* 23 (1928), 475–6, although Legge believed Edmund was summarizing materials written over a lifetime and that much of the work was written for nuns; see her 'Wanted: An Edition of St Edmund's *Merure*', *MLR* 54 (1959), 72–4.

[7] L. E. Boyle, 'The *Oculus Sacerdotis* and Some Other Works of William of Pagula', *Transactions of the Royal Historical Society*, 5th Series 5 (1955), 81–110.

[8] W. A. Pantin, *The English Church in the Fourteenth Century* (Cambridge, 1959), pp. 189–90, first drew attention to the 'definitions and subdefinitions', the 'almost mathematical precision' characterizing the *Speculum* as one of a new group of university-influenced spiritual *summae*.

Augustinians. So, too, is the set of double meditations on the life and death of Christ in the work's later chapters compatible with the relatively unde-manding liturgical responsibilities of the regular canons, presenting as these meditations do a pared-down version of the complex tradition of liturgically oriented meditation.[9] Everything about the work is plain, down to its style, composed as it self-consciously is 'tam breviter quam faciliter et inculte causa vitandi curiositatem verborum, ne quis dimittat sensus interiores sentenci-arum pro curiositate locucionis' ['as briefly as it is written clearly and rudely, in order to avoid verbal elaboration, in case someone lose track of the inner meanings of the sentences because of their elaborate language'].[10]

Yet while Edmund may have written the *Speculum* for Augustinians, I think it more likely he wrote with other readers in mind: whether his two sisters who became nuns at Catesby; recent converts to the religious life at Oxford, where he taught until the early 1220s; or the secular canons at Salis-bury, where he served as treasurer during the early years of Richard Pore's construction of the cathedral, between 1222 and 1234.[11] I thus consider it an open question whether the *Speculum* was written in 1214 or at any time during the next twenty years – the work's possible echoes of Grosseteste's *Templum dei* make the 1220s particularly attractive[12] – and an equally open question for what context and type or types of reader the work was written.

Whether we accept Wilshere's reconstruction of its composition history or not, the work's early history remains a puzzle. There is no thirteenth-century witness to the original work and a gap of several decades between the 1220s and the first manuscripts of the Anglo-Norman *Mirour*, which likely date from after 1250 and are, by their nature, in any case suggestive of new audi-ences and contexts. Presumably the work's circulation was encouraged by Edmund's canonization in 1247. Most manuscripts attribute the work, calling it *Speculum sancti edmundi archiepiscopi*, or alluding to Edmund's shrine at Pontigny.[13] Matthew Paris's verse *Vie de St Edmund*, written for Isabella, Countess of Arundel, dates from 1246–59 and offers a suggestive parallel to the *Mirour* as an early product of the Edmund cult.[14] But this vernacular enthusiasm for Edmund and his book in the century between 1250 and 1350, when most of the surviving Anglo-Norman manuscripts were copied, did

---

9   M. M. Philomena [H. P. Forshaw], 'St Edmund of Abingdon's Meditations Before the Canonical Hours,' *Ephemerides liturgicae* 78 (1968), 35–57.

10   Incipit preceding table of contents in *Speculum religiosorum*, ed. Forshaw (p. 28). Subsequent citations from this work are by paragraph number.

11   For the stages of Edmund's career, see Lawrence, *St Edmund of Abingdon*.

12   Parallels are listed in Grosseteste, *Templum dei*. *Templum dei* itself may be dated to the first half of the 1220s.

13   For the Anglo-Norman translation's titles, see *Mirour*, ed. Wilshere, p. xx.

14   Lawrence, *St Edmund of Abingdon*, pp. 71–82; J. Wogan-Browne, *Saints' Lives and Women's Literary Culture: Virginity and Its Authorizations* c. *1150–1300* (Oxford, 2001), pp. 151–88.

not extend to the *Speculum,* which remained much less widely circulated either than the *Miroir* or its various re-Latinizations, which date from the early fourteenth century on.[15]

Finding a context for the *Speculum* is made at once more difficult and more pressing by the work's combination of contemplative materials that appear 'advanced' with pastoral materials we are accustomed to consider 'basic': a combination that led C. H. Lawrence, Edmund's biographer, to argue the improbable case that this beautifully constructed work is a composite.[16] Reading the work's advocacy of the plain style and its chapters of catechesis, explicitly addressed to a 'laicus vel illiteratus' who does not have direct access to the scriptures (*SR* §25), it is hard to avoid the impression that this work *aspires* to the vernacular, in the sense that it aspires not only to a specialist readership of Anglo-Norman-reading nuns, anchoresses and oblates but to a level of inclusiveness comparable, say, with the broad reach of the verse *Chastel d'amour.* Similarly, watching the work's evolving titles – assuming *Speculum religiosorum* was indeed the work's earliest title – it is hard not to feel that the shift in audience implied by the emergence of the title *Speculum ecclesie* and its vernacular equivalents is not merely a reflection of Edmund's elevation to an archbishopric but a recognition of the general usefulness of this text, to actives as well as contemplatives, lay as well as religious. Despite the text's spiritual ambition, its succinct and carefully simple analyses even of advanced spiritual topics such as contemplation of God in his divinity seem addressed to a far wider readership than is true, say, of the Victorine texts on which Edmund seems to have drawn.

Theories about the work's audience nonetheless have to take into account the fact that the work is explicitly addressed from the outset to *religiosi*, not to the laity:

Videte vocationem vestram (1 Corinthians 1:26). Verbum hoc apostoli precipue competit religiosis, quod ipsos excitat ad vite perfectionem per crebram sui consideracionem. Quociens meipsum considero ex una parte multum gaudeo, ex alia vero multum doleo. Gaudeo plane pro sancta religione; doleo pro mea debili et imperfecta conversacione. Nec est mirum: dicit enim beatus Eusebius in quondam sermone: 'Religionem intrare summe perfectionis est; imperfecte in ea vivere summe dampnacionis est.' Unde religioso summe necessarium est vivere perfecte, id est, ad viam et formam perfectionis tendere. Cum ergo consilio domini religionem ingrediens adhesisti, illud ne deseras si salutem tuam desideras, sed ex toto mundum relinque

---

[15] For the Anglo-Norman manuscripts, see Dean and Boulton, *Anglo-Norman Literature,* §629.

[16] Lawrence, *St Edmund of Abingdon,* p. 122; see also M. D. Legge, *Anglo-Norman in the Cloister: The Influence of the Orders in Anglo-Norman Literature* (Edinburgh, 1958), pp. 93–4.

et quicquid ad eum pertinet, et totum appone conatum summamque dili-
genciam ut perfecte vivas. (*SR* §1–2)

[*Consider your calling* (1 Corinthians 1:26). This statement of the apostle is
particularly applicable to religious, urging them to the life of perfection
through constant reflection upon themselves. Whenever I reflect upon
myself, on the one hand I greatly rejoice, but on the other I greatly sorrow.
I rejoice, simply, because of the holiness of the religious life; I sorrow
for my own feeble and flawed way of living it. And no wonder: for the
blessed Eusebius said in one of his sermons: 'To enter the religious life is
the highest perfection; to live in it imperfectly is the deepest damnation.'
On which account, it is most deeply necessary that a religious person live
perfectly: that is, strive for the way and form of perfection. Thus you, who
with the Lord's counsel have committed yourself to entering the religious
life, do not desert it if you desire your salvation, but completely relinquish
the world and whatever belongs to it and apply all your skill and your
greatest effort to living perfectly.]

The appeal to 'ex toto mundum relinque' in the pursuit of 'vivere perfecte'
clearly belongs to the terminology of the professional religious life, even if the
word 'ingrediens' here may imply a readership of recent converts, whether
oblates or others. Moreover, the work consistently represents its reader as a
religious person actually living the 'perfect' life in separation from the world.
After reflecting on the vileness of the body and the disgusting physicality
that undergirds natural love of parents and siblings (*SR* §11–12) – reflections
typical of medieval works addressed to religious, but deeply inappropriate
to the laity – the reader is instructed, when rising from bed at midnight or
for matins, to think of the thousands who have died that night 'in diversis
periculis, multi in corpore, multi in anima, multis modis in multis locis' ['in
different states of danger, many in body, many in soul, in many ways and in
many places'] (*SR* §14). Both the liturgical setting of this act of recollection
and its exclusiveness belong in the protected setting of a monastery, friary,
or anchorhold.

Given the spiritual exclusiveness of these passages, early in the work, it
is hard to know how to think about the inclusiveness of its prose style, the
conflation of contemplative and pastoral materials under the one roof, and
its later reference to a 'laicus vel illiteratus'. The original context from which
it derived may have been highly specific: say, a single institution housing
Christians of a mixed level of education, some of them technically 'laici', not
'religiosi'. Or Edmund, a career scholar known for his moral rigorism, may
have deliberately written the work for a composite readership, unwilling to
distinguish between what was required of 'religiosi' and of 'laici'. Either way,
the work's claim to importance rests solidly on its skilful integration of a
version of Victorine contemplative thought, shorn of its speculative orientation, with the new pastoral theology and its secular emphases on ethics,
action and belief. Without this novel interaction of different bodies of theo-

logical thought, this incorporation of pastoral theology into contemplative theology, the work would have provided no more than assorted raw materials to the English religious tradition.

This is not the place for a detailed analysis of the complexities of the original work's address. Nonetheless, it bears noting that the emphasis on the pastoral in a work meant for contemplatives is not a sign of incoherence but, in the early thirteenth century, cutting edge, representing the same shift in the presentation of contemplative living we see in *Ancrene Wisse*, with its parallel inclusion of pastoral materials in Parts Four and Five. Crucial to Edmund's deployment of catechetic materials is his desire to further the shift towards 'active' (pastoral, evangelistic, secular) engagements taking place in the contemplative environment of his time, particularly in the wake of the Fourth Lateran Council of 1215 and the arrival in England of the friars, early in the 1220s. The *Speculum* is not a religious rule but a meta-rule: a work intended to shape the lives of those living under a variety of rules, all of whom have in common their adoption of a profession and their pursuit of a single, inner goal, perfection. Rather as the prologue to *Ancrene Wisse* uses a verse of Micah to define 'riht religiun' in a carefully anti-formalist way, as comprised in following the injunction, 'Do wel ant dem wac eauer þe seoluen, ant wið dred ant wið luue ga mid Godd ti Lauerd' ['Do well, and judge yourself always weak; and with fear and with love walk with God your Lord'],[17] so the opening of the *Speculum* reduces the life of 'religiosi' to this single end, defining the goal of perfection as a journey to God possible to undertake within any religious environment.

Simply by refusing to specify the meaning of terms like 'religiosus' or to associate 'perfectio' with any specific practice, the *Speculum* opens the way to the broadest definition of religious living, one capable of incorporating semi-religious such as anchorites, secular priests such as Edmund himself (who never joined a formal religious order), and devout members of the laity. That this is a conscious aspect of the work is shown, for example, by a passage on the *Pater Nosters* used by illiterate contemplatives as a substitute for the liturgy, which criticizes excessive repetition of this prayer, but then turns to those who recite the full office to make much the same criticism: 'Eodem modo de servicio divino intellige ... Nam si corpus tuum sit in choro et labia tua in psalterio, et cor tuum versetur in foro, miserabiliter distractus es et divisus' ['Understand the same about the divine office. For if your body is in the choir and your lips in the psalter and your heart is turned outwards, you are wretchedly distracted and divided'] (*SR* §86). The variety of levels of education alluded to in the *Speculum* seems designed to be as wide as possible.

---

[17] *Ancrene Wisse* ed. B. Millett, Preface 147–8, p. 5; Savage and Watson, *Anchoritic Spirituality*, p. 51.

Yet if the work thus strives for general relevance, it remains spiritually rigorist, identifying its readers with the *perfecti* who will sit in judgement over others on the Last Day and representing the laity's usual route to heaven, via performance of the Works of Mercy, as perilous at best. In Edmund's austere ethical universe, reminiscent of that of one of his sources, Anselm, the salvation even of 'religiosi' is a matter for doubt, dependent on whole-hearted abandonment of the world and a fierce avoidance of the imperfection that leads to 'summe dampnationis'. Despite its insistence that 'divites ... vere', who possess riches but do not love them are better off than 'mendici miseri et falsi religiosi' [wretched beggars and false religious] who are poor but desire to be rich (*SR* §75, 74), the fate of the laity, unless they give themselves wholly over to perfection, remains uncertain indeed.

SOME MIDDLE ENGLISH VERSIONS OF *SPECULUM RELIGIOSORUM*

The puzzling doubleness of the *Speculum*'s audience address marks its textual history in various ways. It helps explain both the work's early translation into Anglo-Norman – probably initially for nuns who were at once 'religiosi' and, as vernacular readers, 'de simple lettrure', as the *Mirour* renders Edmund's 'illiteratus'[18] – and its retranslation into Latin in the early fourteenth century, possibly for secular priests, increasingly anxious to have access to contemplative materials. While it may not justify Wilshere's description of the second, 'B' redaction of the *Mirour* as a 'lay version',[19] it helps account for the increased emphasis placed on catechetical materials at the cost of contemplative ones in this redaction, on which the *Speculum ecclesie* edited by Forshaw was based. It may even help account for the disappearance of the original Latin *Speculum* from the manuscript tradition from the time of its composition until the early fifteenth century.

But the clearest signs of the generativity of the *Speculum* and the complexities of its audience address are provided by the diversity of its Middle English versions. By the late fourteenth century, catechetical materials had come to be firmly associated with the laity and with the universalizing project of vernacular theology: that is, with the acknowledgment that most religious instruction was for the benefit of those who would seek their salvation in the 'world', not by conversion from it. The laity's ability to use contemplative materials was more controversial. Mainstream contemplative works for lay readers written at the end of the fourteenth century, like Walter Hilton's *Mixed Life* or the anonymous *Fervor amoris*, frame limited contemplative programmes that stop short of participation in the contemplation of

---

18 *Mirour*, ed. Wilshere, B.7.3.
19 Ibid., pp. ix–xviii.

the divinity, rather than humanity, of Christ. Except when writing explicitly for religious, Middle English translators could not deny the relevance of the *Speculum*'s pastoral materials to lay readers and the need to address the laity directly. But depending on their stance on the spiritual potential of the lay state, they might take many different attitudes to the work's other materials. Versions of the *Mirror* thus articulate different assumptions about the text they are rendering and its audience, as they do about the implications of its mixture of pedagogical inclusiveness and spiritual exclusivity.

Some versions of the *Mirror* are notably cautious in generalizing the work for a lay readership. Indeed, it is clear that, for translators in general, not only did the word 'religious', despite being defined in apparently spiritual terms throughout the *Speculum*, still have strong institutional affiliations, but that the same was true of 'perfection', despite the fact that the *Speculum* carefully distinguishes between formal religious living and the active pursuit of perfection. The mid-fifteenth-century Thornton version thus limits its address to professional religious, understanding the opening phrase of the *Speculum*, 'Videte vocacionem vestram' to apply only 'till vs folke of religioune'. This version even translates the opening in such a way as to imply that salvation lies only in religious community:

> Þarfore es na turne of þe way bot ane: to come in congregacyone, þat es, to drawe to perfeccione, and als þou will þi saluacyone, to leue all þat es in this worlde and all þat þerto langys and sett thi myghte to lyffe perfitly.[20]

Its concluding words, which address a 'dere syster and ffrende', imply the translation was made for a nun.[21]

Elsewhere, the assumption that certain contemplative models were relevant to all devout people, including the laity, made it possible for such readers to be addressed alongside religious ones. Wynkyn de Worde's 1521 edition of a late fifteenth century translation by Nicholas Bellew does this, not by altering the text but by offering it to readers under a rubric that greatly extends its reach: 'Here foloweth a deuout treatyse conteynynge many goostly medytacyons and instruccions to all maner of people necessary and confortable to the edyfycacion of the soule and body to the loue and grace of god.'[22] This rubric – partly a piece of marketing consistent with that adopted by de Worde in his other contemplative publications – understands the *Mirror* as a 'treatyse' appropriate for those attempting to live the 'mixed' life as defined by Hilton's classic treatise: combining, as the work is said to do, the 'necessary' (catechetic 'instruccions') with the 'confortable' (contemplative 'medy-

---

20 Horstmann, *Yorkshire Writers*, I, 219.
21 Ibid., I, 240.
22 *The Myrrour of the Chyrche*, ed. Wynkyn de Worde (London, 1521), fol. 1a (*STC* 965). This translation is also found in Oxford, Bodleian Library MS e Museo 232.

tacyons') in a work whose contents are diverse enough that 'all maner of people' can benefit.

Slightly more elaborate, the prose *Mirror* in the Vernon manuscript, copied more than a century earlier, perhaps in the 1390s, opens with a quatrain that describes the work's purpose as teaching the way to salvation to all: 'þe Mirour of Seint Edmound i-cleped hit is, / þat techeþ mon to heuene blis.' The contents of this version, based on the 'A' text of the *Mirour*, make no special concessions to lay readers, but the first chapter, 'How Mon schal loken his staat', contains small changes which at first seem casual but whose deliberate effect is to open the work out to a double readership, one religious, the other secular, including lay. Here, the opening argues that Paul's words 'ffalleþ to men of Religion and to alle gode cristene men' and translates 'Videte vocacionem vestram' as 'seoþ þe stat wherto ȝe beoþ clept', rendering 'vocacio' twice, both with the standard vernacularization 'wherto ȝe beoþ clept' and with a noun, the social term 'stat' from the chapter rubric. In the *Mirour*, the speaker feels 'joie pur la seinte religion, dolur e confusion pur ma fieble conversacion' ['joy for the holy religious life, sorrow and confusion on account of my weak way of living it']. Here, she or he feels 'ioye, for þe grete religion and godnesse þat he haþ schewed to me and to monkynde', a clause that (unusually) makes religion into a purely inner quality and that redraws the contrast between 'joie' and 'dolur' in the original, not admitting the professional religious life to be, of itself, a cause of 'ioye' and including all 'monkynde' in the ambit of the work's interest.[23]

The rest of the chapter gives priority to professional religious, but maintains this level of generality. Eusebius's terrifying *sententia* is rendered: 'Cum to religion, is a souereyn perfeccion; not parfytliche liuen is a souereyn dampnacion', omitting from the second clause the crucial 'therein' found in most versions (the *Mirour* has '*nent* parfitement vivre'), so that 'parfytliche liuen' is no longer identified with the professional religious life and failure to do it becomes damnation for all. The final sentence no longer directly addresses 'vus ki vivét en religion' ['you who live in religion'] but remarks to any reader that 'þe beste þing is, whose liueþ in religion, drawe he to þe lyf of perfeccion', a statement that leaves 'alle gode cristene men' to work out their own relation to 'perfeccion' but implicitly encourages them to take 'whose liueþ in religion' as their model. With these few small changes, the entire work becomes recuperable for lay readers as a kind of lay rule, a genre much in vogue at the time Vernon was being compiled. Imageless contemplation and all, devout lay readers are explicitly invited to join contemplatives on the path to perfection.

The de Worde and Vernon modes of adaptation of the *Speculum* for the

---

23 For the quotations in this and the following two paragraphs, see Horstmann, *Yorkshire Writers*, I, 240–1, *Mirour*, ed. Wilshere, A.1.

laity might be termed conservative, in that they keep the original address to religious intact, constituting the work's lay readers as a kind of 'third order' by allowing them to experience the way of life of professional religious in a partly surrogate sense, leaving the absoluteness of their own commitment to 'þe lyf of perfeccion' open. Indeed, Vernon's mild translation of 'E pur ço n'avét turne ke un' ['and for this there is only one way'] as 'þerfore þe beste þing is' saps even the work's address to religious of much of its fierce fervour, suggesting 'þe lyf of perfeccion' as but the 'beste' of a series of legiti-mate choices, not the only path to salvation. Since Vernon itself is full of works announcing such paths – from the A text of William Langland's *Piers Plowman* to the first book of Hilton's *Scale of Perfection* – this acknowledgment of the breakdown through diversification of Edmund's painstakingly unitary model of perfection might be taken as a sign of the times, as the *Speculum* takes its place as merely one amongst an array of devout classics, each with their own suggestions to offer about the spiritual life.

A similar apparent softening of the *Speculum* is evident in one of the two versions of the *Mirror* that seems to be addressed first and foremost to lay readers, *Þe Spore* (or *Prikke*) *of Loue*: the freer but more complete of the two verse versions found in Vernon and its companion, Simeon. The independent prologue to the *Spore* – which replaces both the opening rubric and table of contents and the first two chapters of the *textus receptus* of the *Speculum* – is full of advertisements for the value of the work somewhat reminiscent of the opening rubric in the de Worde version. 'Her beginneþ þe Prikke of loue, / Þat profitable is to soule be-houe', it begins, before invoking the Trinity in a set of formulae that at once construct the work's audience as listeners, not readers, hearing material as useful for them as it is for everyone:

> God þat art of miʒtes most,
> ffader and Sone and holigost,
> Þow graunte hem alle þi blessyng
> Þat herken wel to þis talkyng.

> ffor, lewed and lered, more and lesse,
> Hit wol ow teche holynesse;   [*you*]
> To loue God wiþ fyn chere   [*noble*]
> Hit wol ou teche, my leoue and dere.

> ffor mony a tyme ʒe cone me preye
> Þer-of a lesson ow to seye;
> Ʒoure dulnesse sum what to scharpe
> Ʒe han me preyed for to carpe.

> ffor bisynes of worldli þing
> To monye hit is a gret lettyng,
> And eke ʒor owne frelete,
> Þat makeþ ow ʒeore heui to be   [*before now, anxious*]

Of or-self and зoure liuinge,
Þorw þe ffendes entysynge.
Þerfore þis bok to ow I make
зoure discumfort for to slake,

Þat is cald 'þe spore of loue,'
Þat stureþ or loue to god aboue.
Riht as þe spore makeþ hors to renne,
So schal þis bok sone god ou kenne,

Þat is souereyn holynesse.
зe schul fynde heer-in swetnesse:
Loke зe take herto good hede!   [*what I advise*]
ffor I schal telle зou as I rede.

Þis may be зor halyday werk,
Hit wol a-vayle boþe lewed and clerk.[24]

Although it uses topoi drawn from the professional literature of spiritual counsel – the assumption of intimacy between writer and recipient ('leoue and dere'); the recipient's requests for counsel ('mony a tyme зe cone me preye'); the need to combat ('scharpe') idleness ('dulnesse') with good reading – the prologue's main concern is with the general relevance of the poem it initiates, signified by its use of the vernacular and of verse, as well as by its opening gesture towards 'alle'. The second-person plural pronoun forms bridge intimacy and universality, since they signify both a general address ('lewed and lered, more and lesse, / Hit wol ow teche holynesse') and courtesy towards a lay recipient who is the poem's exemplary target and whose anxieties about her or his spiritual state ('зor owne frelete, / Þat makeþ ow зeore heui to be') are said to have caused it to be made. The poem offers its rendering of the *Speculum* to disperse this 'heui[nes]' – the product of a combination of spiritual 'dulnesse', worldly 'bisynes' and sinfulness, caused by susceptibility to diabolical temptation – by cheering the recipient up through the 'swetnesse' of the experience it provides of the knowledge and love of God. Promising speedy results ('So schal þis bok sone god ou kenne'), the poem also makes modest claims on the recipient's limited free time, presenting itself as 'зor halyday werk': a Sunday book, useful to the writer as well as the recipient ('Hit wol a-vayle boþe lewed and clerk') but transformed from an authoritative *sermo* or *speculum* by a saintly archbishop to an informal 'talkyng', voiced by the poet.

At first sight, this cheerful approach to the *Speculum* might also seem somewhat superficial, as though a work that, in its original form, aspired to incorporate the whole of the diverse lives of its contemplative readers within one frame here shrinks into a general incitement to holiness, written

---

24 *Minor Poems*, ed. Horstmann, 35.3–29.

merely 'discumfort for to slake', to keep the reader 'scharpe'. However, such an impression is shaken by a reading of this beautifully crafted adaptation, which omits all references to 'religion' and 'perfection' (doing away with most of the chapter on the Works of Mercy in which many such references cluster, as well as the chapter on the *Pater Noster* that follows) and cuts most of the final sections on contemplation of God in his divine nature, but retains almost all the rest, lucidly versified and carefully dovetailed with its readers concerns and interests. The poem's largely independent account of the sacraments, for example, besides placing due emphasis on the purely lay sacrament of marriage, gives an impressively integrated account of how the sacraments as a whole work together to build both Christian lives and Christian communities.[25]

Any impression of superficiality is finally dispelled once one recognizes what appears to have been the original institutional context of the *Spore*, the hospital known as the College of the Annunciation of St Mary, in the Newarke at Leicester:

> Contemplacion is to seye:
> Siht of god and his nobleye.
> Þat maiȝt þou se be þin Inwit
> In creature and in holy writ,
>
> And siþen in his owne kynde.
> Of þeose ȝif we wol haue good mynde.
> Þe nobleye of god in his werkes,
> A[lle] men mowe seo, Lewed & Clerkes.
>
> Þou þat neuere seȝe Duyk Henri,
> Þat þe newe werk of Leycetre reised on hiȝ
> Þer-bi maiȝt þou wel wyte and se
> Þat he was lord of gret pouste
>
> Þat hit made of his owne cost –
> I hope he naue þeron not lost.[26]

God can be recognized as 'nobleye' in his works, even though he is invisible, just as Duke Henry can be recognized as 'lord of gret pouste' ['power'] in his construction of 'þe newe werk of Leycetre', even by those who have not seen him. Henry Grosmont, Duke of Lancaster, refounded his father's Hospital of the Annunciation during the 1350s, about twenty-five years after its first foundation and while he was working on his one literary work, the

---

[25] Ibid., 35.586–644.

[26] Ibid., 35.155–68. Here, as elsewhere, I have significantly modified Horstmann's punctuation, substituting for his emendation in line 161 ('Þe nobleye of god [we se] in his werkes') an emendation of my own to the following line, 'alle' for 'as'.

prose *Livre des seyntz medicines*.[27] Henry greatly added to his father's plan by creating, out of a lightly staffed establishment aimed at helping fifty of Leicester's poor, a true, collegiate foundation of a dean, twelve canons, thirteen vicars and six choristers, now supporting a full 100 permanent and temporary inmates (men and women), with impressive buildings 'reised on hiʒ' to match. Evoking this foundation in a context that compares Grosmont directly with God, the *Spore* also locates itself squarely within the spiritual project of the Newarke, which, like all foundations of its kind, fulfilled the founder's obligations to perform the Works of Mercy by feeding the poor and helping the sick, while also preparing those of the poor who became permanent residents spiritually for death in a neo-monastic setting. Written to 'a-vayle boþe lewed and clerk', the poem thus seems to been intended as a carefully calibrated induction into the religious life potentially useful for any member of this mixed college but aimed at the instruction of its poor lay inmates in particular. Far from a diminishment of Edmund's original intentions, the *Spore* represents a direct continuation of his project of opening the category of 'religiosi' as widely as possible.[28]

In the *Spore*, as in the prose version of the *Speculum* in the Vernon manuscript, laicization of the work nonetheless seems to coincide with real shifts, not only in the status of the laity, but also in soteriology, as what I elsewhere call the 'misericordist' tendencies of much late medieval vernacular religious thought take hold and the doors of heaven, or at least purgatory, seem to swing more and more widely open: a process analysed with penetration and uncertainty in *Piers Plowman*.[29] Yet the softening of the *Speculum*'s exclusivism characteristic of some Middle English versions is emphatically not present in the second version of the *Mirror* directly written for the laity: the full prose version in Oxford, Bodleian Library MS 416 and two other manuscripts, to which I turn in closing. Here, the universalizing of the work's address is immediately compensated for by its uncompromising determination to

27 See W. M. Ormrod, 'Henry of Lancaster, first duke of Lancaster (*c*. 1310–1361)', *ODNB* (accessed online January 2008); A. Hamilton Thompson, *The History of the Hospital and New College of the Annunciation of Saint Mary in the Newarke, Leicester* (Leicester, 1937).

28 The passage also potentially dates the work to after Grosmont's death (understanding 'I hope he naue þeron not lost' as 'I am sure he came to no spiritual harm by it'), once John of Gaunt had finished the building work and late enough that few of the poem's first audience had seen Grosmont, who was buried in the college at his death in 1361. A date *c.* 1370 or later, less than two decades before Vernon was compiled, seems likely. Despite positive references to 'þe ffrere sarmounyng' and 'ffreres prechinge' (271, 510), the poem was likely written by a canon or priest of the college, since the earlier of these passages distinguishes 'our' preaching from that of the friars: 'Alle þinges þat we of prechen, / Summe of þeos poyntes forsoþe þei techen' (280–1).

29 '*Piers Plowman*, Pastoral Theology and Spiritual Perfectionism: Hawkyn's Cloak and Patience's *Pater Noster*', *Yearbook of Langland Studies* 21 (2007), 83–118.

uphold the spiritual standards the *Speculum* outlines, subjecting everyone to the perilous path of perfection:

> 'Se ȝe ȝoure clepinge'. Þis word of þe apostel bilongeþ to eueri cristene man and womman þat wol be saued. 'Se ȝe', he seiþ, 'wharto ȝe ben clepud'. And þat he seiþ forte sturen ȝou to perfeccioun. And þerfore whanne Y þenke on my self bi day or bi nyȝt, in þat on half ich haue gret ioye and þat oþer gret sorwe: ioye for þe goodnes of God; sorwe for my febele lif. And þat is no merueile, for ich haue gret enchesoun. For, as seiþ seint Anselme in a sermoun þat he made: 'To come to Cristis lawe, þat is souereyn perfeccioun; nouȝt to lyue perfiȝtliche is souereyn damnacioun'. And þat is but on lyue, in congregacioun, and þat draweþ þe to þe wei of perfeccioun. As þou wolt þi sauacioun, lef al þat is in þis world and al þat þer to longeþ and set al þi power forte lyuen partiflich.[30]

'Eueri cristene man and womman þat wol be saued' can translate 'religiosi' (Anglo-Norman 'gent de religion') here because the 'clepinge' to which Paul calls his readers is no longer that institutional thing, 'religion', but the universal mandate of 'Cristis lawe' (a second translation of 'religion' in the passage) which governs all alike under 'þe goodnes of God' (a third translation). 'Cristis lawe' is likely a variation of the Wycliffite term 'Goddes lawe', used formulaically to describe the scriptures in vernacular works from the 1380s on, while the phrase 'eueri cristene man and womman þat wol be saued' bridges the emphasis on good will in reformist spiritual texts of the period and the Wycliffite emphasis on predestination (*wol* also has the future sense of *shall*).

The elect readership the latter phrase hails in theory belongs to any spiritual estate but in practice is determinedly conceived of as lay. The clause 'þat is but on lyue' [i.e., the 'wei of perfeccioun' consists of a single possible way of life] 'in congregacioun', may seem to suggest otherwise, but 'congregacioun' here cannot refer to monastic congregations, for the work makes a determined effort to avoid mentioning 'religion' and several times repeats its general address to 'eche cristene man' (see especially its partly independent exposition of the Creed in Chapter 13). The implied reader of the chapter on the *Pater Noster* (Chapter 17) does not sing the full office in the choir, but is told to 'don þin offis in þin herte deuoutlich'. In the chapter on the Works of Mercy (Chapter 16), a 'religiosus' who worries over the impossibility of performing these works from a monastic cell is replaced by a generic sick person: 'But now miȝtow seien, þat art in bodili disese, "I haue no power to ȝeue mete ne drinke, ne cloþinge, ne herberow [etc.]".' Only at the end of the chapter, which distinguishes between true and false versions of poverty, do

---

[30] Oxford, Bodleian Library MS 416, fols. 111a–b. I thank Natalie Huffels and Blair Morris for their initial transcription of the text in this manuscript, which has much aided my study.

we meet 'false men of religioun' among those who, while not being materially rich, are still not spiritually poor, since they 'louen hem [riches] and bleþeli wolden haue hem'; and, at last, 'holi men of religioun þat ben uerrei pore'.[31] Even the hierarchy of the church fares badly. In the *Speculum's* exposition of the clause of the *Pater Noster* 'sicut in celo et in terra', a list of the celestial and earthly orders of the saved includes a careful listing of the spiritual and temporal estates:

> Dominus papa, cardinales, archiepiscopi, episcopi, abbates, priores, et omnes eorum subditi; scilicet archidiaconi, decani, presbiteri et omnes ordines sacri; reges, principes, comites, barones, divites, pauperes, clerici, laici. (§82)
>
> [Our lord the pope, cardinals, archbishops and bishops, abbots and abbesses, priors and prioresses and those subject to them; archdeacons and deans, parsons and priests and all holy orders; kings and princes, counts and barons, poor and rich, clerics and lay.]

The equivalent passage here first inscribes the requirements all must meet for salvation, then ruthlessly cuts most of the spiritual estates listed in the *Speculum* out of the picture:

> þe ordres of man don þi wil þat ben in erþe: þat is to sein, þo that þorʒ bapteme and bileue and oþer goode uertues ben comen to Cristis religioun, of what state so þei ben, maidens or oþer: prestis and alle þe holi ordres; kynges and princes, erles and barouns, riche and pore, clerkes and lewede.[32]

'Alle þe holi ordres' are still present, but their importance is vastly diminished.

Unlike *Þe Spore of Loue*, it does not seem possible to locate the Bodley 416 version of the *Mirror* in a specific institutional context. But the literary and codicological context of the version is extremely rich, too much so, indeed, to be more than alluded to here. This version is one of a group of texts circulating in a London/West Midlands milieu in the last years of the fourteenth century, alongside works such as *Pore Caitif*, the *Pater Noster of Richard Hermit*, the 'E' version of *The Visitation of the Sick*, *The Life of Soul* and *Book to a Mother*, all of which have reformist, in some cases Wycliffite, tendencies.[33] As the phrase, 'Cristis religioun' in the passage just quoted suggests, the version has

---

31 Oxford, Bodleian Library MS 416, fols. 124a–125a (Chapter 13), 131b (Chapter 17), 126a–127b (Chapter 16).

32 Oxford, Bodleian Library MS 416, fol. 130a.

33 See A. J. Fletcher, 'A Hive of Industry or a Hornets' Nest? MS Sidney Sussex 74 and Its Scribes', in *Late-Medieval Religious Texts and Their Transmission*, ed. A. J. Minnis (Cambridge, 1994), pp. 131–56; Hanna, *Pursuing History*, pp. 35–47; A. Moss, 'A Merchant's Tales: A London Fifteenth-Century Household Miscellany', *YES* 33 (2003), 156–69.

a particularly close relation with its main companion in Bodley 416, *Book to a Mother*, a work which lays out a radical lay agenda thoroughly congruent with this version of Edmund's thought. *Book to a Mother* combines the suspicion of monasticism that was coming to be associated with Wycliffism in the last decades of the fourteenth century with a desire to appropriate key monastic themes for lay purposes: starting with the term 'religioun' itself, but including the idea of the rule, the call to perfection and the maintenance of high spiritual standards by anyone who hopes to be saved.[34] Although it retains a place for 'true' monks and nuns amidst its suspicion that few such exist, *Book to a Mother*, more explicitly than the Bodley *Mirror* but to the same effect, displaces the monastic orders by arguing that all the spiritual ground with which they are associated can best be occupied outside the institutional context of monastery or convent.

How so? For the very reason Edmund alludes to in distinguishing between vocation and conversation, the call to perfection and the failure to live what one professes, and that *Ancrene Wisse* also evokes in its early discussion of 'riht religiun': the potential association between religious profession and spiritual formalism or hypocrisy, the sins that lie behind the 'suvereine dampnation' that is the improperly lived religious life. On some level, fear of formalism and hypocrisy lies at the root of the *Speculum* tradition, with its insistence on the general ethical and theological principles that lie behind all types of religious profession and consequent implied downgrading of specific religious rules. For all its radicalism, its refusal to acknowledge the significance of any religion but 'Cristis religioun', the Bodley version of the *Mirror* represents an authentic, late fourteenth century endpoint of this tradition.

---

[34] See N. Watson, 'Fashioning the Puritan Gentrywoman: Devotion and Dissent in *A Book to a Mother'*, in *Medieval Women: Texts and Contexts in Late Medieval Britain: Essays for Felicity Riddy*, ed. J. Wogan-Browne et al. (Turnhout, 2000), pp. 169–84.

9

Terror and Pastoral Care in *Handlyng Synne*

Robert Hasenfratz

Handlyng Synne is a scary text. It and its source, the *Manuel des Péchés*,[1] present the consequences of sin and improper or incomplete confession in stark, often terrifying terms: priests and holy men with uncanny powers for detecting mortal sin,[2] strangulation by invisible hands (877–976, 2221–352, 3156–242, 6377–492), sudden death in mid-sin (877–976, 2697–722, 3356–96, 4703–32, 11,719–54), the horrific desecrations of sinners' corpses or graves (1547–82, 1741–862, 7983–8080, 8747–78, 11,083–126), pleas for release from tormented phantoms (2221–352, 3556–620, 10,403–96, 11,011–66), lurid visions of hell (1369–486, 2221–352, 2473–590, 3156–242, 3243–310, 4369–514, 5237–312, 6637–722, 10,403–96), avenging demons, often armed with hooks or knives (1252–84, 2473–590, 3156–242, 4369–514, 7727–882, 8161–274, 8446–570, 8747–78, 8821–84, 11,853–89), etc. At times the author, Robert Mannyng of Brunne, makes the case quite directly; in the last section, on the conditions of confession, for example, he does not beat around the bush: 'Ne forhele

---

[1] Written circa 1303 by Robert Mannyng of Brunne, in all probability a Gilbertine canon, *Handlyng Synne* is a Middle English adaptation of the Anglo-Norman *Le Manuel des Péchés*, composed in England between 1250 and 1270, perhaps by William of Waddington. For the known facts of Robert Mannyng's life see R. Biggar, 'Robert Mannyng', in the *ODNB*, pp. 522–3. After a brief prologue (ll. 1–146), *Handlyng Synne* treats the Ten Commandments (ll. 147–2990), the seven deadly sins (ll. 2991–8586), sacrilege (ll. 8587–9500), the seven sacraments (ll. 9501–11,310) and confession – twelve properties of shrift, eight graces and mistakes to avoid in making confession (11,311–12,638). Part of the *Manuel* was later translated into Middle English prose: see K. Bitterling, *Of Shrifte and Penance: The ME Prose Translation of 'Le Manuel des Péchés'*, edited from St John's College, Cambridge, MS G.30 (Heidelberg, 1998). A. Bennett, in 'A Book Designed for a Noblewoman: An Illustrated *Manuel des Péchés* of the Thirteenth Century', in *Medieval Book Production: Assessing the Evidence*, ed. L. L. Brownrigg (Los Altos Hills CA, 1995), pp. 163–75, argues that at least one version of the *Manuel*, Princeton University Library, Taylor Medieval MS 1, a rare illustrated copy, was prepared for an identifiable patron, Joan Tateshal of Lincolnshire.

[2] *Handlyng Synne*, ll. 10,166–256 and 12,171–260. All citations from *Handlyng Synne* will be taken from the edition by I. Sullens (Binghamton NY, 1983); references will be by line number in the main body of the text. For a useful critique of this edition, see R. Biggar's review in *Speculum* 62 (1987), 969–73.

[conceal] nat þy mysdede: / Goddes veniaunce shalt þou drede' (11,709–10). The necessity, even efficacy of fear also forms a conscious element of many of the illustrative *exempla*. In the account of the evil squire of King Conrad, Mannyng stresses his pathological lack of fear in the face of a potentially lethal illness. This squire, guilty of extortion, treason and sacrilege, has a kind of manly courage in the face of death that dooms him to hell. In fact, he is initially described in positive chivalric terms: 'of body vaylaunt, [valiant] / Yn armes was he a doghty squyere' (4374–5). But when King Conrad, on a visit to his sick bed, acting as surrogate confessor, urges him to repent, the squire refuses to be afraid:

> Y wlde nat be fownde so vyle
> Þat myn herte were yn swych peryle
> To repente me for a lytyl syknes.
> But 3yf y were yn harder stres,
> 3yf y for drede askede a prest,
> Þat shame al day shulde be me nest [next]
> Þat y were afered of þe ded [death].   (4403–9)

This foolhardy courage ultimately damns the squire, who has a fitful vision of angels and devils visiting his bedside with books of his good and bad deeds respectively. Mannyng greatly expands and heightens the power of this *exemplum* (this last speech for example does not appear in the *Manuel*), finishing it with the squire's despair as he realizes that it is too late to repent:

> Twey brennyng knyues þey out drowe
> And seyde 'do we oure dede nowe.
> Do we swyþe [quickly] and noght we dwelle,
> And haste we vs wyþ hym to helle.' (4489–92)

Unlike the squire, who puts off his repentance until it is too late, these demons, ironically, seem to be immune to procrastination, getting on with their jobs with admirable speed. The grim humour of the scene is framed by the fact that the tale illustrates the deadly sin of sloth and thus displays the horrors of hell to those who would postpone their confessions.

Later in the same section, 'slow' priests who neglect the chastising of their flocks are reminded of their awesome responsibilities and of the terrors they will face at judgement day: 'For hem he schal at þe assyse [judgement] / Be ponysshed before þe hygh iustyse' (4831–2). The text then moves to address parents who fail to chastise their children; to illustrate this point, the text provides an *exemplum* illustrating the dangers of not terrifying children with discipline, one which paraphrases Solomon's advice: 'Wyle 3e þat 3oure chylder be aferd, / 3euyf hem þe smert ende of þe 3erd [rod, stick]' (4861–4).[3]

---

3   Though Solomon is cited as the source for this sentiment, the paraphrase is broad

In the tale, reminiscent of Goethe's 'Erlkönig' in its violent sentimentality, a young boy, prone to swearing because of his father's lax discipline, takes ill and dies in his father's arms. Before his death, the five-year-old has terrifying visions of demons surrounding him:

> blake men, blake
> Are aboute me, to take
> Me wyþ hem wyle þey lede.
> Y ne shal skape for no need. [for no necessity, not at all] (4887–90)

Clearly, the *exemplum* aims at maximum pathos to drive home the point that fear of punishment is necessary, indeed urgent, in the education of children as in the training of the Christian adult penitent.[4]

Does this deployment of fear, guilt and shame[5] in the penitential system imply an infantilization of the believer? T. N. Tentler suggested as much when he argued that the system of penance was created, in part, to serve as a system of social control through the creation of a 'culture of guilt'.[6] With respect to the *Manuel des Péchés* specifically, a recent commentator, U. Schemmann, has taken a sharply opposing view, arguing against Tentler that the *Manuel* in fact aims at a far higher form of lay education than even basic confessional manuals for priests, producing not cringing parishioners, but intelligent, independent ones:

enough that several verses from Proverbs may be intended. Among the possibilities are (1) Proverbs 13. 24 ('He that spareth the rod hateth his son: but he that loveth him correcteth him betimes'), (2) Proverbs 22. 15 ('Folly is bound up in the heart of a child, and the rod of correction shall drive it away') or (3) Proverbs 23. 13–14 ('Withhold not correction from a child: for if thou strike him with the rod, he shall not die. Thou shalt beat him with the rod, and deliver his soul from hell').

4 In his study of Mannyg's *exempla*, F. Kemmler remarks that 'An author using illustrative narratives as part of his argument ... can select a particular emotive force that will dominate the composition of his narrative – fear, pity (laughter of) relief, etc. However, though he is *idealiter* free to select any emotive force, he is, nevertheless, *realiter* under certain constraints imposed upon him by the tradition in which he works': *Exempla in Context: A Historical Study of Robert Mannyng of Brunne's 'Handlyng Synne'* (Tübingen, 1984), p. 182. A majority, but certainly not all, of Mannyng's illustrative narratives are arguably governed by the emotive force of fear. A few rely on humour (see for example the account of the slap-stick demon, ll. 9264–311) or comforting visions of heaven or divine grace (see for example the vision of St Macarius, ll. 1917–96) or the redemptive powers of music, ll. 4743–68.

5 For a discussion of Mannyng's complex deployment of shame in the Dancers of Colbeck section, see M. Miller, 'Displaced Souls, Idle Talk, Spectacular Scenes: *Handlyng Synne* and the Perspective of Agency', *Speculum* 71 (1996), 606–32.

6 T. N. Tentler, 'The Summa for Confessors as an Instrument of Social Control', in *The Pursuit of Holiness in Late Medieval and Renaissance Religion* (Leiden, 1974), pp. 103–26 (p. 123).

it shifts responsibility from the confessor to the penitent himself. By devoting a large part to teaching him what kind of behaviour constitutes a sin and why sinning is something hateful, it makes the lay person aware of the difference between morally good and bad behaviour and of the dangers the latter would imply for his soul's destiny after death.[7]

At this stage, it may be difficult decide between these two rather extreme views especially since penitential fear and doctrinal sophistication need not necessarily exclude each other.

Nevertheless, *Handlyng Synne* appears to be a text that relies on basic fear, its rhetoric working often by coercion. If, however, confessors and preachers actually believed in the reality of purgatory and hell, as they obviously did, would they not be guilty of gross malpractice if they omitted the peril of sin to dwell on sweetness and light? *Handlyng Synne* itself has stern warnings for priests[8] who neglect the care of their parishioners' souls.

Suspicion of the coercive motives in such penitential literature may be conditioned by the intense politics of fear in the early twenty-first century and thus may seem to map contemporary concerns all too crudely onto theological controversies of the twelfth and thirteenth centuries. Yet generations of medieval theologians themselves wrestled with the problem of fear,[9] and particularly with the potentially corrosive effects of controlling believers through mere fear of hell and punishment. The Bible itself has seemingly quite contradictory things to say about fear, generally rendered in Latin as *timor*. In Proverbs 1. 7, fear, specifically the fear of God, is a positive good: 'timor Domini principium scientiae' ['the fear of God is the beginning of wisdom'],[10] and Psalm 18. 10 states that 'timor Domini mundus perseverans in saecula' ['The fear of the Lord is holy, enduring for ever and ever']. In 1 John 4. 18, however, fear seems to be the polar opposite of love:

> timor non est in caritate, sed perfecta caritas foras mittit timorem, quoniam timor poenam habet. Qui autem timet non est perfectus in caritate. Nos ergo diligamus, quoniam Deus prior dilexit nos.

---

[7] U. Schemmann, *Confessional Literature and Lay Education: The 'Manuel dé Pechez' as a Book of Good Conduct and Guide to Personal Religion* (Düsseldorf, 2000), pp. 52–3.

[8] For an analysis of Mannyng's dual audience (priests and layfolk), see K. Greenspan, 'Lessons for the Priest, Lessons for the People: Robert Mannyng of Brunne's Audiences for *Handlyng Synne*', *Essays in Medieval Studies* 21 (2004), 109–21.

[9] A number of disciplines in and outside of the humanities have recently been taking a keen interest in emotions, and with respect to medieval emotions, the scholastic philosophy offers the possibility of gaining insight into contemporary categories of emotion. For a foundational study, see B. Rosenwein, *Communities of Emotion in the Early Middle Ages* (Ithaca NY, 2006). For a convenient summary of work on emotion (particularly fear) in evolutionary psychology, see J. Tooby and L. Cosmides, 'The Evolutionary Psychology of the Emotions and Their Relationship to Internal Regulatory Variables', in *Handbook of the Emotions*, ed. M. Lewis et al. (New York, 2008).

[10] See also Proverbs 1. 29, 9. 10 and Psalm 110. 10.

[Fear is not in charity: but perfect charity casteth out fear, because fear hath pain. And he that feareth, is not perfected in charity. Let us therefore love God, because God first hath loved us.]

The struggle to reconcile these contradictory passages began in the psalm commentaries of Augustine and Cassiodorus, but eventually blossomed into a full-blown scholastic topos, codified in Peter Lombard's *Sententiae*[11] – the most important theological compendium of the high Middle Ages – and later examined at length by Aquinas.[12] In fact, R. W. Southern uses this evolving 'theology of fear' as the example *par excellence* of scholastic thought. He sees it as a symptomatic of the

> step-by-step progress ... characteristic of the scholastic mode of advancing by stages of ever greater clarification of terms and refinements in understanding of the biblical texts and their relationship to the ascent of any individual towards God.[13]

Southern traces the theology of fear from its beginnings in the biblical commentaries of Augustine and Cassiodorus, to Anselm of Laon's crucial recasting of the problem, which in turn was taken up by a number of theologians before it was codified finally in Peter Lombard's *Sentences* under the title 'Plena timorum distinctio'. The forging of the 'system' started with verbal analysis and ended with a graded and ascending set of definitions:

> This combination of analysis of words, relating these words to actual experiences, and arranging a progression from one state to another, provided a perfect scholastic exercise: it required the analysis of concepts, the identification of the experience associated with these concepts, and the tracing of a movement from one to another. When all these aspects of the problem had been closely analysed and integrated into a single system, the scholastic task was completed, and the texts were ready for use in a pastoral context.[14]

Southern suggests that the first sixty years of this developing analysis reveals a 'steady advance' that was 'relatively simple', but that a vast array

---

11 P. Lombard, *Sententiae in IV Libris Distinctae*, 2 vols., Spicilegium Bonaventurianum, IV (Rome, 1971–81), II, 192–8. The 'plena timorum distinctio' is found in Book III, Distinctio XXIV, chapters 4–9. For a recent account of the central importance of the *Sentences*, see P. W. Rosemann, 'Peter Lombard', in *A Companion to Philosophy in the Middle Ages*, ed. J. J. E. Gracia and T. B. Noone (Oxford, 2005), pp. 514–15.

12 Thomas Aquinas, *Summa Theologiae*, XXXIII, ed. W. J. Hill (Cambridge, 2006), 2a2æ, 19. Aquinas had forged many of his most important positions on fear in his commentary on the *Sentences*: *Scriptum super libros sententiarum magistri Petri Lombardi Episcopi Parisiensis*, 4 vols., ed. M. F. Moos and P. Mandonnet (Paris, 1929–47).

13 R. W. Southern, *Scholastic Humanism and the Unification of Europe*, I (Oxford, 1995), p. 129.

14 Ibid., p. 127.

of complications were taken up later.[15] In this formative period, though, fear was resolved into an ascending scale of four types: natural fear, servile fear, initial fear and chaste or filial fear.[16] Natural fear, the emotion we share with animals, was thought to be an almost instinctual fear for bodily safety and one's possessions. Servile fear, perhaps the most interesting category, came to designate pure fear of punishment (*timor poene*) or of hell (*timor gehenne*), which drives believers from sin. Initial fear, probably so named because it was thought to be the beginning of wisdom or at least of an ascent to a higher form of fear, contained equal parts of fear of punishment and love, usually the love of justice. The last and highest category, pure (*castus*) or filial (*filialis*) fear began to merge with love: the believer, out of love for the Father, fears his absence or giving offence to him. With this fear, advanced believers acted like children of God, not his abject slaves.[17]

Again and again, *Handlyng Synne* attempts to arouse servile fear – the fear of punishment and hell – in its listeners and readers. And yet many twelfth-century theologians who grappled with the theology of fear, even in the early, relatively straightforward period of development, harboured profound misgivings about the efficacy of servile fear, in particular. The roots of these doubts about servile fear go back to Augustine, whose earlier division of fear into two diametrically opposed types in his commentary on 1 John 4. 18 cemented the adjectives *servilis* and *castus* into place. In the later four-fold system, the qualifier *servilis*, though in the scholastic context describing a potentially higher, more positive form of fear, retained its pejorative force.

In general, as Landgraf's detailed analysis shows, the earliest commentators were certain that *timor servilis* was undesirable: 'Es sei nun sofort darauf hingewiesen, daß von Anfang an lediglich der *timor mundanus* und *servilis* als schlecht bezeichnet wurden' ['One should point out that from the beginning only earthly fear and servile fear were designated as evil'], mainly because they lacked love.[18] Another potent objection was that servile fear merely inhibits the evil act but not the will to commit such an act. Stephen Langton (1150–1228), for example, who concerned himself with fear in a number of treatises but particularly in his *Summa Quaestionum Theologiae*, argues that

---

[15] Ibid., p. 129.

[16] For a detailed survey of the evolution of the *topos* see A. M. Landgraf, *Dogmengeschichte der Frühscholastik, Vierter Teil: Die Lehre von der Sünde und ihren Folgen*, I (Regensburg, 1955), pp. 276–385. See also *Fear and Its Representations in the Middle Ages and Renaissance*, ed. A. Scott and C. Kosso (Turnhout, 2002). For an analysis of the theology of fear in a vernacular English text, see E. J. Johnson, '"In Dryz Dred and Daunger": The Tradition and Rhetoric of Fear in *Cleanness* and *Patience*' (unpublished PhD thesis, University of York, 2000).

[17] These basic definitions only hint at the intricate lines of argument and counter-argument revolving around whether Christ experienced any forms of fear, how fear affects the will, or whether fear will exist in heaven, etc.

[18] Landgraf, *Dogmengeschichte*, p. 292.

Seruilis enim timor non potest cohibere uoluntatem interiorem, set exteriorem, quia lex cohibit manum et non animum. ... ergo seruiliter timens uult peccare opere exteriori ex eo quod in eo uiuit uoluntas sic peccandi.

[Therefore servile fear cannot restrain the interior will, but only the exterior, because the law restrains the hand not the heart. ... therefore the person fearing in a servile way wants to sin in the external act because the will to sin thus lives in him.][19]

Though Langton goes on to parse the operation of the will even more intricately later on, he stands by the conclusion that *timor servilis* merely stops the hand without changing the heart.[20] In his commentary on 1 John, he makes it clear that servile fear, though a gift of the Holy Spirit, has no power to save:

Timor seruilis est cum quis tantum timore gehenne uel etiam temporalis pene uiuat facere peccatum; et talis timor est donum spiritus sancti, et ita bonum, set tale bonum quo nullus meretur uitam eternam.

[Servile fear occurs when someone is in such great fear of hell or likewise of temporal punishment that he avoids committing sin; and such fear is a gift of the Holy Spirit, and is thus good, but such a good by which no one would merit eternal life.][21]

Langton here is only slightly more sceptical of the power of servile fear than Peter Lombard's classic formulation in the *Sententiae*:

Timor autem servilis est, ut ait Augustinus, 'cum per timorem gehennae continet se homo a peccato', 'quo praesentiam judicis et poenas metuit; et timore facit quidquid boni facit: non timore amittendi aeternum bonum quod non amat, sed timore patiendi malum quod formidat. Non timet ne perdat amplexus pulcherrimi sponsi, sed timet ne mittatur in gehennam. Bonus est iste timor et utilis', licet insufficiens, per quem 'fit paulatim consuetudo justitiae'. Et succedit initialis timor, quando 'incipit quod durum erat amari'; et sic incipit 'excludi servilis timor a charitate'. Et succedit deinde timor castus sive amicabilis, 'quo timemus ne sponsus tardet, ne discedat, ne offendamus, ne eo careamus. Timor iste de amore venit. Ille quidem servilis est utilis, sed non *permanens in aeternum* ut iste.' 'Timor divinus comes est per omnes gradus.'[22]

[Servile fear occurs, as Augustine said 'when a person holds himself back from sin for fear of hell', 'where he is afraid of the immediate punishments of the Judge; and in fear does whatever good he does: not through fear of losing an eternal good which he does not love, but in fear that he must

---

19 R. Quinto, 'Die *Quaestiones* des Stephan Langton über Gottesfurcht', *Cahiers de l'Institut du Moyen-Âge Grec et Latin* 62 (1992), 77–165 (p. 139).
20 See Landgraf, *Dogmengeschichte*, pp. 382–3.
21 Quinto, 'Die *Quaestiones* des Stephan Langton', p. 117.
22 Peter Lombard, *Sententiae*, Book III, Dist. XXIV, cap. 4, ll. 6–18 (II, 193).

suffer evil of which he is terrified. He does not fear that he will forfeit the embrace of the most handsome Bridegroom, but fears that he will be sent to hell. This kind of fear is good and useful', although insufficient, through which 'the habit of justice is made little by little'. And it leads to initial fear, when 'that which was harsh begins to be loved', and so 'servile fear begins to be shut off from love'. And at length this leads to chaste or friendly love, 'in which we fear that the Bridegroom may delay or depart because we offend, and that we will be cut off from him. This fear comes from love. That servile kind of fear is in fact useful, but will not remain in heaven.' 'Divine fear is present through every stage.']

Thus for Peter Lombard, the only function of servile fear is to lead, bit by bit, to initial fear, a higher form which embraces the love of right rather than merely avoids sin through fear of pain and punishment. Though it is useful and can lead to good effects, it is in itself impermanent and 'insufficiens'.

Of course, this high scholastic philosophy, with its careful definitions and its subtle, ascending ladder of fears, might seem to be worlds away from the vernacular theologies in the *Manuel des Péchés* or *Handlyng Synne*, where the visceral fear of hell is employed as a powerful tool to lead listeners to proper confession. Yet, the complex theology of fear that I have just outlined did filter into pastoral literature, mainly, I believe, through penitential manuals, handbooks on preaching and sermons.

Few scholars know better than the honorand the intricate pathways that lead from the high theology of the twelfth-century schools of Paris to Latin manuals of pastoral care and finally to Middle English texts intended for complex lay audiences.[23] In this process of translation, carefully argued definitions and distinctions were inevitably elided, simplified and adapted, as Tentler points out:

> The academic tradition that fed pastoral literature, therefore, had to be interpreted judiciously. Theological technicalities, scholastic disputes, and well-intentioned subtleties could be helpful, or irrelevant, or even harmful. And good pastoral care would choose what was helpful and avoid the rest.[24]

This process can be traced in part through the works of Raymond of Penyafort and Thomas of Chobham (*c*.1160–1236).

Some penitential manuals incorporated the theology of fear in rather indirect ways. Raymond of Penyafort in his *Summa de Paenitentia*, for example,

---

[23] Besides the masterful notes in Bella Millett's definitive edition of *Ancrene Wisse*, see vol. I, 'Institution Context', pp. xxiv–xxix, and 'Sources and Analogues', pp. xxix–xxxvi, as well as '*Ancrene Wisse* and the Conditions of Confession', *English Studies* 80 (1999), 193–215.

[24] T. N. Tentler, *Sin and Confession on the Eve of the Reformation* (Princeton, 1977), p. 234.

clearly knows about the division between servile and filial fear,[25] and the fear of hell receives brief, though prominent mention at the beginning of his discussion of contrition and its causes:

> Causae inductivae sunt sex: cogitatio, et ex ea pudor de peccatis commissis; detestatio vilitatis ipsius peccati; timore de die iudicii et de poena gehennae; dolor de amissione caelestis patriae et multiplici offensa Creatoris.[26]

> [Causes leading [to contrition] are six: [1] thought, and from it shame for sins committed; [2] hatred of the baseness of sin; [3] fear of the Day of Judgement and [4] of the punishments of hell; [5] pain at the loss of the heavenly home and [6] at the many offences against the Creator.]

Raymond goes on to count the hopes that contrition brings with it: 'spes triplex, scilicet: veniae, gratiae et gloriae' ['three hopes, namely: (hope of) mercy, grace and glory'].

Arguably beneath this list lie generations of theological thought about fear: 'cogitatio' puts the subsequent fear beyond the natural because of its rationality, while the fear of last judgement and hell clearly represents servile fear. Finally the pain of losing heaven and offending God resembles Peter Lombard's version of filial fear closely. In general, though, the problematic nature of servile fear as well as its progressive quality disappears completely in Raymond's account – fears of last judgement and hell are simply two of six causes of life-giving contrition.

As a student at the University of Paris at the end of the twelfth century, Thomas of Chobham certainly knew about the evolving debate on fear since he reproduced the graded set of definitions of it in his so-called *Summa Confessorum*, a work which attempts to provide confessors access to sophisticated theological and legal learning. In a section that parses carefully which of the seven gifts of the spirit[27] is actually a virtue, Thomas concludes that some types of fear are virtues,[28] though others are not: 'illa dona non sunt virtutes que pertinent ad speculationem, scilicet donum scientie et donum intellectus et donum sapientie non sunt virtutes' ['Those gifts are not virtues which pertain to observation; it is clear that the gift of knowledge and the gift

---

25 Raymond of Penyafort, *Summa*, cols. 823–4: 'Pura quoad intentionem, ut non ad vanam gloriam vel hypocrisim vel timore servili, sed timore filiali fiat, et sine omni fictione.' ['(Confession should be) pure with respect to intention so that (it is not made) because of vainglory or hypocrisy or servile fear, but is performed with filial fear, free from all fabrication'].
26 Raymond of Penyafort, *Summa*, col. 804.
27 The fear of the Lord or *timor Domini* is the last of the seven gifts of the spirit. This *topos* is based largely on the list in Isa. 11. 2–3: *sapientiae, intellectus, consilium, fortitudo, scientia, pietas* and *timor Domini*.
28 Derived ultimately from Greek philosophy, the four cardinal virtues are *prudentia, iustitia, temperantia* and *fortitudo*.

of perception and the gift of wisdom are not virtues'].[29] Like Peter Lombard, Thomas divides fear into four types: natural fear, servile fear, initial fear and chaste or filial fear. In general only the last two types of fear can be said to be active virtues. Servile fear, however, he does not count a virtue:

Timor servilis est quo homo per rationem videt penam sequentem, et propter illam solam penam abstinet a malo, non propter aliquem amorem iustite. Iste timor bonus est in se et non est virtus, sed sepe introducit virtutem.[30]

[Servile fear occurs when someone sees coming punishment through his rational faculty, and because of that punishment alone abstains from sin, not for any love of justice. This fear is good in itself and is not a virtue, though it often leads to virtue.]

For Thomas, though, servile fear, however positive its effects may be, is a complex enough category to include mortal sin. Both human and mundane fear, usually defined as 'natural' fears we share with animals can, if they rise to the level of rationality, lead to damnation. He calls these two rational forms of human and mundane fear companions (*comites*) of servile fear:

Timor humanus est quo aliquis homo timet pelli sue. Timor mundanus est quo aliquis homo timet damnum rerum temporalium. Isti autem timores si ex natura surgant naturales sunt: si oriuntur ex ratione dicuntur timores serviles. Vix tam potest contingere quod timor mundanus possit esse sine motu rationis circa damnum rerum temporalium. Si autem propter istos timores dimittatur bonum vel fiat malum uterque timor per accidens[31] peccatum mortale est.[32]

[Human fear occurs when someone fears for his skin. Mundane fear occurs when someone fears the loss of temporal things. Moreover, these two fears if they are born of nature belong to the category of natural fear: if they arise from reason they are called servile fears. It can scarcely happen that mundane fear could occur without the operation of reason concerning the loss of temporal things. If however good is renounced because of these two fears or evil is done then both forms of fear are in effect mortal sins.]

Servile fear, then, emerges as a complex, mixed category for Thomas: it is good in itself and can lead to virtue but is in fact not a virtue itself and, furthermore, certain of its subtypes are mortal sins. It is a form of fear which can lead up the ladder or down. In this sense its only real good is that it can, once left behind, lead to higher forms of fear which begin to merge with love. Initial fear represents this key transition from fear to love: 'Timor autem

---

29 Chobham, *Summa Confessorum*, p. 40.
30 Ibid., p. 41.
31 I.e., because of their accidental qualities and effects, not their essence.
32 Chobham, *Summa Confessorum*, p. 41.

intialis est scilicet quo ex una parte timetur pena, ex alia parte amatur iustitia. Virtus est propter amorem iustitie' ['It is evident, however, that initial fear occurs when one fears punishment on the one hand and loves justice on the other. It is a virtue because of its love of justice.'][33] If perfect love casts out fear, of course, then initial fear can itself only be an imperfect, lower form of fear awaiting perfection in chaste or filial fear. In fact, Thomas makes his most important contribution to the theology of fear in this last category by introducing a new three-fold subdivision of its types: the fear of being separated from God, the fear of giving offence to God and the fear arising from reverence in the awe-inspiring presence of God. According to Thomas, only this last type will survive eternally in heaven. Building on the work of other thinkers, then, Thomas further systematizes and dramatizes the ascending quality of the types of fear.

As I have already implied, this careful parsing of fear, debated and refined in the schools, was not destined to survive fully intact in pastoral literature. In addressing the practical needs of preachers in his *Summa de arte praedicandi*, for example, Thomas of Chobham himself significantly simplifies his account of the theology of fear. In a section on the two types of preaching (*de diuisione predicationis*), he says plainly that preaching can either produce fear or love in listeners, finding this division in a number of sometimes obscure passages from the Old Testament. The last example is perhaps the most interesting. Taking the prohibition in Deuteronomy 24. 6 against swearing on either the upper or lower millstone as a starting point, he remarks that

> Per inferiorem molam intelligitur timor, per superiorem intelligitur amor, quia inter has duas molas, id est timorem et amorem, semper debet moli[34] christianus, ut semper uno oculo habeat respectum ad timorem gehenne et alio oculo habeat respectum ad amorem patrie. … Quilibet igitur predicator, hec duo debet in sermone suo commiscere, ut semper ex una parte incutiat auditoribus timorem Dei propter penas inferni, et ex altera parte inuitet eos ad amorem Dei propter glorie premium.[35]

> [By the lower millstone fear is understood, by the upper millstone, love, because a Christian must always operate between these two millstones, that is fear and love, so that he has a view to the fear of hell with one eye and a view to the love of heaven with the other. … Therefore every preacher should mix these two in his sermons so that he always strikes fear of the punishments of hell into his listeners on the one hand and invites them on the other to the love of God because of the reward of glory.]

Clearly, Thomas imagines that initial fear with its mixture of low fear and

---

[33] Ibid., p. 42.
[34] Note Thomas's use of paranomasia here: *moli* 'to work' plays on the similarity of *mola* 'millstone'.
[35] Chobham, *Summa de Arte Praedicandi*, p. 28.

high love is the most suitable goal for lay listeners. He goes on to devote a section to methods of inviting listeners to the love of God through the seven works of mercy ('Quomodo auditores inuitandi sunt ad amorem Dei' ['How listeners are to be encouraged to the love of God']),[36] but a much longer and more vigorous section to terrifying audiences ('Quomodo auditores absterrendi sunt' ['How listeners are to be deterred by fright']),[37] which rehearses the various pains of hell.

In their pastoral versions of the theology of fear, Raymond of Penyafort and Thomas of Chobham dispense with the formal graded system of ascending types. Thomas's adaptation, by far the more interesting from my point of view, opts instead for a powerful binary of love and fear. Thomas obscures the scholastic model of fear further by reversing the order of these two: love first sketched fairly lightly and fear second in heavy and frightening detail. Crucially, Thomas makes no attempt to give a complex and potentially confusing picture of servile fear in creating his powerful push-pull approach.

It stands to reason that nearly all penitential texts must in some way harness the fear of punishment as part of their pastoral mission, but the question remains whether or not this theology of fear in its high or vernacular versions forms anything more than a very general or atmospheric context for understanding *Handlyng Synne*. A very strong case can be made that it does. Part of the *Manuel des Péchés*, not translated in *Handlyng Synne*, relies directly on the vernacular version of the theology of fear, and shadows Thomas of Chobham's approach closely; this section, often called the 'Petit sermon',[38] forms part six of the *Manuel* in a majority of the manuscripts and was possibly a somewhat later addition to the text.[39] Though an editor has called it a 'Poème sur l'amour de Dieu et sur la haine du péché' ['Poem concerning the love of God and the hatred of sin'], it might more accurately be described as a poem about the competing importance of love and fear (not hate). The 'Petit sermon' survives as a separate poem[40] which redacts the contents of

---

[36] Ibid., pp. 28–32.

[37] Ibid., pp. 32–53.

[38] After many years of lamentation on this score, there is still no satisfactory edition of the *Manuel des Péchés*. In his edition of *Handlyng Synne* for the Roxburghe Club (London, 1862), F. J. Furnivall provided a full edition of the *Manuel* based on British Library MSS Harley 273 and 4657, but reprinted a partial edition – only those portions of the Anglo-Norman text which Mannyng made use of – in the later version of *Handlyng Synne* for the EETS OS 119 (London, 1901).

[39] E. J. Arnould, in his still indispensable study, *Le Manuel des péchés: étude de littérature religieuse anglo-normande* (Paris, 1940), numbers this section among 'parties non authentiques ou suspectes', p. 205.

[40] I shall rely on the edition of the independent form of the 'Petit sermon' edited by P. Meyer, 'Notice du MS Rawlinson Poetry 241', *Romania* 29 (1900), 1–84 (pp. 5–21). The 'Petit sermon' appears as ll. 7793–8482 in Furnivall's 1862 edition. For a list of manuscripts and editions, see Dean, *Anglo-Norman Literature*, no. 636.

part VI of the *Manuel* in a somewhat different order.[41] Very much a sermon in verse,[42] it can be divided into roughly three sections: (1) a definition of love, listing two reasons for loving God, (2) an analysis of fear (a reason for hating sin) divided into three types: the fear of sudden death, the fear of last judgement and the fear of hell and (3) a closing section which returns to love, repeating the two reasons from section one and adding a third. E. J. Arnould notes that 'Petit sermon' relies heavily on the theology of fear I have mapped out above:

> L'amour tel que le comprend le *Petit sermon*, bien que très supérieur à la crainte, ainsi que notre auteur le souligne, n'est pas non plus parfaitement désintéressé: il ressemble beaucoup à la 'crainte filiale' dont parlent les Pères.[43]

> [Love as the *Little Sermon* understands it, although vastly superior to fear as our author emphasizes, is not entirely selfless: it resembles very much the 'filial fear' of which the Fathers speak.]

In the beginning of section two, the author of the 'Petit sermon' thinks of love and fear as two emotions, one superior to the other, driving the believer towards a good life:

> La premere dount jeo vous di
> Qui pecché fet estre haï,
> Et la meindre, c'est amour
> Et l'autre est parfite poür;
> Ceux deux gardeyns ad Dieux
> Pur bien garder ces amys.
> Poür lour fet pecché lesser
> Et amour vertuz enracer;

---

41 The version of this section of the *Manuel* in Cambridge, University Library, Mm.6.4, for example, begins immediately with the section juxtaposing love and fear: 'Dous choses ad deu establiz / Pur meuz garder tuz ses amis. / En l'alme chescun chretien, / Ky enprent garde, il fet bien. / La premere chose ce vus di / Ke fet peche estre hay / Ce est de deu parfite pour. / L'autre si est uerray amur' (fol. 67v). The 'Petit sermon', then may diverge from part VI of the *Manuel* more or less radically in organization and emphasis.

42 Arnould stresses its stylistic and thematic dependence on sermon literature: 'on peut y discerner les parties essentielles qui, d'après les *Artes Praedicandi* devaient constituer le sermon: texte et thème, division, subdivisions et rappel de celles-ci entre chaque point, exposé clair et 'autorisé' de chacune les parties, 'récitation', conclusion et prière finale' [one can recognize the key parts which according to the *Manuals of Preaching* the sermon must have: text and theme, division, subdivisions with a summary of the subdivisions accompanying each point, presented clearly and 'authorised' by each of the parts, recapitulation, conclusion, and final prayer], and offers it as 'un excellent exemple du genre parénétique populaire' [an excellent example of the popular moralising genre], *Manuel des Péchés*, p. 206.

43 Arnould, *Manuel des Péchés*, p. 208.

Poür lour fet d'enfer fuer,
Amour lour fet au ciel fuer.[44]

[I will tell you the first means as well as a lesser one which brings
about a hatred of sin, the one is love and the other is perfect fear;
God has established these two guardians to protect those souls.
Fear makes them abandon sin, and love makes them embrace
virtues; fear makes them flee hell while love makes them come
to heaven.]

The opposed emotions of love and fear have a push–pull effect here, but
they are in some ways so closely allied as to be two aspects of the same
force. This fear is certainly not servile, as Arnould pointed out: it is 'parfit', a
close mirror image of love. When the author of the 'Petit sermon' goes on to
explore fear more fully, he enumerates the three principal types of fear, 'neist
en coer de homme / Qui bien en memorie les a' ['born in the heart of man,
who wisely keeps them in his memory']:[45] namely, (1) 'hidour de mort subite'
['horror of sudden death'], (2) 'del destresse del juggement' ['of the anguish
of the judgement'] and (3) 'd'enfer le orible feu' ['(of) the horrible fire of
hell'].[46] He then explores each separately at some length. These are precisely
the kinds of fear that are conjured up again and again in *Handlyng Synne*.

In the longer discussion of the terrors of the last judgement, the poet of the
'Petit sermon', somewhat like Mannyng in his *exemplum* of the courageous
sinner (see above), implies that a lack of fear can itself lead to damnation:

Et qui de ceo n'ad nulle doute
Jeo di que en alme ne voit goute,
Car en munde ne'st coer si hardi
Ne par pecché si emmorti,
Que bien pensat de ceo jour,
Que ne trembleroit de poür.[47]

[And whoever has no fear, I say that he will see no drop [of mercy]
in his soul, because there is no heart on earth so courageous, nor
deadened so much by sin that considers carefully the events of
that Day who would not tremble with fear.]

He continues with a description of the 'grantz dolours' ['great pains'][48] of the
damned, before arriving at the last of the three fears, the terror of hell. In this
section, the presentation of fear starts to rival the complexity of the scholars,

---

[44] 'Petit sermon', ll. 327–36.
[45] Ibid., ll. 340–41.
[46] Ibid., ll. 344, 346 and 348.
[47] Ibid., ll. 551–56.
[48] Ibid., l. 557.

beginning with the recognition of the salutary benefits of fear for Christians incapable of giving up sin for love:

> Molz fait ceo poür bien
> A chekun feble crestïen
> Que pur amur ne veut lesser
> Le dur servage del peccher.[49]

> [This fear accomplishes much good for the weak Christian who does not want to abandon out of love the hard servitude of the sinner.]

The fear of hell is most effective obviously as a remedial therapy. Its inferiority to love and its insufficiency in itself becomes crystal clear in the following lines:

> De yceste treble poür
> Nous delye par sa douceour
> Jhesu le fiz seynte Marie,
> Qu'en sa amour si ferm nous lye
> Que pecché heom pur s'amour;
> Et nyent soulement pur poür,
> Car poür ne sauve alme mye
> Si ele n'eit amour en compaignie,
> Mès amour ad le poer,
> Tot saunz poür, l'ame sauver,
> Mes poür ait home retraire
> Quant il ad talent de mal faire.
> Amour fait pecché en despit
> Et Dieux servir de coer parfit
> A poür aver ne put suffire.[50]

> [From these three fears Jesus Christ, the son of the Virgin Mary, frees us in his great kindness, and embraces us – we who hate sin for his love – tightly in his love; and (we hate sin) not only because of fear, because fear does not save the soul at all if it is not accompanied by love. Moreover, love has the power, completely without fear to save the soul. But fear makes man draw back, when he has the desire to do evil. Love defies sin and makes one serve God with a perfect heart. To have fear cannot suffice.]

Though he does not imagine fear as a ladder with many rungs as the scholastic philosophers do, there is a sense in which the poet's conception of fear, like that of Thomas of Chobham, acknowledges the benefits of fear while recognizing that it falls short of virtue: Thomas wrote that

---

[49] Ibid., ll. 627–30.
[50] Ibid., ll. 635–49.

Servile fear occurs when someone sees coming punishment through his rational faculty, and because of that punishment alone abstains from sin, not for any love of justice. This fear is good in itself and is not a virtue, though it often leads to virtue.[51]

In some ways, the author of the 'Petit sermon' takes the problematic nature of servile fear further than Thomas in ending the last section with a description of the joys of heaven.[52]

Handlyng Synne, as we have seen, evokes the same kinds of fear in its readers as does the 'Petit sermon'; indeed, one might consider the 'Petit sermon' as the absent theory for the actual praxis of the text. Yet, unlike the 'Petit sermon', in only one instance does *Handlyng Synne* question the efficacy of fear directly and unequivocally: in the penultimate section on the twelve conditions of confession. In the first point, that confession be voluntary or 'Wyþ gode wyl and herte fre',[53] believers are warned not to put off their confessions until a point of crisis or death:

> Abyde nat tyl þou most nedely,
> For þan hyt ys wiþ fors & maystry.
> Þou shryuest þe þan for drede,
> Nat for loue but more for nede.[54]

This statement in many ways represents a breathtaking reversal of the entire orientation of *Handlyng Synne* with respect to the horror of sudden death, hell and damnation. In the *exemplum* of Conrad's squire, with which I opened this essay, the squire erred tragically by *not* acting out of a healthy fear which could have saved his soul. In adapting the *Manuel*'s fuller treatment of this point, Mannyng condensed greatly the Biblical exemplum of Achan,[55] spun out in fuller narrative detail in the *Manuel*, and mentions Achan briefly as a man who confessed only because he was caught and afraid of punishment. Fear and compulsion actually destroy the efficacy of the confession. In the Biblical account, Achan was stoned: fearful, red-handed confession has no power to save.

Why does *Handlyng Synne* reverse itself so violently on this point? It seems possible to me that the undesirability of a fearful confession mentioned in the first condition of confession represents something like the ghost limb of the

---

51 See note 32.
52 Thomas begins with love but ends with a much lengthier and terrifying description of the fear of hell and last judgement.
53 *Handlyng Synne*, l. 11,360. The *Manuel* (ed. Furnivall) at this point reads 'Sans force & necesité, / Mes par ta bone volunté' ['without compulsion and force, but of your free will'], ll. 9612–13. See B. Millett, '*Ancrene Wisse* and the Conditions of Confession' for the development of this *topos*.
54 *Handlyng Synne*, ll. 11,367–11,370.
55 In the *Manuel*, ed. Furnivall, the name appears as 'Achor' (ll. 9,634 and ff.) and as 'Acor' in *Handlyng Synne* (l. 11,364).

'Petit sermon', which immediately preceded the conditions in the *Manuel*. Having omitted the 'Petit sermon' in adapting *Handlyng Synne*, however, Mannyng's warning about unforced confession falls somewhat flat.

In conclusion, from the point of view of high scholastic philosophy as well as its adaptations in the pastoral literature, *Handlyng Synne*, more than the *Manuel*, seems to push its readers and listeners away from sin and towards confession mainly by conjuring up a vivid and compelling form of servile fear, rather than pulling them towards God by love. In practice, it was easier and perhaps more realistic for confessors, preachers and penitential texts like *Handlyng Synne* to strike fear than to inspire love in the hearts and minds of their listeners. No less an authority on medieval preaching than G. W. Owst was inclined to this view:

> In a rude and turbulent world like that of the Middle Ages, the more sensitive in the preacher's audiences might well be tamed and uplifted, nay, even educated by frequent references to the appeal of the beautiful around them. … But the pulpit, as we have already remarked, was not much given to the kindred emotions of love and sweetness. It preferred generally the themes of denunciation and terror.[56]

In this regard, *Handlyng Synne* may betray a pragmatic attitude toward the capabilities of lay believers. Though it would be far too simplistic to claim that its 20,000 plus lines merely attempt to frighten readers into virtue, looking over the collection of *exempla* as a whole, a remarkable number of them do end in sudden illness, death, hell or demonic attack. *Handlyng Synne* arguably has little interest in producing independent, dispassionate parsers of motive in its readers; instead, it attempts to instil a kind of fearful introspection by means of penitential instruction coupled with thousands of lines of often wildly vivid narrative.

---

[56] G. W. Owst, *Literature and Pulpit in Medieval England: A Neglected Chapter in the History of English Letters and of the English People*, 2nd edn (Oxford, 1961), pp. 47–8.

10

Prophecy, Complaint and Pastoral Care in the Fifteenth Century
Thomas Gascoigne's *Liber Veritatum*

Mishtooni Bose

In his commentary on St Matthew's gospel, Thomas Aquinas identifies two purposes of prophecy: confirmation of the faith and the correction of morals. In his view, the second task 'is never complete, nor will it ever be'.[1] There is some continuity between this statement and Benedict XVI's recent assertion that a certain 'prophetic-charismatic history traverses the whole time of the Church. It is always there especially at the most critical times of transition.'[2] Such statements indicate the necessity, and indeed the inevitability, of prophetic discourse as an essential element in the evolution and continuous reform of the Church. But 'prophecy' has always been a multivalent term requiring nuanced taxonomy, and different levels of institutional privilege have been granted to its various modes over time. Kathryn Kerby-Fulton has recently argued for the existence of a fundamental antagonism between 'the revelatory and the scholastic' during the high and late Middle Ages, seeing them as 'rivals for the prize of theological illumination ... with contempt for each other's methods'.[3]

Revelation was only one of the prophetic modes, however, and scholastic theologians retained an important role for a different kind of prophecy among their professional duties. Most pertinent for the concerns of this essay is what such theologians understood as *prophetia comminationis*, 'the prophecy of denunciation', a prominent mode of discourse among the Old Testament prophets, which typically took the form of the denunciation of lax mores and calls to repentance. *Prophetia comminationis* was one of the forms identified by Aquinas in his treatise on prophecy and charismata in the *Summa Theologiae*.

---

[1] '[A]d corrigendos mores numquam deficit, nec deficiet prophetia': *Super Evangelium St Matthaei Lectura*, ed. P. R. Cai, OP (Turin, 1951), 924 (p. 145).

[2] Joseph Cardinal Ratzinger (now Benedict XVI), 'Foreword' to N. C. Hvidt, *Christian Prophecy: The Post-Biblical Tradition* (New York, 2007), p. viii.

[3] K. Kerby-Fulton, *Books Under Suspicion: Censorship and Tolerance of Revelatory Writing in Late Medieval England* (Notre Dame IN, 2006), p. 189.

In this he was following the taxonomy established in the *Glossa Ordinaria*, which had stated that denunciation was 'significative of the divine wrath' ['quae fit ob signum divinae animadversionis'].[4] The exegesis of scriptural examples of *prophetia comminationis* became a fundamental resource for the rhetoric of late medieval ecclesiastical reform, even among theologians who contested the validity of other prophetic modes.[5] As sanctioned by scripture, and by scriptural exegesis, the prophecy of denunciation became a standard rhetorical feature in the works of both avowedly orthodox writers – such as Thomas Gascoigne, the subject of this essay – and those whose ideas were hereticated. As I will show in this essay, examination of the prevalence and significance of the prophecy of denunciation focuses attention on the extent to which, under the umbrella of reformist thinking, orthodox and heterodox alike shared the same *auctoritates*, rhetorical strategies and many substantive concerns.[6]

The tradition of prophetic denunciation that would eventually produce Gascoigne had been notably enriched by John Wyclif who, like Aquinas and other doctors, understood prophecy to take several different forms. In *De vaticinacione seu prophetia* (written by 1382), one of several works in which he discusses the case of Hildegard of Bingen, Wyclif began by asserting that in the opinion of the saints, it was 'the duty of an evangelical teacher to prophesy' ['spectat ad officium doctoris evangelici prophetare'].[7] For the *doctor evangelicus*, however, evangelical teaching necessitated that an important distinction be drawn between the modes of prophecy attributed to Merlin and Hildegard – that is, the genre of enigmatic utterance, or prognostication, that did not depend for its vocabulary or rhetoric on the words of scripture – and the authoritative prophesying in which he intended to engage 'on the basis of more faithful evidence' ['fideliori evidencia']: this was denunciation, a genre that derived its authority, its vocabulary and its characteristic discursive modes from the language of the Old Testament prophets, and had its foundation in exegesis of the prophetic books.[8]

---

4 *Summa Theologiae* 2a2ae q. 174 ad 1, in *Summa Theologiae XLV: Prophecy and Other Charisms* (2a2ae 171–8), ed. R. Potter, OP (Cambridge, 2006), pp. 68–9.

5 On the different kinds of prophecy and the derived authority of the exegete, see for example D. Watt, *Secretaries of God: Women Prophets in Late Medieval and Early Modern England* (Cambridge, 1997), pp. 19–22.

6 Although the immediate concerns of this essay are temporally at some distance from those addressed in Bella Millett's writings, my reading of a reform sermon in its historical context is offered as a scholarly *hommage* to her explorations of an earlier period of Church reform, and particularly to her work on the Lambeth and Trinity homilies, during the early phase of which I was privileged to be her colleague.

7 John Wyclif, *De vaticinacione seu prophetia, in Opera Minora*, ed. J. Loserth (London, 1913), p. 165/3–4.

8 Ibid., p. 165/7.

Wyclif wastes no time in modelling the kind of prophesying in which, he believed, an evangelist not only could, but should, engage. In the treatise's opening lines, he identifies laxity on the part of the clergy as the origin of sin among the people, and stipulates that the clergy should be vigilant in watching over the church, like shepherds guarding their flock. This standard topos is buttressed with reference to Ezekiel 33.7: 'et tu fili hominis specu-latorem dedi te domui Israhel' ['So thou, O son of man, I have made thee a watchman to the house of Israel'], the first reference to scripture in Wyclif's treatise.[9] Later, Isaiah and Daniel feature as part of Wyclif's expanding reper-toire of castigation, as he develops an argument concerning reform of the church's temporalities. Thus, Wyclif saw himself as functioning within an established and authoritative castigatory tradition, and it was the distinc-tive rhetoric of this tradition that was central to his self-appointed role as the reformist scourge of his contemporaries. Wyclif's distinctions between different modes of prophecy serve as a particularly apposite introduction to the particular concerns of this essay because they show him functioning within an established ecclesiastical tradition to which many clergy of unques-tioned orthodoxy had contributed before him, and would continue to do after his time. Indeed, his approval and use of the prophecy of denunciation is a good example of the institutionally normative aspects of much of his rhetoric and thought.[10]

From the amount that has been written about the circulation and influence of prophecy on political and cultural life, in England and elsewhere, during the fourteenth and fifteenth centuries, it is clear that Wyclif's pragmatic and polemical distinction between prognostication and castigation, important as it is for our purposes here, was not sufficiently nuanced to do justice to the variety of discursive modes and genres that might be have been classified as prophetical during the late Middle Ages. In addition to the enigmatic fore-telling ascribed not only to Merlin but also to figures such as Thomas of Erceldoune and St John of Bridlington, prophecy took the millenarian forms famously associated with Joachim of Fiore, and formed part of the apocalyptic discourses on which *Piers Plowman* has been said to draw.[11] Prophecy was one

---

9   I give the Latin as it appears in the texts under discussion, with translations from the Douay-Rheims Bible.

10   For discussion of the institutionally conservative aspects of Wycliffism, see Kerby-Fulton, *Books Under Suspicion*, pp. 205–33 (a discussion that particularly focuses on attitudes to revelatory prophecy); F. Somerset, '*Eciam Mulier*: Women in Lollardy and the Problem of Sources' and K. Kerby-Fulton, '*Eciam Lollardi*: Some Further Thoughts on Fiona Somerset's "*Eciam Mulier*: Women in Lollardy and the Problem of Sources"', in *Voices in Dialogue. Reading Women in the Middle Ages*, ed. L. Olson and K. Kerby-Fulton (Notre Dame IN, 2005), pp. 245–60 and 261–78 respectively.

11   Kerby-Fulton, *Books Under Suspicion and Reformist Apocalypticism and Piers Plowman* (Cambridge, 1990); M. Reeves, *The Influence of Prophecy in the Later Middle Ages:*

way in which a woman might achieve charismatic authority, *a fortiori* because of her marginal status in relation to institutions of learning and the processes of discernment.[12] The Great Schism influenced the later prophetic interventions of Catherine of Siena and was a period during which the charisms of Bridget of Sweden gradually earned the institutional validation signified by canonization.[13] Other forms of prophecy flourished during the same period and afterwards. For example, the studies of Lesley Coote and others have shown how important prognostication remained in England during decades when politics were dominated by a number of interlocking and unresolved issues such as the legitimacy and robustness of the Lancastrian regime, relations with France, and the Wars of the Roses.[14] But the prophecy of denunciation was a more firmly embedded mode in the Church's discursive repertoire, and was institutionally privileged, denoting as it did possession of the intellectual capital acquired through the study of scripture. Neither as cryptic and useful to secular politics as the prophecies of Merlin, nor as provocatively aslant from institutional authorization as female prophecies, scriptural castigation in the idioms of Jeremiah, Ezekiel or Isaiah was less obviously *outré*, institutionally and ideologically, than other forms of prophecy, but it was distinguished by its ubiquity and longevity. And one of the most substantial pieces of evidence for the longevity of this form of prophecy in the service of a reformist *mentalité* in late medieval England is the subject of the present essay: the *Liber Veritatum* ('Book of Truths') compiled by the Oxford theologian, Thomas Gascoigne, between *c.* 1434 and his death in 1458.[15] Gascoigne's

---

A Study in Joachimism (Oxford, 1969); R. Nissé, 'Prophetic Nations' and L. Coote and T. Thornton, 'Merlin, Erceldoune, Nixon: A Tradition of Popular Political Prophecy', *New Medieval Literatures* 4 (2001), 95–115 and 117–37 respectively.

12 Kerby-Fulton, *Books Under Suspicion*, p. 204. On female prophets, see Watt, *Secretaries of God*; *Prophets Abroad: The Reception of Continental Holy Women in Late-Medieval England*, ed. R. Voaden (Cambridge, 1996); D. Elliott, *Proving Woman: Female Spirituality and Inquisitional Culture in the Later Middle Ages* (Princeton, 2004).

13 On prophecy per se during the Great Schism, see R. Blumenfeld-Kosinski, *Poets, Saints and Visionaries of the Great Schism, 1378–1417* (University Park PA, 2006), pp. 165–200. Blumenfeld-Kosinski quite justifiably classifies Bridget and Catherine as 'saints and visionaries' rather than as prophets, but, equally justifiably, such a distinction is not always made in current scholarship, and is not in the present essay.

14 L. Coote, *Prophecy and Public Affairs in Later Medieval England* (York, 2000); T. Thornton, *Prophecy, Politics and People in Early Modern England* (Woodbridge, 2006); *Prophecy: The Power of Inspired Language in History 1300–2000*, ed. B. Taithe and T. Thornton (Stroud, 1997).

15 On Gascoigne, see C. von Nolcken, 'Gascoigne, Thomas', in *ODNB*, 21: 587–9; A. B. Emden, *A Biographical Register of the University of Oxford to AD 1500* (Oxford, 1989), pp. 745–8; W. Pronger, 'Thomas Gascoigne', *English Historical Review* 53 (1938), 606–26 (I): 54 (1939), 20–37 (II). On his place in intellectual life, see R. M. Ball, *Thomas Gascoigne, Libraries and Scholarship* (Cambridge, 2006) and 'The Oppo-

Liber is an enormous work, extant in two large manuscripts (Oxford, Lincoln College, MSS Lat. 117 and 118), each of which contains over 600 folios.[16] Ostensibly a compendium of *distinctiones* for use by preachers, the *Liber* is in fact a commonplace book in which, under many headings arranged alphabetically, the Yorkist Gascoigne complains at length about what he saw as the decay of pastoral care in Lancastrian England.[17] The registers of Gascoigne's complaints shift between precise vignettes of particular churchmen whom he held responsible for the fostering of abuses (whether because they were careerists themselves, or because they had promoted them), and a more general analysis of contemporary wrongs in the idiom of lamentation.[18] In such passages, Gascoigne channels the voice of Ezekiel, imitating and duplicating the process whereby the prophet had in turn channelled the voice of God. As the book unfolds, the voice of Ezekiel alternates with those of Jeremiah, Hosea, Elijah or Job, all of whom are read through the commentaries of St Jerome, whom Gascoigne also co-opted as a prophetic prototype. Thus, scriptural and exegetical voices combine to produce a polyphonic, prophetic idiom that resonates throughout this extremely long work.

Gascoigne's reading of English affairs during the first half of the fifteenth century is particularly remarkable for its plangent intensity. Winifred Pronger, the first substantial modern commentator on Gascoigne, acknowledged that 'he is perhaps most commonly pictured as a fifteenth-century corruption of Jeremiah – an isolated student in a dingy cell, pouring out bitter lamentation over the worldly successes of others, and inveighing against the vices of his age'. However, she also asserted that, however compelling, such a persona was deceptive, because 'in reality, he was a learned scholar and practised

---

nents of Bishop Pecok', *Journal of Ecclesiastical History* 48 (1997), 230–62; J. Catto, 'Theology after Wycliffism', in *The History of the University of Oxford, II: Late Medieval Oxford*, ed. J. I. Catto and R. Evans (Oxford, 1992) pp. 263–80 (especially pp. 271–2, 274).

[16] The full manuscript remains unedited. For convenience, I have used the (very) select printed edition, *Loci e Libro Veritatum. Passages selected from Gascoigne's Theological Dictionary Illustrating the Condition of Church and State 1403–1458*, ed. J. E. Thorold Rogers (Oxford, 1881): henceforth *Loci*.

[17] On the particular compilatory tradition to which the *Liber* is a late contribution, see C. von Nolcken, 'Some Alphabetical Compendia and How Preachers Used Them in Fourteenth-Century England', *Viator* 12 (1981), 271–88. As on Nolcken's discussion of the Wycliffite *Floretum* and *Rosarium* show, this was yet another scholastic genre in which, methodologically at least, Wycliffites were part of the institutional mainstream.

[18] I discuss some of the vignettes, and Gascoigne's criticisms of the contemporary church, in 'Thomas Gascoigne's Biographies', in *Recording Lives in England in the Later Middle Ages*, ed. J. Boffey and V. Davis, Harlaxton Medieval Studies XVII (forthcoming, 2009) and 'After the Wycliffite Controversies: Religious Thought and Political Practice in Thomas Gascoigne's *Liber Veritatum*', *Cultural and Social History* 6 (forthcoming, 2009).

administrator, with lively personal prejudices and equally absorbing hobbies. He should not be accepted, neither should he be rejected, as a prophet.'[19] I disagree with this conclusion, choosing instead to endorse a more recent description of Gascoigne as the 'self-appointed prophet of doom for the Church of his day'.[20] Gascoigne was indeed a prophet in the scripturally derived mode endorsed by Wyclif; and, as had proved the case for so long with Wyclif, such a self-appointed role was not at odds, but rather at one, with that of the scholar-administrator. To depict Gascoigne as a 'prophet of doom' is not to trivialize him, but rather to recognize the usefulness of his distinctive, vigorous conception of an evangelical priesthood, since it suggests that the temper of English religious thought remained resiliently, and even characteristically, reformist in the decades following the Wycliffite controversies.

Both Gascoigne's concerns, and the prophetic discourse through which he articulated them, are clearly enunciated in one of his longest and most explicit dissertations on the subject of reform, which takes as its text the opening verse of Psalm 136, 'Super flumina Babilonis illic sedimus et flevimus dum record-aremur Syon' ['Upon the rivers of Babylon, there we sat and wept: when we remembered Sion'].[21] Examination of this lengthy dissertation shows the extent to which, in his view, a reformist mentality required modes of rhetoric and thought embedded in, or otherwise derived from, the language of the scriptural prophets. As we will see, this emphasis in turn shows how capacious a discourse orthodox reform remained in England during this period.

Thorold Rogers, Gascoigne's nineteenth-century editor, speculated that *Super flumina* may have been 'a *concio ad clerum*, a discourse addressed to the University [of Oxford]', and found it 'very instructive, not only as a specimen of an elaborate fifteenth-century sermon, but as a statement of the condition of the Church at the time in which it was composed'.[22] Whether *Super flumina* was actually preached, or whether it remained a draft or model, it is certainly structured as a 'modern' or scholastic sermon; that is, in Siegfried Wenzel's words, it is 'based on a single word, phrase, or sentence – the "theme" – out of which the preacher develops a long verbal structure by distinguishing several meanings of his verbal base and dividing and developing it according to rhetorical principles'.[23] Thus, Gascoigne established the *flumina* as a theme on which he could play his own extended variations.

---

19 Pronger, 'Thomas Gascoigne', II, 29.
20 J. Harris, 'Publicising the Crusade: English Bishops and the Jubilee Indulgence of 1455', *Journal of Ecclesiastical History* 50 (1999), 23–37 (p. 24).
21 *Loci*, pp. 53–99; henceforth *Super flumina*. In the discussion that follows, I give page numbers in the main body of the text for the reader's convenience.
22 Ibid., p. lxxxi.
23 S. Wenzel, *Preachers, Poets and the Early English Lyric* (Princeton, 1986), p. 62.

Central to the coherence of the dissertation is the plural noun *flumina* (waters), which enables him to organize the sermon as a treatment of 'seven great evils, like seven rivers' ['septem magna mala, tanquam septem flumina'], from which 'innumerable evils derive, like streams from rivers' ['sicut rivuli a fluminibus dirivantur'] (53). For Gascoigne, 'Babylon' was the equivalent of 'confusion' (55). Just as the Israelite tribes lamented their fate when they were taken from Jerusalem into Babylonian captivity, so, Gascoigne urges, should the sons of the celestial Jerusalem lament the seven well-springs of evil by which the Church is beset. In the *divisio*, or *partitio thematis*, with which the organizing principles are announced, Gascoigne briefly outlines the seven kinds of corruption: first, irregular conduct in the ordination and institution of bishops, rectors and officers; second, the absences of rectors from their parishes; third, the holding of pluralities, whether in the form of churches or offices, by individuals; fourth, the appropriation of tithes by those who are not the curates of parishes; fifth, the abuse of absolution; sixth, the abuse of indulgences; and finally, the abuse of dispensations and licences (53).

Gascoigne's fundamental concern was that the word of God was not being heard, and parish priests, who should be the chief mediators of the word, were neglecting their duties. So in his protheme, as throughout the rest of the sermon, he is concerned to delineate the character of a good pastor, and thence to explain his duties to his parish and to the rest of Christendom. The protheme contains simple dichotomies ('O quot mala destruxit bonus pastor et quot bona induxit!' ['Oh, how many evils a good priest destroys, and how many blessings he brings about!'] 54) as much as it draws on exegesis: Joseph, son of Jacob, is the first named example of a good rector, in that he did many good things in Egypt, destroyed evils and prevented others (54). But Gascoigne develops the protheme by exploring in greater depth, and with a higher degree of subtlety, the cognate affiliations between *pastor* and *pascere* (54–5): when Jesus says 'Feed my sheep' ['Pasce oves meas'], the feeding has to be understood as taking the form of preaching, prayer, and the leading of an exemplary life, central to which is the administering of the sacraments. Even the possessive adjective *meas* is vital: in nurturing, the priest should at all times carry out God's will, and not simply his own, towards the parishioners. This in turn entails nurturing others for the glory of God, and not for one's own selfish ends.

Gascoigne here broaches a theme that runs throughout the whole discourse: 'Peter nurtured as a pastor, rector, leader of the people [dux populi], when he said: "Thou, Lord, who knowest the hearts of all men, show which of these two thou hast chosen"' ['Tu, Domine, qui nosti corda omnium, ostende quem tu elegeris': Acts 1. 24] (55). His central theme is that God alone can validate the sincerity of the good priest. Correct discernment of the will of God is thus the foundation of sacerdotal duty. It follows that a state of affairs in which, as he believed, temporal affairs were constantly prevailing over spiritual ones, and in which injudicious ordinations took place through cronyism or careerism, was bound to be the fundamental cause, as well as the effect, of sin.

Priests were inevitably caught up in this chain of responsibility, and one of their gravest sins was to be the cause of sin in others through the omission of castigation, as well as the active commission of depravities. Thus Gascoigne imagines a wicked priest acknowledging on the day of his death that his soul will be punished eternally because of all the evils committed by those entrusted to his care (66). And all of these evils had to be corrected not only through reformation but through lamentation ['plangendum est et reform- andum', 55]. He even commands a priest to lament (*luge*) because he could not know for certain whether others had sinned, and had thus incurred eternal punishment, because of his own selfish incompetence ('luge pro peccato ... Luge ergo, luge coram illo Domino' ['Lament for your sin ... Lament, there- fore, lament in the presence of the Lord', 82–3]). This is a theme he would take up later when arguing that the priest's reformation of a single parish would have beneficial effects for the entire church ['Mundant ecclesiam qui reformant parochiam suam vel diocesim'] (58). This reformation also had to occur within the individual, with the repentant priest behaving as St Paul did after his conversion, throwing himself as zealously into evangelizing, teaching, and defending the faith as he had formerly dedicated himself to eradicating it (77).

Having established these fundamentals in his introduction, and reprising them elsewhere, Gascoigne devotes most of his disquisition to describing and castigating the seven 'rivers of confusion' that, in his view, afflicted the delivery of pastoral care in England. A close reading of the ensuing exeget- ical polemic shows how centrally Gascoigne positions biblical prophecy, and commentary on the prophetic books, in order to synthesize a vehemently reformist voice from their combined rhetorical resources. As might be expected, his sources range much further than simply the prophets: Acts and the Pauline Epistles are also important to his argument, as are Bede, Augus- tine and Gregory. But his principal *auctores* are the prophets Isaiah, Ezekiel and Jeremiah, together with Jerome's commentaries on these books. Together, these prophetic voices perform a variety of counter-cultural, choric functions, including the crucial one of enabling Gascoigne to re-imagine the roles of a committed priest. Thus when building his image of the properly disinter- ested rector, attentive only to God's will and not to worldly ambition, he uses the lamentations of Solomon in Ecclesiastes, God speaking to Jeremiah (57) and Pharoah's appointment of the exceptional Joseph (57).

A similar choric cluster of prophetic voices occurs in a passage towards the end of Gascoigne's explication of the first river of confusion (62). Here, like those of *pastor*, the etymology and morphological affiliations of *rector* are what concern him. For what does it mean to 'rule' (*regere*) in this context? In part, it requires being so concerned for the salvation of others that one is willing to suffer punishments in the cause of justice against tyrants: and here he adapts the words of Jeremiah 2. 34 ('in alis tuis inventus est sanguis animarum pauperum et innocentum' ['in thy skirts is found the blood of the souls of the poor and innocent']) with which the zealous priest should castigate landowners whose wealth is derived from the labour of the poor. A little further on, he recalls another prophet from III Kings 20. 39, who exhorts: 'Custodi virum ipsum, quia si lapsus fuit, erit anima tua pro anima ejus' ['Keep this man: and if he shall slip away, thy life shall be for his life'] (62): that is, if a man falls into sin because of a negligent priest, the priest's soul will also be punished. Gascoigne then resummons Ezekiel to amplify his point. Thus, no fewer than three prophets are marshalled in this passage alone to script the words and deeds of an exemplary rector, and the context in which he is to understand his vocation.

Later in the sermon, Gascoigne selects the book of Jeremiah in order to emphasize that God delivers warnings against those who take his grace for granted (76), and Ezekiel in order to urge the importance of penance (76). A little further on, Isaiah (78) is used as a warning against priests who wrongly say that sinners are just in the eyes of God, and a comparable gloss on the same situation is provided by Ezekiel, in which God curses those who give life to souls that do not live, and kill those that are not dead (78). The catena of quotations from the prophets culminates in a brief passage from the Apocalypse, and one from the prophet Malachi in which God promises to curse the blessings of misguided priests on sinners (79).

For Gascoigne, an orthodox stance is practical, but plangent rather than pragmatic. Prophets provided not only teaching and examples, but also the affective modes of imprecation and lamentation. Thus, in the face of complacency and ignorance, the Church should pray like the prophet in Psalm 24. 17: 'Deliver me from my necessities' ['De necessitatibus meis, eripe me, Domine!'] (80). Likewise, a prophetic lament is recommended as normative behaviour for the penitent (82–3) as Gascoigne too enjoins lamentation on his clerical readers, who are urged to adopt the affective postures of the child-bearing woman in Jeremiah 4. 31: (Fac ergo, poenitens! Luctum … qualem luctum facit mater pro unigenito mortuo [82]: ['Therefore, O penitent, lament as does a mother whose only son has perished']).

The fundamental work of a curate (*opus curati* [58]) was to evangelize, to provide testimony of God's judgements, and to make God's wishes manifest to his people through his words and through the example of his life. These duties in turn conferred on him the twofold role of *speculator* (that is, the vigilant watchman, well-read in the scripture and patristics, and in the book of nature, 'libro naturarum, seu in noticia rerum'), and *annunciator* (58): he should first discover God's will, and then impart it to the ignorant. And for this reason, in Acts 20. 20, St Paul describes his preaching as a form of 'annunciation' (58). Gascoigne adds the prophet Ezekiel as a model of one whom God appointed to the role of both *annunciator* of His word and *speculator*; and Jerome's commentary on this enables Gascoigne to build the argument that he who is appointed to be a *speculator* must for much of the time be quiet and grieve (*quiescere et dolere*, 58) in the face of what he sees, and have nothing on his conscience that might be a source of corruption to others. Thus, says Gascoigne (drawing on the same passage that Wyclif had employed at the beginning of *De vaticinatione*), Ezekiel sat and brooded for seven days, considering what he might say, and sorrowed over those whose sins he had to reveal and rebuke. When those seven days had come to an end, the word of God said to him: 'So thou, O son of man, I have made thee a watchman to the house of Israel: therefore thou shalt hear the word from my mouth and shalt tell it them from me' ['Fili hominis! Speculatorem dedi te domui Israel et audies de ore meo verbum, et annunciabis eis ex me': Ezek. 33. 7]. A further example for the latter-day priest is Uriah the prophet, who prophesied against Judah and was forced to flee into Egypt when King Joachim sought to put him to death. He did not escape Joachim's assassins, however, and his dead body was cast 'into the graves of the common people' (Jer. 26. 21–3). Nevertheless, Gascoigne very necessarily adds, the preacher should not worry unduly about the outcome of his words, but should follow the advice of Augustine and leave that to the judgement of God (59). The cumulative force of these examples is the construction of a clerical identity that is always potentially, and sometimes explicitly, counter-cultural; and in the conclusion to this essay I will consider the implications of such a provocative stance for our understanding of the latitudes of religious orthodoxy, at least as this was envisioned by Gascoigne. But first it is necessary to consider further how he utilizes prophetic voices in order to model the levels and kinds of insight, discernment and patience that the orthodox priest needs to have at his disposal; and this emerges with particular clarity in a discussion of sacerdotal duties in the sacrament of confession.

At the core of Gascoigne's invective against the misuse of this sacrament, here and elsewhere in the *Liber*, is a fundamental distinction between what takes place *vocaliter* and that which is true *realiter*. Whatever a priest says, it is impossible for a vocal absolution to override what God knows *realiter* about an individual's life; and alms alone cannot achieve anything without a positive turning away from one's sins (79). He must wisely interrogate and seek out, with arguments and evidence taken from scripture and the doctors, the correct way to direct a particular penitent, and the modes of behaviour that he should avoid (84). Reason, and not the will of the confessor alone, must establish whether or not absolution in particular cases is justified (84). On the same principle, indulgences should not be given unless they have been authorized by God, and once more it is the priest's hard task to discern what God's will is in individual cases (87). A prophetic voice is used to discriminate between human and divine roles here, as Gascoigne quotes Daniel, who urged Nebuchadnezzar to cancel out his sins by doing good, since it was at least possible that this would lead God to forgive his sins ['Peccata tua elemosinis redime; forte remittet tibi Deus peccata tua': Dan. 4. 24] (87). Likewise

John the Baptist (88) had eloquently warned against complacency among the Pharisees and Sadducees, lest they should feel assured of forgiveness without performing penance themselves (Matt. 3. 9).

When Gascoigne wishes to inveigh against half-hearted penitents, he ventriloquizes his warning through the words of God in the book of Jeremiah (15. 1) on the men of Jerusalem: 'If Moses and Samuel shall stand before me, my soul is not toward this people' ['Si steterunt Moyses et Samuel coram me, non est anima mea ad populum istum'] (90). And it is fitting that almost the last word in this long and passionate sermon is given to God inveighing in Isaiah 3.9 about the shameless display of sins in Jerusalem and Judah that recall those flaunted in Sodom.

As an encapsulation of Gascoigne's thought, *Super flumina* provides a fresh vantage-point from which to assess the impact of the Wycliffite controversies on intellectual life in England during the period in which he received his intellectual formation. Kantik Ghosh has argued that 'a polarization had been achieved between "Lollardy" and "orthodoxy", one which gave both sides of the confrontation a more definite identity … Lollardy … changed fundamentally the nature of [the Latinate academic-ecclesiastical establishment] and its traditional liberties.'[24] Yet the sermon that we have examined at length suggests that the picture was more complex than one of absolute, or even relative, polarization. It is certainly true that in *Super flumina*, no less than throughout the rest of the *Liber*, Gascoigne introjected and replayed anxieties that had been sustained throughout generations of English churchmen regarding the efficacy and unity of the Church both nationally and internationally. In his clerical subjectivity, long-established ecclesiastical dialectics between charisma and conformity were given full play. But the fact that they were long-established is an important one. Robert Lerner has pointed out that different forms of prophecy, which he classifies as 'the visionary, the Biblical, the astrological, and the pseudonymous', had long been part of the Church's discourse of reform.[25] 'Even in the thirteenth century', he observes, 'the need for clerical reform was emerging as an important prophetic theme. Sometimes … stress on the need for reform was barely distinguishable from outright anticlericalism.'[26] He also points out that in pre-Reformation Germany – an instructive comparator for Gascoigne's England – '[n]umerous Latin and vernacular prophecies … expressed deep dissatisfaction with the state of the Church, warnings of coming chastisement for the corrupt clergy,

---

[24] K. Ghosh, *The Wycliffite Heresy. Authority and the Interpretation of Texts* (Cambridge, 2002), pp. 212–13.

[25] R. Lerner, 'Medieval Prophecy and Religious Dissent', *Past and Present* 72 (1976), 3–24 (p. 8).

[26] Ibid., p. 15.

and hopes for religious reform in the future'.[27] Nor was such prophecy necessarily an indicator of heresy. His first example, Meister Theodorius, issued a prophecy in 1463 that 'was addressed to and read by orthodox Germans of different walks of life'.[28] It is in a similar context that we should assess the rhetorical choices made by Gascoigne, as distant from Wyclif as Theodorius was from Huss, when he was fashioning his distinctive clerical persona. It is an unsurprising fact in itself that Wyclif and Gascoigne should draw on the same *topos* from Ezekiel when assembling their arguments about clerical duties. Such an example merely shows them to be representatives, from different generations, of the same clerical culture. Nevertheless, having taken stock of the rhetoric and arguments of *Super flumina*, it is necessary that we conclude by examining more closely the implications of what I suggested briefly above, namely that, notwithstanding its grounding in scriptural exegesis, Gascoigne's conception of the clergy was that of a counter-cultural force whose charisma depended precisely on a delicate relationship with the institution it sought to serve.

Gascoigne's definition of the task of preaching fully articulated his view that the role of the priest must meld with the persona of the prophet: preaching, he stated in *Super flumina*, must take place even if others cavil and contradict, and even if they behave in a worse manner than when they first heard the word of God. The work of annunciation had to go on, he argued (buttressing his views with those of Peter Lombard and Gregory on Ezekiel) whatever the consequences, and it had to happen, in the manner of prophecy, *'oportune et importune'*, that is, to those who wished to hear it and to those who did not. It is easy to see how Gascoigne's uncompromising stance here could look like an actively dissenting position: he modulates from this manifesto into an explicit criticism of a particular piece of ecclesiastical legislation aimed at the regulation of preaching: Archbishop Thomas Arundel's *Provincial Constitutions* (1407–9) which, in his view, had been excessively driven by fear of the worst that could happen.[29] Summarizing the first of the *Constitutions*, Gascoigne correctly states that Arundel had ordained that no one should preach in the province of Canterbury without a licence (61). If only, he adds, bishops were as assiduous in cultivating skilful, knowledgeable preachers, as they were in implementing this legislation and using it as another opportunity to make money. He then gloats over what he regarded as the particularly apposite manner of Arundel's death from an obstruction in the throat. In the light of such statements, his observation that Christ had risked death rather

---

[27] Ibid., p. 20.
[28] Ibid., p. 6.
[29] For a recent appraisal of the regulation of preaching in the *Constitutions* which emphasizes their continuity with previous legislation – an aspect not considered by Gascoigne – see I. Forrest, *The Detection of Heresy in Late Medieval England* (Oxford, 2005), pp. 66–8.

than keeping silent or refraining from rebuking others (61) shows just what is at stake in the application of the term 'counter-cultural' to some of the positions he adopted.

The pose adopted by Gascoigne is that of a scourge at once embroiled within, and at some remove from, the institution that causes him such concern. He addresses the bishops of his day as if he were himself a latter-day prophet with privileged insight ('Annuncia, O episcope! ... et adducite [homines] ad Jesum, quia hoc est opus vestrae professionis' ['Announce, O bishops! ... and lead men to Jesus, for this is the task of your profession']) (61). Moreover, his contrasting model of a good bishop was divided between the image of St Paul and a bishop from a much more recent period: Robert Grosseteste 'of blessed memory' (*sanctae memoriae*, 64). Grosseteste had the singular merit of being a man about whom Gascoigne and Wyclif were in perfect accord, and this fact in turn illustrates both the synchronic and diachronic latitudes of English orthodox reform during and well beyond Wyclif's time. Although the name of Grosseteste was thus capable of uniting two very different English churchmen in the forms of Wyclif and Gascoigne, he was hardly an uncontroversial rallying figure. Rather, he was one of a group of several prominent churchmen – such as Ockham, Fitzralph and Wyclif himself – with markedly ambivalent reputations derived from their contributions to ecclesiastical controversies. For centuries after his death, Grosseteste would continue to inspire the English reforming imagination, sometimes in unexpected ways. One of his castigatory sermons (Sermon 14, *Dominus noster*) survives in a manuscript from the 1420s, compiled by John Maynsforth, who was then a Fellow of Merton College, Oxford. This manuscript (Oxford, Bodleian Library MS 52) also contains Wyclif's *Tractatus parvus de schismate*, at the end of which Wyclif's authorship is openly acknowleged, followed by the parting flourish ' ... et deo gracias' ['Thanks be to God']. In this provocative manuscript, Wyclif's reforming voice survives after the end of the Schism, and *a fortiori* after the promulgation of the *Constitutions* that had been designed not only to regulate preaching but also to restrict the dissemination of his works. For Maynsforth, an Oxford theologian from the same generation as Gascoigne, it was more important to assemble an anthology of texts that traced and emphasized the continuities in English reformist thought and polemic.[30]

As examples such as this enable us more precisely to understand the complex texture of intellectual life in England during the fifteenth century, so a figure such as Gascoigne begins to look less idiosyncratic. It is possible to claim that, rather than suffering the trauma of ideological polarization in

---

[30] Anne Hudson surveys the evidence for the continued reading of Wyclif's works in England after Arundel's *Constitutions* in 'The Survival of Wyclif's Works in England and Bohemia', item XVI in A. Hudson, *Studies in the Transmission of Wyclif's Writings* (Aldershot, 2008). I am grateful to Professor Hudson for letting me read this essay prior to publication.

the aftermath of the Wycliffite controversies, the English ecclesiastical estab-lishment during this period was one that characteristically did its thinking in a variety of reformist modes. According to this reading of the period, when we open the *Liber*, we hear a particularly trenchant voice from a thickly populated *longue durée* of reformist thought that had generated its own inner dialectics, together with its own pragmatic methods of containing them.

11

Pastoral Concerns in the Middle English Adaptation of Bonaventure's *Lignum Vitae**

Catherine Innes-Parker

The influence of St Bonaventure on the devotional climate of the thirteenth to fifteenth centuries is well known.[1] His own writings circulated widely, and the tradition of affective devotion was also developed in many texts attributed to him, such as the pseudo-Bonaventure *Meditationes Vitae Christi*. Both Bonaventure's own writings and those attributed to him were translated into numerous vernacular languages and circulated throughout Europe. One such text is Bonaventure's *Lignum Vitae*, which was translated into at least five vernacular languages, and also had a strong influence on the iconographic tradition of manuscript illumination and artistic representation throughout the late Middle Ages. Nevertheless, this text has remained neglected in its original Latin and virtually unknown in its vernacular versions.

The *Lignum Vitae* was written between 1257 and 1267, when Bonaventure was minister general of the Franciscan Order. It was intended as a spiritual exercise in meditation on the life of Christ for a sophisticated audience of Franciscan friars familiar with the biblical, patristic and devotional texts and traditions upon which it draws. Although there are numerous vernacular translations, there is only one surviving Middle English version of *Lignum Vitae*, *Þe passioun of oure lord*.[2] This version is extant in two copies, St John's College Cambridge MS G.20 and New York, Columbia University MS Plimpton 256, both mid- to late fifteenth century. It is not attributed to

* I wish to thank the Social Sciences and Humanities Research Council of Canada and the University of Prince Edward Island for the generous funding which made the research for this paper possible. I also wish to thank my research assistants Qeturah Tersteeg and Jennifer Tasker for their patient and careful work.

1 See, for example, Michael G. Sargent's extensive bibliography and detailed introduction to Love, *Mirror* (2005), especially the introduction, pp. 2–23.

2 Other than the sole Middle English version, the earliest English translation seems to be an early printed edition, found in *The Soliloquies Meditations and Prayers of St Bonaventure*, printed in London, 1655 (BL 4404.aa.27).

Bonaventure, and has not generally been recognized as a version of *Lignum Vitae*.[3] In part, this is because *Þe passioun of oure lord* is more than simply a translation; much of the Latin text is expanded and its central metaphor is adapted in such a way as to radically alter its application expressly for a lay audience. Indeed, the alterations are extensive enough that one must describe the translator as the Middle English author, rather than simply an adaptor.[4] The identity of the Middle English author is unknown, although he seems to have been a member of an order which included pastoral duties to lay people in its mandate; the only clue to his identity comes in the opening words of the final prayer, where he seeks Christ's advocacy to the Father, to give the seven gifts of the Holy Ghost 'to me and to alle my freendis þat y am bounde to preie fore' (fol. 111v).[5] Nevertheless, it is clear throughout the text that his

---

3   Marie du Bel Amour Hamelin identified it as a version of *Lignum Vitae* in her dissertation, 'The Middle English Devotional Pieces: "The Passioun of Oure Lord" and "The Tretijs of Loue": Edition and Commentary' (unpublished PhD dissertation, Fordham University, 1962). However, her identification remained unnoticed, although the online catalogue description of Plimpton 256 has included it, and a notice of the dissertation is included in the file on Plimpton 256 at Columbia University. My thanks to Consuela Deutschke, Manuscript Curator, Columbia University, for drawing this and other articles about this manuscript, to my attention.

4   See my article, '*Þe passioun of our lord*: A Middle English Adaptation of Bonaventure's *Lignum Vitae* in St John's College, Cambridge, MS G.20', *FMLS* 47:3 (2007), 199–206. This article forms an introduction to my transcription of the text from St John's MS G.20, in three sections: '*Þe passioun of our lord*, edited from St John's College, Cambridge MS G.20', *FMLS* 47:3 (2007), 207–22; '*Þe passioun of our lord*, Branches IX–XII, Sections 33–48: Edited from St John's College, Cambridge MS G.20', *FMLS* 44:1 (2008), 1–11; '*Þe passioun of our lord*, Prologue and Branches I–IV, Sections 1–16: Edited from St John's College, Cambridge MS G.20', *FMLS* 44:2 (2008), 276–94. I wish to thank the Masters and Fellows of St John's College, Cambridge, for permission to publish these transcriptions, and Dr. Jonathan Harrison, Collections Manager, St John's College Library, for his cheerful assistance throughout the years of my research there. All references to *Þe passioun of our lord* will be from MS G.20, cited by folio number. I have used St John's MS G.20 as the base for my study of the text because its dialect, spelling and punctuation appear to be closest to the original. In particular, the punctuation of St John's G.20 is used to guide the reader through various points of meditation, to indicate where one should pause and reflect upon particular details. Plimpton 256 is incomplete, lacking the first folio of the text.

5   The manuscripts are little help. Nothing is known about the provenance of St John's MS G.20, but Plimpton 256 was copied by a London scribe writing in the third quarter of the fifteenth century, during the reign of Edward IV, see Linda Ehrsam Voigts, 'A Doctor and His Books: The Manuscripts of Rober Marchall (d.1477)', in *New Science Out of Old Books: Studies in Manuscripts and Early Printed Books in Honour of A. I. Doyle*, ed. Richard Beadle and A. J. Piper (Aldershot, 1995), pp. 249–323 (p. 262 and n. 67). Hamelin identifies the language of the text as 'essentially that of the Midland standard literary English of the late fourteenth century', but states that specific linguistic features are characteristic of the Oxford district. The cumulative effect of both linguistic and rhetorical style, she argues, indicate

reworking of Bonaventure's original is rooted in his pastoral concerns for his readers.

The controlling metaphor of the text is the Tree of Life, based on Apocalypse 22. Bonaventure uses the tree as both a structural and mnemonic device. In the prologue, he urges his readers to carry the cross of Christ in both body and soul, until he can say with Paul, 'with Christ I am nailed to the cross' ['Christio confixus sum cruci'] (Gal. 2. 20). Such an identification with Christ crucified is achieved by one who contemplates Christ's life and works

> with such vividness of memory, such sharpness of intellect and such charity of will that he can truly say with the bride: A bundle of myrrh is my beloved to me; he will linger between my breasts.[6]
>
> [tanta *memoriae* vivicitate, tanto *intellectus* acumine, tanta *voluntatis* caritate … quod veraciter illud sponsae proferre potest eloquium: *Fasciculus myrrhae dilectus meus mihi, inter ubera mea commortabitur.*][7]

To cultivate such contemplation, Bonaventure has gathered this bundle of myrrh from the forest of the gospel and bound it together with 'simple, familiar and unsophisticated terms' (p. 120) ['verbis … simplicibus, consuetis et rudibus' (p. 67)], not because his audience is unfamiliar with the gospel stories, but to focus their attention on the relevant details (to which he refers very briefly in each chapter before moving straight to the meaning which he wishes his readers to draw from them). Having arranged his bundle of myrrh into an imaginary tree, he instructs his readers to picture the tree in their minds, describing its twelve branches, arranged into three groups of four, focusing respectively on Christ's nativity and life; Christ's passion; and Christ's eternal reign. Each branch has four sections (or chapters) directing the reader to contemplate a particular event from the gospels, for a total of forty-eight chapters. Bonaventure describes the tree, with its fruit, leaves and flowers, in some detail.

The Middle English author retains the structural metaphor of the tree, but changes the tree from a mnemonic device to a metaphor that defines not only

---

that the text originated in a 'learned center', supporting 'the conjectural ascription of the text to Oxford' ('Middle English Devotional Pieces', pp. xxxii–xxxiv). As to the identity of the author, she suggests that he is 'certainly a cleric, orthodox and zealous' writing in 'the tradition of the preaching friar' with a special interest in Franciscan devotion. She admits that, although suggestive, these indications are not conclusive, and speculates that the author might, perhaps, have been 'a friar chaplain attached to a noble family' (ibid., p. lvii, n. 36).

6 Bonaventure, *The Soul's Journey into God; The Tree of Life; The Life of St Francis*, tr. Ewert Cousins, Classics of Western Spirituality (Mahwah NJ, 1978), p. 119. All translations of the *Lignum Vitae* are from this edition, cited by page number within the body of the chapter.

7 *Doctoris Seraphici S. Bonaventurae Opera Omnia* (Quarracchi; 1882–1902), VIII, 67. All future references will be by page number, in the body of the chapter.

the text, but the process of writing and reading it. Furthermore, it focuses on Christ's passion as the central part of the text. The Middle English author drops the references to the bundle of myrrh from the Song of Songs and to the tree of life from Apocalypse 22, introducing instead the metaphor of two faggots of wood in an extended treatment of Paul's words; 'I am crucified in þe cros, wiþ oure lord ihesu crist' (fol. 67v).[8] The true disciple who would conform to Christ's crucifixion

> schulde alwey bere in his mynde þe werkis of ihesu crist. And he schulde in his bodi bere contynuel penaunce .... For it bihoueþ þat he schulde bere in his herte a vagat of þe werkis of ihesu crist bi ofte remembraunce of him; and in his fleisch anoþir fagat of a cros of mortificacioun of his fleische, aftir the ensaumple of ihesu crist þat mortifiede his fleish in þe cros, and þanne may he seie y am crucified wiþ ihesu crist. (fol. 67v)

As Bonaventure has gathered the bundle of myrrh for his readers to trigger their meditation, the Middle English author explains that

> For to asemble and gadere to gideris þese fagatis, þe werkis of þe passioun þat ihesus crist suffride in þe cros; y haue entrid in to forest of þe holi gospels, and so ferforþli [thoroughly] y haue souȝt and cerchid [searched] þis forest; þat y haue asemblid þese fagatis, and maad of hem a tre of xij braunchis. (fol. 67v)[9]

---

8 The metaphor of the cross as two pieces of wood that must be kindled into devotion through penance and meditation on the passion is found in *Ancrene Wisse* Part 7: 'Forte ontended ow wel, gederið wude þerto wið þe poure wummon of Sarepte, þe burh þe spealeð "ontendunge". ... "Lauerd," quoð ha to Helye, þe hali prophete, "lo Ich gederi twa treon." Þeos two treon bitacnið þet a treo þet stod upriht, ant þet oþer þe eode þwertouer, o þe deore rode. Of þeos twa treon ȝe schulen ontende fur of luue inwið ower heorte. Biseoð ofte towart hem; þencheð ȝef ȝe ne ahen eaðe to luuien þe king of blisse, þe tospreat swa his earmes toward ow, ant buheð as to beoden cos duneward his heaued. ... ȝef þe soðe Helye, þet is, Godd almihti, infint ow þeose twa treon bisiliche gederine, he wule gestnin wið ow, ant nomifalden in ow his deorewurðe grace' ['And so as to kindle yourselves well, gather wood for it with the poor woman of Sarepta, the city which means "kindling." ... "Lord," she said to Elijah, the holy prophet, "See, I gather two pieces of wood." These two pieces of wood signify the one upright piece of wood, and the other that went across it on the dear cross. With these two pieces of wood you will kindle the fire of love in your heart. Look often toward them. Consider if you ought not to love the King of joy easily, who so spreads wide his arms toward you and bows down his head as if to be kissed. ... if the true Elijah, that is God almighty, finds you busily gathering these two pieces of wood, he will lodge with you, and multiply in you his precious grace'] (*Ancrene* Wisse, ed. Millett, I 7.244–55, p. 151; Savage and Watson, *Anchoritic Spirituality*, p. 195).

9 Compare the original: 'To enkindle in us this affection, to shape this understanding and to imprint this memory, I have endeavored to gather this bundle of myrrh from the forest of the holy Gospel, which treats at length the life, passion and glorification of Jesus Christ' (pp. 119–20) ['Ut igitur praefatus in nobis accendatur,

After describing the tree, its branches, leaves, flowers and fruit in terms similar to the Latin, he concludes:

> So þat þou schalt fynde riȝt delitable sauour, and þou schalt fynde it upon euerych of þese braunchis, whann y hadde founde þis tree in þe forseid forest, y bare it out of þe forest and took it to þe lay peple þat ben of rude vndirstonding for to ȝeue hem foorme to lyue aftir þe foorme of þe werkis of ihesu crist, and for to teche hem þe foorme of þer feiþ and of her bileeue, and for to norische hem in deuocion. (fol. 70r–70v)

Here, the Middle English author explicitly reveals the pastoral nature of his enterprise: he writes for lay people of simple understanding in order to 'teach them the form of their faith' and 'nourish them in devotion', through reading or hearing the text.

The relationship between the Middle English author and his readers is thus quite different from that between Bonaventure and his audience of Franciscan friars. Bonaventure presents himself as a guide, but one who has simply selected and ordered what his audience already knows in order to focus their contemplation, providing examples of contemplative prayer which encourage his readers to move beyond the text to more complex meditation. He takes for granted that his audience is familiar with the gospels and themes such as the concept of *imitatio Christi*, the soul's marriage to Christ, the imagery of the Song of Songs and the apocalyptic imagery of the Book of Revelation. He also expects them to identify and understand theological concepts such as the relationship between intellect, memory and will, and the function of the imagination in contemplation. In sum, Bonaventure expects his audience to be familiar with contemplative theory and practice, able to use and understand his text on a sophisticated level.

The Middle English author makes no such assumptions. He omits all material relating to the Apocalypse and the Song of Songs and adds long passages expanding upon the gospel stories for those who are not familiar with them; he also omits specifically theological terminology, while adding explanations of certain concepts that are important for his readers to understand, tying them to familiar liturgy and sacraments. He modifies his role as author, although he retains Bonaventure's pastoral focus. But he is not merely a guide: he is the teacher/author and his readers are those of 'rude understanding' who require him to mediate between the gospel and themselves. He creates a close metaphorical tie between himself, the book, and the reader through the image of the cross, which he bears by composing the book, and they bear by reading the book which is, itself, the tree of the

affectus, formetur cogitatus imprimatur memoria, ex sacri Evangelii silva, in qua de vita, passione et glorificatione Iesu Christi diffuse tractatur, colligere studui hunc myrrhe fasciculum' (p. 67)].

cross.[10] The composition of the text is as much a part of his pastoral duties as the prayers that he is bound to pray for his charges.

Indeed, the Middle English author sees his work more as a work of instructional meditation than a contemplative text. This is very clear from his alteration of the concluding paragraph of the prologue in a passage which immediately precedes that quoted above. Bonaventure concludes simply:

> Arise, then, O soul devoted to Christ, and examine diligently, consider attentively and mull over carefully each of the things that are said about Jesus. (p. 125)

> [Expergiscere proinde, anima Christo devota et singula, quae de Iesu dicuntur, diligentius discute, attente considera et morose pertracta. (p. 70)]

Bonaventure assumes the reader's ability to examine and contemplate the material that the text presents.

The Middle English author, however, assumes that his reader will need guidance to fully contemplate the material in his text, and while the reader may at times be able to feel devotional 'savour' without it, he assumes that the reader will be reliant upon the text for his or her devotional practice:

> O þou deuout soule, if þou fynde not sauour in þis sweet fruy3t ihesu crist such as y haue seid to þee, haue recourse to þat book þat schal schewe to þee þis fruy3t. (fol. 60r)

Unlike the readers of Bonaventure's Lignum Vitae, the readers of *Þe passioun of oure lord* are beginners.

Consistent with the rudimentary needs of his readers, many of the changes that the Middle English author makes to the text are intended to clarify the biblical text upon which the meditations are based. Sometimes, these expansions seem to be intended simply to provide details with which the readers might not be familiar. Most of the time, however, the Middle English author uses the specific points that he adds to the text to instruct and encourage his readers in their devotion.

There are three kinds of alterations made by the Middle English author that are significant in preparing his audience for the central purpose of meditation upon Christ's passion. While the kinds of changes discussed here continue throughout the text, for the sake of focus, I have concentrated on the first four branches, dealing with Christ's nativity and life. In these preparatory chapters, the Middle English author's pastoral concerns are particularly clear.

First, he adds references to the liturgy and the liturgical calendar. Second, he expands Bonaventure's treatment of the sacraments. Third, he alters

---

10 See Innes-Parker, 'A Middle English Adaptation', pp. 203–4.

Bonaventure's theological discourse. Together, the effect of these alterations is to provide a link between private devotion and public worship, between the sacraments of the church and private meditation. They also focus the attention of the reader on the humanity of Christ and his place in the Trinity. Finally, they provide models for the reader's meditation and response to Christ's love, particularly as that love is displayed in the passion.

The Middle English author often links the details of the gospel stories to specific portions of the liturgy, creating a link between private and public devotion. For example, he expands upon Bonaventure's treatment of the Visitation, adding the detail that it was the Virgin who composed the Magnificat and expressly locating it in the context of the liturgy: 'þe sweet song þat holi chirche vsiþ to singe at euensong' (fol. 73r). He also includes Elizabeth's song, 'þou art blessid aboue alle wommen and þe fruyȝt of þi wombe moost blessid' (fol. 73v), which Bonaventure omits, implicitly connecting the passage to the familiar recitation of the *Ave Maria*.[11] Similarly, the Middle English author explicitly reminds the reader that the song which the angels sang at Christ's birth is 'þe song þat þe preest in þe bigynnng of þe masse seiþ in þis wise; *gloria in excelsis deo, and in terra pax hominibus bone voluntatis*' (fol. 75r). The reader is also reminded that Christ was offered at the temple on what we now call 'candilmasse day,' which is so called 'for in þat day was offrid þat blessd lord þat came doun from heuene to liȝtne al þe world' (fol. 78r), and that Simeon's song is 'þat blessid song þat þe chirche vsith to singe. *Nunc dimittis seruum tuum domine secundum verbum tuum in pace*' (fol. 78r).

By specifically linking the text to the reader's experience of the liturgy, the Middle English author begins to bridge the gap between public and private devotion. A second, and more important, bridge is found in the Middle English author's concern that his readers have an appropriate understanding of the sacraments, particularly baptism and the Eucharist. For example, he adjusts the focus of the story of Christ's baptism while retaining the essential outline of the chapter. Christ's example is not to 'practice what he preached,' as in Bonaventure, but to give example of the things which we must do to save our soul, but which he had no need of.[12] And, although he himself had

---

[11] See Gunn, *AW From Pastoral Literature.* pp. 67–8 on the use of the *Ave Maria* by the laity.

[12] Similarly, in Chapter Five, on the circumcision, Bonaventure states that the circumcision was the first example of Christ's pouring out his blood for sinners. The circumcision is also a model of humility; Bonaventure explains that, in his humility, Christ wished to conform to his forefathers in every way, even to the extent of being circumcised. The Middle English author expands only slightly, but in so doing he changes the focus. Christ, he explains, had no original sin. However, he wished to take on the likeness of a sinful man, and so he was circumcised to show his likeness to us in his humanity. Therefore, he concludes, the devout reader should not try to take on the outward appearance of good and holy men through pride or hypocrisy.

no need of baptism, Christ's pure flesh having been baptized in water gives the water the power to cleanse the soul from original sin. Having grounded the efficacy of baptism in Christ's own actions (as he later will with the Eucharist), the author moves to three benefits of baptism and meditation upon it. First, the baptized soul receives the Holy Ghost by grace, as the Holy Ghost descended upon Christ in the form of a dove. Second, baptism leaves an imprint upon the soul so that God knows the soul as his daughter in whom he is well pleased, as the voice of the Father approved his beloved son, in whom he is well pleased. Third, baptism opens the gates of heaven to the soul, as the heavens opened after Christ's baptism.

The Middle English author here retains Bonaventure's trinitarian language but shifts the emphasis to the presence of the Trinity in the soul. His concern that his readers have an appropriate understanding of the Trinity is also evident in the story of the Transfiguration. Typically, the Middle English author both simplifies and explains the events on the mountain, expanding the story slightly, but omitting the presence of Moses and Elijah and focusing on Christ's transfigured body, which prefigures his glorious body in paradise. He explains that the apostles were given 'certein knouleche' of the persons of Father, Son and Holy Ghost: the bright cloud revealed the Holy Ghost, and the voice from heaven revealed the Father, and his approval of his transfigured son. In response, rather than contemplating the secrets of God through strength and virtue, as Bonaventure counsels his readers, the devout soul is to behold God's great courtesy in showing so clearly that the three persons of the Trinity are one perfect God.

The Middle English author is also concerned that his audience grasps the exact relationship between Christ's humanity and his divinity, and the place of the incarnate Christ in the Trinity. One important issue is the relationship implied by the terminology of God engendering the Son. This issue is tackled in Chapter One, 'Jesus begotten of God'. The Latin text begins this chapter simply: 'When you hear that Jesus is begotten of God, beware lest some inadequate thought of the flesh appear before your mind's eye' (p. 126) ['Cum Iesum audis ex Deo genitum, cave, ne mentis tuae oculis infirmum aliquid carnalis cogitationis occurat' (p. 71)]. Bonaventure then goes on to summarize the 'coeternal, coequal, and cosubstantial splendour' ['coaeternus, coaequalis et consubstantialis splendor'] which emerges 'from the Eternal Light'

Again, in Chapter Seven, on Christ's submission to the law, he expands Bonaventure's statement that the Virgin Mary observed the law of purification, although she was herself entirely pure. The Middle English author first explains the law of purification, 'þat comaundiþ alle wommen on child bed of a sone; þat þei schuld dispende þat tyme [forty days] for to rest hem and purifie hem'. He then affirms that the virgin had no need for purification, since she had conceived without the knowledge of man, nor of rest, since she bore her child without any pain, sorrow or labour.

['aeterna luce'] and through which the Father created and governs the world. Once again, he assumes his readers' familiarity with the terminology and concepts he presents. The Middle English author does not. He is particularly concerned that his readers not misunderstand the concept of engendering, telling them to beware of having 'so symple and lewde vndirstonding, þat þe fadir engendride þe son bi fleischly engendring' (fol. 70v), because anyone who has that 'fantasy' has neither clean nor pure heart and does no reverence or worship to God. He is also concerned that his readers understand that Christ's engendering does not imply a temporal distinction between Father and Son, explaining at length that the Father and the Son are two people but only one substance, and only one God. He alters Bonaventure's metaphor of light, explaining instead that although we see the sun in the heavens and feel its light and heat on earth, we do not imagine that there are two suns; further, we know that when the sun was created, its clearness (or light) was engendered. In the same way, he concludes, there is only one God, who appears in two persons.[13]

Similarly, the Middle English author radically simplifies Bonaventure's description of the Incarnation in Chapter Three. The Latin explains that in the instant that Mary gave her consent, the power of God overshadowed her, Christ's body was formed, his soul created, and both were joined to the divinity in the person of the Son, making the Son both God and man, maintaining the qualities of each. In the Middle English, however, while Mary is still 'brennyngli embracid' by the Holy Spirit, it is the Son of God (not the power of God) who 'in þe same tyme discendid and schadewid him in hir.' The theological explanation of how the power of God became simultaneously God and man in the creation of the body and soul of Christ becomes simply 'and [he] took mankinde in þe foorme of man' (fol. 72v).

The Middle English author's concern with his readers' understanding of the Incarnate Christ and the complexity of Christ's simultaneous humanity and divinity is one with his focus on the passion. Nowhere, perhaps, is this clearer than in his treatment of the Last Supper and the Eucharist which it symbolizes and establishes. The Middle English follows the original fairly closely in its comparison of the lamb upon which the disciples dined to the 'sweete lombe ihesu crist' (fol. 85v), and in Christ's example of humility, love and compassion in eating with his disciples and washing their feet. However, he expands upon Christ's generosity in offering his body and blood, connecting it specifically to the passion, which will be described in

---

13 Although the Middle English author simplifies both the discussion and the metaphors here and elsewhere, these are, nevertheless, quite complex and sophisticated theological concepts which he is trying to convey to his readers. It is possible that some of his alterations may have to do with concerns about heresy – if so, further research may be helpful in recovering some of the context in which the text was written.

the next section of the text, beginning with Chapter Seventeen, the Betrayal. Bonaventure employs the language of sacrifice and sacrament, referring to Christ's body as our 'viaticum and sustenance'. The Middle English author, on the other hand, explains that just as one gives a gift to friends as a remembrance when one leaves them, so Christ gave us not gold or silver or any earthly gift, as worldly friends do, but the most precious gift of his body.

At this point the Middle English author departs radically from the original, explaining in detail how we have Christ's remembrance before us at the mass in the likeness of bread in the priest's hands. He asserts that the soul should have 'certein bileeue þat it is his verri bodi þat same þat was born of þe virgine marie, and þat for oure loue hangid on þe cros, and such as he is now in þe glorious blis of heuene' (fol. 86v). In order to have this faith, he explains, one must not believe any of one's wits, for all the wits are deceived: sight is deceived, for it seems to see bread but truly sees the body of Christ; taste is deceived because it seems to eat bread, but truly eats the body of Christ; touch is deceived, for it seems that one holds bread, and yet one holds in one's hands the body of Christ.

The Middle English author moves on to the difficult problem which he has posed for his readers: how can it be that the bread held in the priest's hands is the true body of Christ? Here we see most clearly his concern for his audience, simple lay folk of rude understanding, who need to understand such a mystery, but cannot comprehend the complex theology of the doctrine of transubstantiation.[14] He explains to his readers that God has given such virtue to the words that the priest says over the bread that 'þe virtu of þo wordis chaungiþ and translatiþ þe substaunce of breed in to þe substaunce of þe blessid bodi of ihesu crist' (fol. 86v). He continues:

> And þis is a vertu aboue alle oþire vertuis, þat god haþ ȝeuen to þese v wordis; *hoc est enim corpus meum*. And whanne þe preest haþ seid þese wordis ouir þe breed; þe substaunce of þe breed is turned in to þe verri substaunce of þe verri bodi of ihesu crist. (fols. 86v–87r)

He concludes by reminding his readers that this gift was given so that we should always have Christ present with us.

The Middle English author also radically alters Bonaventure's concluding address to the devout soul. Bonaventure urges the soul who is invited to such a banquet to run with all his desire, crying out with the prophet David, 'As the stag longs for springs of water, so my soul longs for you, O God!' (p. 139) ['Quemadmodum desiderat cervus ad fontes aquarum, ita desiderat anima

---

14 Again, it is not clear how much of this has to do with combating heresy, rather than simply explaining theological doctrine to lay people. In either case, however, the author's concern that his readers understand the doctrine of transubstantiation is sincere.

mea ad te, Deus' (p. 75)].[15] The Middle English author, however, exhorts his readers:

> O þou deuout soule þat wolt neiȝe [draw near] to þe table of ihesu crist, and wilt receyue and herborewe [shelter] þe precious bodi of ihesu crist in to þi bodi; first biholde and serche þou well þi conscience if þer be eny filþe or synne þer ynne. For if sche be founde foul wiþ deedli synne; þou receyuest him to þi iugement and dampnacion. (fol. 87r)

Once again, the Middle English author refers his readers to the practical application of the text to the salvation of the soul, rooting it firmly in the liturgy of the mass and its spiritual implications. And, by removing the reference to the soul who longs for God, the Middle English author reduces the ecstatic, mystical tone of the original. Yet he does not exclude the intimacy of the soul with God; rather than thirsting for God, the devout reader receives and harbours the body of Christ in the unity created by physically absorbing Christ's body in the form of the eucharistic bread into his or her own body.[16]

Through references to the liturgy, the sacraments and important theological motifs such as the Trinity and Christ's place in it, the Middle English author bridges the gap between public and private devotion; between ecclesiastical instruction and personal belief; between participation in the Church, and participation in Christ. But simple understanding is not the point. Understanding must lead to devotion, and in order to exemplify this, the Middle English author presents his readers with role models and allegorizes details of the gospel stories as metaphors for the soul's devotion to Christ. For example, understanding Christ's simultaneous divinity and humanity leads the soul to worship Christ as both God and man. Such worship is exemplified by the gifts of the Magi. Where Bonaventure simply urges his readers to emulate the three kings through worshipping Christ as both God and man with gold, frankincense and myrrh, the Middle English author speaks specifically and at length of what these three gifts symbolize. First, he describes the gifts of the kings and their significance:

> Aftir þat þei presentiden him wiþ ȝiftis eueriche bi himself [each one presented him with gifts]; bi whiche ȝiftis þei schewiden þat he was verry god and verri man, and verri king of heuene and erþe. For eche of hem presentid to him wiþ encence [incense], in signifiynge þat he was god; for to god oonli, longiþ þe present of encens.

---

15 Psalm 41. 2.

16 This is an example of another characteristic of the Middle English author. While he retains the affective element of the text, the Middle English author never uses affective language for its own sake; rather than evoking a heightened affective response, he is concerned with instructing his reader how to use the affective response for the benefit of the soul.

Aftir eche of hem made him a ʒift, and a present of mirre; in signifiyng, þat þei knoulechiden [made known, or acknowledged] him a deedli man, for mirre kepeþ þe deed bodi þat it schal not rote [rot.]

Aftir þat, eche of hem maden him an offringe of gold, in signifiyng; þat þei knoulechiden him verri king of heuenee and of erþe. For to a king men ʒeuen preciose ʒiftis as golde; þat is þe moost preciose metal þat is.

(fol. 76v–77r)

Then he urges the reader to give these same gifts to acknowledge Christ as true God and true man, king of heaven and earth, offering up his or her heart as incense, for as incense rises to heaven, so too the devout thoughts of the heart rise up to God. The gift of the reader's body is like myrrh, for as myrrh is bitter, so too is bodily penance, which God makes sweet through grace.[17] Finally, the reader is to present all his or her most precious temporal goods to God, like the gold which the kings gave to Christ, and so acknowledge him as king of heaven and earth, worshipped above all things.

The gift of myrrh reminds us of the first faggot of wood in the prologue, the penance of the body. Penance is also the focus of the particularly fine chapter on the temptation in the wilderness. The Middle English author, typically, takes a practical approach to the gospel story. After reminding the reader that the devil came to tempt Christ after forty days of fasting in the desert, when he was weakened by hunger, the Middle English author outlines the three temptations, not by retelling the story, but by referring to the particular sins with which the devil attempted to deceive Christ: gluttony (representing temptations of the flesh), pride, and covetousness. He also changes the language describing Christ's response: unlike Bonaventure, the Middle English author does not describe Christ as victorious over the devil. Rather, Christ does not consent to the temptation – an important distinction for the lay reader, who is counselled to be 'miʒti and vertuouse' against the temptations of the fiend, 'and in no wise consente to him'.[18] The Middle English author acknowledges that the soul will often feel in peril of being overcome by weakness; then he or she must run to Christ and seek his help through prayer, 'for if þou calle him deuoutli, he wole not suffre þee to perische' (fol. 81v).

---

17 The metaphorical connection between myrrh, penance, and bitterness made sweet is developed more fully in *Ancrene Wisse*, ed. Millett, I 6.335–431, pp. 140–2 (Savage and Watson, *Anchoritic Spirituality*, pp. 184–7).

18 A similar change is found in the prologue, where, in the description of the eighth branch, Bonaventure refers to Christ's victory in the cross. The Middle English author expands, explaining that Christ's victory is not only over *the* enemy, but over *all his enemies* (fol. 70r) – including, as the rest of the text will show, the enemies/temptations that the devout soul is likely to encounter.

Indeed, it is in the direct address to the reader that the Middle English author departs most significantly from the original text. Here he presents Christ not as an example of resisting temptation, but of penance. Christ washed himself by baptism before his fast; so too the devout soul should be washed with the water of contrition and confession before fasting or doing any other penance, in order to be clean before God. As Christ fasted in the wilderness, the reader should fast far from the abundance of delicate food. Finally, the devout soul should fast or do penance, 'in þe most secreet wise þat þou miȝtist' where Christ alone will see. 'For if þou faste or do penaunce for to be seen of þe world; þou shalt neuere haue oþire mede [reward]' (fol. 81v). This is a distinct contrast to Bonaventure's advice to share in Christ's silence, prayer and fasting in order to search into the secrets of solitude with Him.

Here, again, the Middle English author has followed his pattern of expanding the biblical story. The response of the soul is also shifted: Bonaventure's meditative silence, prayer and fasting are replaced by the practical application of contrition, confession and penance; and Bonaventure's contemplative searching of the secrets of solitude becomes the solitary enactment of penance, for the eyes of Christ alone. Returning to the gist of the original at the end, the Middle English author retains the soul's recourse to the one who has compassion on our weakness, but focuses not on Christ's victory but on the devout prayer of the soul, confident that his saviour will not allow him to perish.

Christ's modelling of the virtues of the soul is, of course, found throughout the text. In the chapter on the flight into Egypt and Jesus's teaching in the temple at the age of twelve, the Middle English author expands Bonaventure's treatment of the three virtues of poverty, patience and obedience which Christ showed in his flight to Egypt, taking what is, in the original, a simple list and allotting a full paragraph to each virtue. Then, instead of counselling the reader to follow Jesus and Mary into Egypt in contemplation, he advises that the soul should be followed by the three virtues which Christ has displayed, focusing on the benefits to the soul of emulating the virtues that Christ has modelled.

But Christ is not the only model for the soul. In the same chapter, Mary is a model for the reader's sorrow as she grieves at the loss of her son in Jerusalem, and for joy as she finds him again, but although Bonaventure assumes that the reader's meditation will merge into tears of devotion, he gives few details. The Middle English author's treatment of the meditative section of this chapter, however, is so altered as to be nearly unrecognizable. He expands upon the reader's following of Mary in Jerusalem as she seeks her son, not in order to elicit an emotional response, but as a model for the soul who seeks Christ in his or her heart:

And also y counceile þee þat þou ceesse not to seke ihesu crist til þou fynde him in þin herte bi contemplacioun eiþer bi grace; lijk as his modir souȝt him bodili in ierusalem. For þou schalt euere be in sorewe til þou fynde him in þin herte; riʒt as his blessid modir þat myʒt no counfort neiþer ioie [joy] haue til sche hadde founde him. And of þat be þou sure, þat aftir þat þou hast founde him; greet ioie and counfort schal be in þin herte.

(fol. 79v–80r)

Here, the soul seeks to heal sorrow, not to feel it more intensely, and sorrow is healed by finding Christ in the heart. Once again, the author focuses on the specific benefits to the soul of contemplating the events of Christ's life: Mary's seeking Christ in Jerusalem exemplifies the soul's seeking Christ in the heart, and her finding Christ in the temple models the joy and comfort that the soul will feel when Christ descends into the temple of the heart. Significantly, although the author counsels and provides models for meditation throughout the text, he emphasizes here that Christ can be found in the heart either by contemplation or by grace, a theme that is developed throughout the text as meditation is accompanied by prayer.

Even this brief comparison of the opening chapters of the Middle English *Þe passioun of oure lord* with the original *Lignum Vitae* shows that the Middle English author is not merely clarifying and adapting the text for a lay audience of 'simple' understanding. Rather, the Middle English author makes significant changes to the text based on his perception of his audience's devotional needs and the kind of meditation that he wishes to inspire in his readers. First, he uses his expanded gospel stories to link the private devotion provided by his book to the familiar public devotion of the liturgy and the liturgical year. In so doing, he provides a bridge between the familiar and the new, as well as between public and private.

This connection between public and private then extends into the treatment of theological motifs. While the Middle English author is not concerned with scholarly and arcane theological language or theory, he is very concerned that his audience understand the broader theological issues that tie private devotion to the teachings of the church, particularly in the context of the sacraments. He is especially concerned that his audience understand the manifestation of Christ's humanity both in his life and in the larger picture of his relationship to the Father and his place in the Trinity. Finally, he prepares his readers for the central section on the passion with a careful explanation of how the body of Christ, given at the Last Supper and offered up on the cross, is not merely represented, but actually present in the eucharistic elements of bread and wine.

Nevertheless, with all its attention to bridging the space between public and private devotion, this text is meant to instruct the reader in private prayer and meditation. The careful instruction of the soul enables the reader to experience the sweetness of Christ through the reading of the book which reveals to them the tree of life which bears Christ as its fruit. In other words, the book itself will enable its readers to bear the two faggots of wood that will conform them to Christ's crucifixion as it guides the reader through meditation on Christ's life, passion and eternal reign, fostering the love of Christ in the heart. This is truly a book to which the reader can return again and again, to find savour in the sweet fruit of the tree of life, Jesus Christ.

12

Prayer, Meditation and Women Readers in Late Medieval England: Teaching and Sharing Through Books

C. Annette Grisé

The connections made in Bella Millett's important article '*Ancrene Wisse* and the Book of Hours' between pastoral instruction for anchoresses and the development of extra-liturgical devotional manuscripts for those who held an 'intermediate position between *literati* and the illiterate'[1] illustrate the ways in which many readers benefited from vernacular devotional texts originally written for pious women. Starting from *Ancrene Wisse* through to the end of the Middle Ages there developed a large programme of pastoral instruction through vernacular devotional texts aimed at semi-religious and religious women, attested to even by the manuscript history of thirteenth-century instruction for anchoresses. Through its elucidation of the distinctions between the inner and outer rule *Ancrene Wisse* also establishes two interconnected pastoral functions of Middle English devotional texts: to regulate external behaviour and to reform interior cognitive processes. Three key genres of devotional texts for female religious provided pastoral care for their readers: guides for religious living, treatises on spiritual topics and devotional exercises such as passion meditations. I will argue that as a supplement to interpersonal and community pastoral care led by male religious, pious women participated in an intermediate system of peer-to-peer care, sharing and teaching (in contrast to the caring and preaching performed by monks and priests) through vernacular books. In this way readers taught through their own examples, shared their manuscripts, and made use of the practices of translation and recording their devotional practices as both a form of spiritual exercise and a way to share these experiences with their peers. A small group of manuscripts associated with the Bridgettine monastery Syon Abbey is particularly helpful in considering the ways in which women participated in teaching and sharing through devotional texts.

The devotional texts written for the nuns of Syon by their brother monks

---

[1] Bella Millett, '*Ancrene Wisse* and the Book of Hours', in *Writing Religious Women*, pp. 21–40 (p. 31).

and those at Sheen carefully coached their readers in how to approach the texts written for them. These texts offer an astonishing amount of instruction on reading, praying, meditating, and sometimes contemplating. They work hard to guide their unlearned readership (i.e., illiterate in Latin, literate in the vernacular, some with monastic training, some without) in practising devotions, as they offer the useful service of providing devotional texts for this audience.

The nuns were encouraged to keep themselves busy with a variety of devotional practices. For example, Richard Whytford's *Dyuers holy instrucyons and teachynges* provides a satisfactory overview of the devotional practices expected for the nuns:

> Lection, and redyng or heryng of good holy bookes and auctorysed werkes is a good occupacion. Study and lernyng, and also techynge is a good occupacion, meditacion of holy scripture is a holy occupacion. Applie thy selfe therunto, & use thy selfe therein. For the occupacion of redynge and meditacion shall teche the what to fle, and avoyde, and whyther thou shuldest intende and passe. By redynge and lernynge thy wytte and understandynge shall increase. And moche mayst thou profet therby if thou worke & do therafter. Prayer also is a singuler good occupacion, use them interchaungeable, nowe from one unto an other, and so wythout werynes thou shalte go forth with great ease pleasure, and profete in all them, that is to say in bodely labours, in redynge, in meditacion, in prayer and contemplacion.[2]

This passage expands *lectio divina* to contain all kinds of devout activities, all kinds of spiritual practices that can be undertaken by a wide range of devout readers. A similar understanding of devotional practices is to be found in the *Dyetary of Ghostly Helthe*[3] in a chapter titled 'How we should give ourselves to diverse ghostly exercises':

> bycause our mynde whiche is moche subject unto vanyte whyles we ben in this lyfe, abydeth never longe in one state. Therfor we must dryve away ydelnes by dyverse chaunge of good exercyses. As somtyme by good hande worke and convenyent bodyly labour. Somtyme in prayer somtyme in study or redynge of scrypture or of some good workes of holy doctours, somtyme in meditacion and contemplacion yf ye can attain therto. (f. A.v.b)

I have not come across any direct references encouraging the Syon nuns to write: rather, their public representation centres on their role as readers of devotional texts, addressed by the monks who prepare devotional texts for their use. The exercise of reading was represented as an active one in the best-known texts from Syon, *The Myroure of Oure Ladye* and *The Orcherd of*

---

2   *STC* 25420, fol. lxix.
3   *STC* 6833, possibly not a Syon text but certainly emulating them.

Syon: it is likened to sewing a coat, walking in an orchard; it is figured as a means to saying the Lady Office more devoutly, or more generally as a way to work actively on reforming one's soul, just as one examines one's reflection in a mirror. In this way Syon texts demarcate the role of reader and writer: nuns read, monks write. As those responsible for the pastoral care of the Syon nuns, the monks and priests of the Bridgettine monastery and its Carthusian neighbour Sheen put their writing skills to great use: they lived the creed of preaching with their hands to the nuns in the books they produced for them. In fact, Richard Whytford turned the *praedicare manibus* of Syon into a cottage industry in the 1530s, recycling many of the manuscripts he wrote for the nuns (and other friends of the abbey) into printed devotional books for those who could afford to buy them.

Despite the delimited roles assigned to the Syon nuns and those respon-sible for their pastoral care, by the fifteenth century writing was not only a professional and clerical skill; it could also be used as a devotional activity. In Durham University Library MS Cosin V.iii.16 there is a reference to female religious writing, but it is figured as a past practice rather than a present one. This manuscript comprises principally Latin sermons and some mystical extracts from Bridget of Sweden and Mechthild of Hackeborn. In the middle of the volume is found a letter in English, addressed to '[w]elbiloued susturs in our lord Jh[es]u Crist'.[4] It is likely that this volume is written in the hand of William Darker, a Syon brother,[5] and the subject matter also suggests a Brid-gettine association. In this letter, the only selection written in the vernacular in the manuscript, we find writing subscribed as a devotional activity in a romanticized vision of female monasticism 'in the olde tyme':

> Thou women of religioun used contynuelly devoute preier and contempla-cioun, wasshe and grete abstynence, with other vertues afor rehersid: never unoccupied as in redyng, studying, writyng, siwyng, wasshynge, delfyng or herbys settyng or sowyng with other, little seen or never seen out of her place. (fol. 118r)

Although the sisters addressed in the letter are not directly encouraged to write, the ancestral models presented here read and write as well as perform manual labour. The women of religion mentioned here are unnamed: within the manuscript context they are the familiar female visionaries excerpted in the Latin passages comprising the rest of the volume, such as Mechthild of Hackeborn and Bridget of Sweden. The sisters are encouraged to maintain their bookishness and their books in the final address:

---

4   The letter is found in Durham University Library MS Cosin V.iii.16, fols. 118 r–v.
5   See Ann M. Hutchison, 'What the Nuns Read: Literary Evidence From the English Bridgettine House, Syon Abbey', *Mediaeval Studies* 57 (1995), 205–22 (pp. 221–2), and Bell, *What Nuns Read*, p. 174. Hutchison and Bell cite A. I. Doyle's opinion on examining the manuscript.

Wherfor susturs awake and take god hede to thies writynges that be
ordeyned for you and oftymes rede hem and kepe hem clene and hole and
when tyme shall require, repayre hem as a chefe tresoure for youre sowlys
and se in eny wyse ye do theraftur. (fol. 118v)

These illustrations reveal that the act of reading could be merged with the act
of practising devotions: reading about devotions and devotional experiences
became a devotional experience. In some ways this letter does not seem to fit
well with the rest of the texts in the manuscript, since the other Latin materials seem more suited for a male clerical audience; however, I suggest that
the letter represents a kind of artifact for the use of books by nuns, or perhaps
as a testament to nuns' uses of books and the dissemination of texts to nuns.
The opening of the letter stands as a strong witness to textual transmission
between nuns:

> Welbiloved susturs in our Lord Jhesu Crist: Aftur dew saluting knowe ye
> that of such goostly writynge as our susturs have with ys we sende you
> yt consailing and wishing you for ever esse of oure mede to lere thies be
> comoun emong you and yif copy of them to others of religioun that dwell
> nygh you. (fol. 118r)

Felicity Riddy and others have demonstrated the close textual connections
of the female devotional subculture of late medieval England.[6] Devotional
collections associated with Syon provide us with similar examples of this
activity; moreover, they illustrate some of the very few extant examples of
women writing in manuscripts as part of this devotional subculture. From
the evidence it is clear that the Syon nuns made extensive use of devotional
manuscripts. As scholars have noted, the Bridgettine rule and statutes were
very generous with regard to the reading practices of their members; for
the Syon nun, reading was an essential part of her day. Yet, although the
Bridgettines were a learned order, in England there is little or no evidence
of the presence or training of female scribes in contrast to what occurred

---

[6] This has become a burgeoning field which cannot be summed up in a footnote.
A. I. Doyle was the first to put a great deal of effort into this topic, while Felicity
Riddy's article made significant advances for the subject. Other important work
has been done by such scholars as Krug and Erler: A. I. Doyle, 'A Survey of the
Origins and Circulation of Theological Writings in English in the 14th, 15th and
early 16th Centuries' (unpublished PhD thesis, University of Cambridge 1953);
'Book Production by the Monastic Orders in England (*c*. 1375–1530): Assessing the
Evidence', in *Medieval Book Production: Assessing the Evidence*, ed. L. L. Brownrigg
(Los Altos Hills CA, 1990), pp. 1–21; and 'Books Connected with the Vere Family
and Barking Abbey', *Transactions of the Essex Archaeological Society* n.s. 25 (1958),
222–43; F. Riddy, '"Women Talking About the Things of God": a Late Medieval Sub-
Culture', in *Women and Literature*, pp. 104–27; M. C. Erler, *Women, Reading, and Piety
in Late Medieval England* (Cambridge, 2002); and R. Krug, *Reading Families: Women's
Literate Practice in Late Medieval England* (Ithaca NY, 2002).

in continental monasteries. In my extensive research on Syon's vernacular manuscripts and texts I have come across only two possible extant examples of a Syon nun as scribe, which I would like to discuss here in the context of another Syon-related manuscript. I am interested here in what kinds of devotional compilations and miscellanies nuns owned and shared, and how the devotional exercises espoused in these manuscripts might lead to other forms of sharing and teaching – especially through women writing down their devotions for others.

Fifteenth-century nuns' manuscripts most often were collections of devotional pieces: from longer meditation sequences, lives of saints, various Hours, and instructions on holy living, to short prayers and sayings in the vernacular and Latin. I am especially interested in this essay in prayers and meditations – popular texts which provide materials for devotional practices. From the extant evidence we can assume there was a very strong interest on the part of female religious in meditations and prayers, and that collections of these kinds of texts were useful resources for nuns.

An excellent example of this kind of collection is a compilation owned by Clemence Tresham, a nun at Syon in the first half of the sixteenth century. Durham University Library MS Cosin V.v.12 contains both Latin and Middle English meditations and prayers. The manuscript holds a collection of nocturnes written in 1495 by Sir John Cressener of Norfolk and titled *The Sawter of Mercy* as well as a version of Jordan of Saxony's *Meditations on the Life and Passion of Jesus Christ*.[7] This is the only copy we have of Cressener's work, which is described in the colophon:

> The sawter of mercy here endyd is. Why it is so callyd marke ye a right: in euery verse mercy expressyd ys, dayle to sey it put to your myght. The ordyr of thys sawter ys thys. There be viij nocturnes: in euery nocturne be thre psalmes in the name of the blyssid trinite. In euery psalme be v versys betokennyng the v wondes of cryste. On sonday be seyde the fyrst nocturne, on monday the seconnde nocturne and so furth be rew, so that the viii nocturne be seyde on saturday after euensong. (fols. 9v–10r)

This text offers the reader an original set of daily devotions that, combined with the passion meditation found in the manuscript, express one of the most popular aspects of late medieval devotional interests: Christ's life and death, and especially a devotion to the wounds of Christ.[8] The excerpts from the psalms provide solid, orthodox devotional materials for the use of the

---

7   On this manuscript see Bell, *What Nuns Read*, Syon A.16; Krug, *Reading Families*, p. 192, Erler, *Women Reading, and Piety*, p. 148, and Hutchison, 'What Nuns Read', pp. 214–15, n. 48.

8   Thomas H. Bestul provides a number of good examples of late medieval vernacular meditations in his article 'Chaucer's Parson's Tale and the Late-Medieval Tradition of Religious Meditation', *Speculum* 64 (1989), 600–19.

reader, not stepping outside the kinds of devotions already available but supplementing them with an additional, similar set. The vernacular frame of meditating on the Trinity and Christ's wounds is a brilliant nod to current devotional trends while still maintaining the conservative nature of the Latin meditations. This continues into the rest of the manuscript as well. An intermediary section of prayers, 'approximat[ing] to a memoria'[9] follows the Sawter of Mercy (fols. 10r–18r), beginning with a prayer to Christ's wounds, then a series of prayers to popular angels and saints and concluding with a prayer to Catherine of Siena (Katerine of Sene) (fols. 17r–18r) – a favourite saint at Syon and the subject of the important translation of her visionary account, *The Orcherde of Syon*, which ends the section of prayers.

In the passion meditation we see a similar dynamic at work. The Augustinian Jordan of Saxony, sometimes known as Jordan of Quedlinburg, wrote the popular passion meditation in the middle of the fourteenth century which is found here written in Middle English with Latin prayers. This text was printed in Latin on the continent twice in the incunable period,[10] followed by Richard Pynson's printed Latin edition of the *Meditationes Iordani de vita et passione Iesu Christi*[11] in 1513. This meditation is considered a more comprehensive piece than the *Sawter*, offering a detailed account of Christ's life and passion as the remedy to all the reader's needs and wants. It is appropriately morbidly obsessed with details, training the proper affective response from the reader to the passion story.

How did the unique versions of these texts end up in this manuscript? It is very possible that the vernacular translation of Jordan of Quedlinburg's text was made from a continental incunable, since they were published at approximately the same time Cressener wrote his *Sawter*, but further research is necessary to determine where Pynson's edition fits into this picture. As for the *Sawter of Mercy*, there is an Elizabeth Cressener who was Prioress at Dartford at the time the text was written. No one has discovered evidence to support a possible familial connection to John Cressener, although it is an intriguing possibility since it would connect the meditation's author with the Dominican community while the manuscript itself is connected with the Syon community, supporting the model of transmission offered in the letter in MS Cosin V.iii.16. The use of meditations and prayers for personal devotional reading for nuns seems to be widespread, offering writers and scribes like Cressener and the translator of Jordan of Quedlinburg's text the opportunity to influence the devotional activities of their charges (or possibly family

---

[9] Quoted from the online description for Durham University Library MS Cosin V.v.12 Devotionalia s. xv/xvi.

[10] Jordan of Quedlinburg, *Meditationes Iordani de vita et passione Iesu Christi* (Antwerp, 1487, 1491).

[11] Jordan of Quedlinburg, *Meditationes Iordani de vita et passione Iesu Christi* (London, 1513); *STC* (2nd edn), 14789.

members), and then through the further transmission of the works, the activities of other female religious.

Another fascinating example of this kind of transmission occurring as a result of strong audience demand is the different printed editions of William Bonde's *The Directory of Conscience*. Originally written for the Syon nuns, this text goes through three different editions addressed to different readers. The 1527 edition describes the original context for the writing of the text and relates that it was printed at the request of another male religious. The 1534 edition is addressed to a general audience, while the 1535 edition includes a prefatory letter addressed to a nun of Denny who had diligently requested a copy of the text from Bonde through a mutual friend.[12] This letter demonstrates that nuns wanted variety in their devotional activities, eagerly seeking out new devotions. Female religious were able to receive pastoral instruction through devotional texts and manuscripts and sought new and current materials for their devotional practices. Male religious scribes did their best to supply this demand.

Another important manuscript associated with the Syon nuns also contains prayers and meditations in the vernacular and Latin suitable for personal use by nuns: London, Lambeth Palace Library, MS 546.[13] Veronica O'Mara has noted that this manuscript, which has texts and pieces written in several hands (including a Syon favourite, William Darker from Sheen), also contains a colophon from one 'wreched syster' to her 'good deuote syster' at the end of the Lambeth Devotion:[14]

> Good syster of your charyte I you pray remember the scrybeler when that ye may with on Ave Maria or els thys swete word Jhesu have marcy on my wreched syster whose name by the marcy of god I trust shall be wrytyn in the boke of lyfe. Good deuote syster I pray you to lerne thys lesson well of your master our Sauyour Cryst Jhesu that sayth lerne of me for I am mylde and meke in hart and pray for me that I may do and have the same.
>
> (fol. 55r)

---

12 For more information on this example see my forthcoming chapter '"Moche profitable unto religious persones, gathered by a brother of Syon": Syon Abbey and English Books', in *Syon Abbey and Its Books*, ed. A. Walsingham and E. A. Jones (Woodbridge, forthcoming).

13 For manuscript information see Bell, *What Nuns Read*, Syon A.29, as well as V. M. O'Mara, 'A Middle English Text Written by a Female Scribe', *Notes and Queries* 235 (1990), 396–8, and more recently S. Schwamb, 'Introduction to Lambeth MS 546, fols. 1–7r: The Fifteen Places Mary Visited after Christ's Ascension', *ANQ* 18 (2005), 20–31. O'Mara includes the full text of the colophon from the female scribe, p. 397.

14 Named such by Hope Emily Allen, who includes the text in her *Writings Ascribed to Richard Rolle* (New York and London, 1927), pp. 343–4: referenced by O'Mara, 'Middle English Text', pp. 396–7. I am grateful to Stephanie Morley for drawing my attention to O'Mara's article, which also includes the text of the colophon, p. 396.

This fascinating manuscript merits further study as a representative of late medieval devotional production and reception: it is a collection of several prayers and meditations written in several hands (including one identified female one) and then bound together. The collection illustrates important late medieval devotional trends such as meditations on Christ's life and passion, the cult of Jesus' name and an interest in the Virgin Mary. Many of the prayers and meditations offer similar materials to other such contemporary items but may provide a slightly new frame or lens. For example, the first treatise in the manuscript is a short passion meditation set within the context of Mary visiting fifteen places associated with Christ (an early version of the Stations of the Cross[15]), providing a slightly 'new' perspective on the tradi- tional passion meditation, but one which would still be familiar enough to the audience. The second treatise, 'The Fifteen Sorrows of Our Lady', continues the Marian theme of the collection but moves from the third-person narra- tion of the first treatise to a first-person address to the Virgin. There are also some prayers to the Virgin later in the manuscript (fols. 52v, 79v–80r), three of which are in written in the hand of our female scribe. The remaining two lengthier treatises in the manuscript, the 'Golden Litany' (fols. 34–51) and the 'Lambeth Devotion' (fols. 53–5), address Christ in second-person narration: the former offers a meditation on the life and passion of Christ while the latter focuses the reader's attention on the redemptive nature of the wounds of Christ. Other entries offer the reader practical prayers to be said before and after communion, or on one's deathbed, for example. The manuscript must have been a useful resource of contemporary devotional materials for its reader(s).

Moreover, Lambeth 546 offers some significant comments on our two areas of concern. As well as giving us an example of a female scribe the manuscript also illustrates details of textual transmission and models of pastoral care involving men and women preaching and teaching respectively. The opening treatise on the Fifteen Places discusses the way in which this devotion devel- oped out of the Virgin Mary's visitations to the 'steeds' where her son had spent his last hours:

> And syth she went a bought from one place to an other so longe tyl she had goon alle the xv statiouns rounde a bought. And it is to know the virgyn mary was contynually after her Sonnys ascension. Besyde Jerusalem uppon the mownte of Syon ther had sche her dwellynge and her sell. And ther Seynt Johan the evangeliste songe oftyn tymes masse before her in the same yerys. who that þeyse. xv steedys wolle dayly go in his harte with a perfight mynde and trew entendaunce: then yeveth he to the virgyn mary. and to her blessyde son. fulle gretely pleasaunce. For that in hem be closyd alle the Passion of oure lorde Jhesu. (fols. 1v–2r)

---

[15] See Schwamb, 'Introduction to Lambeth MS 546' for a full discussion of the sources and traditions of this text.

In the first place this passage is important for describing the way that Mary turns her walk and remembrance into a devotional exercise. It is shown as a natural progression from her sorrowful reminiscences to an affective meditation on Christ's passion as told from the perspective of his mother. The close connection between the subject matter and the point of view is meant to enhance the affective experience. In the second place the text provides a fine example of very early Christian pastoral care in the figure of John the Evangelist. He plays a notable role here singing mass before Mary: in fact his role is viewed as the culmination of the devotional process as he brings 'pleasaunce' to Mary and Christ through his ministering. Although Mary may develop the Lambeth Devotion herself (according to this account), she still needs John's supervision and ministry – the pastoral care shared in textual devotions does not replace that provided by priests.

The other example comes from the prologue to the Golden Litany (fols. 29–33): it begins by recounting a familiar type of narrative of a holy woman named 'Mawdlene' who prayed to God to know the best way to worship him; Christ appears to her, shows her his wounds and tells her that reading and saying the Golden Litany every day will bring about great spiritual profit. She complies and is granted the gift of the stigmata. This promotion for the Golden Litany mentions five times the actions of reading and saying the devotion daily, illustrating literally the effects it had on Mawdlene and suggesting the positive effects it can have for all who perform the devotion. The tale of the iconic female visionary who is granted a special grace and then shares it with others for their spiritual benefit was also used in the preface to the 'Fifteen Oes' and also reminds us of Julian of Norwich's petitions and subsequent visions. Here the text gives not only the (brief) visionary account that acts as an endorsement but also the accompanying meditations that proved so beneficial to the holy woman, so that the reader can also participate in the devotional practice – just as was shown for the Lambeth Devotion.

In the Golden Litany we are also given two pastoral figures who parallel Mary and John: the holy woman and Christ. Mawdlene plays a similar role to Mary, while Christ offers advice – not masses – not only to Mawdlene but also to subsequent practitioners of the devotion. He offers the context for the devotion, demonstrating that enhanced knowledge of the materials will enhance the performance and providing an allegory for the meditation process:

> For as oftyn as þu or any other whyth herty deuocion saye or rede thys goolden letany havyng mynde on my passion: so often þu dost anoynte my wondys with swete salues and preciouse oyntmentes in such wyse þat I can not denye nothyng þat þu ryghtfully desyrest of me for thy sylf or for any other of þy frendis lyvyng vpon erthe or for any soulys lyvyng in the paynes of purgatori. (fols. 30v–31r)

This frame again places us within the context of devotions to the passion and specifically the wounds of Christ: the reading process and devotional practice are figured as putting salve or ointment on the wounds, an active, maternal role.

Lambeth 546 thus shows us women taking active roles in their devotions – as healers, scribes, visionaries, witnesses and practitioners. We also see the significance of the role of the male spiritual guide or mentor providing guidance and pastoral care to religious women. While the men can sing the mass and preach, the women teach by their examples and offer their own devotional practices for the use of the reader: female religious teach and share instead of preaching and caring.

In writing down the Lambeth Devotion our female scribe can minister to her fellow readers. It is similar to male translators and scribes preparing pastoral instruction and devotional materials for female religious readers, yet in this case it is framed as a devotion performed by a woman, written down by a woman for a female audience. Another excellent example of women writing down devotions for women is found in Oxford, Bodleian, MS Holkham Misc. 41, which Erler identifies as a Syon manuscript.[16] The *Feitis and the Passion of Our Lord Jesu Christ*,[17] found only in MS Holkham Misc 41, is a fairly conventional set of meditations written by a female religious for someone she terms her religious sister (which is itself a convention of the genre, although it is usually a male religious who writes to his female spiritual charge, as Richard Rolle and Walter Hilton had done years before). In the preface the writer addresses herself to the reader:

O myn sustir preie my lord god the Trinite that for his great bounty, and for his endeles mercy, haue mercy and pite on me sinful and make me a good woman. For ful ofte sinne and wrechidnes withdrawith my gosteli syht from his glorious presence. And therefore yow and othere of his special children, I preie to purchace me sum grace of that benigne lord in whom al grace is in.[18]

---

16 Erler, *Women, Reading, and Piety*, p. 143. On the Holkham manuscript see Catherine Innes-Parker, 'Anchoritic Elements of Holkham Misc. 41', in *Anchorites, Wombs and Tombs: Intersections of Gender and Enclosure in the Middle Ages*, ed. E. Herbert MacAvoy and M. Hughes Edwards (Aberystwyth, 2005), pp. 172–81, and 'Bodleian Library MS Holkham Miscellany 41 and the Modelling of Women's Devotion', in *Readers, Reading, and Reception in Medieval English Devotional Literature and Practice*, ed. C. Annette Grisé, Susan Uselmann, and Kathryn Vulić, *Disputatio* (Turnhout, forthcoming). Earlier work on the manuscript is by William F. Pollard, 'Bodleian MS Holkham Misc. 41: A Fifteenth-Century Bridgettine Manuscript and Prayer Cycle', *Birgittiana* 3 (1997), 43–53; and Josephine Koster Tarvers, 'Gender, Text, Critic: The Case of Holkham Misc. 41', *Medieval Perspectives* 14 (1999), 229–41.

17 The text has not been fully edited; however, Alexandra Barratt includes a partial edition as 'A Collection of Prayers: *The Faits and the Passion of Our Lord Jesu Christ*', in *Women's Writing in Middle English* (London, 1992), pp. 207–18.

18 Oxford, Bodleian, MS Holkham Misc. 41, p. 3. The manuscript folios are not numbered, but a later hand has included pagination; I have used the pagination for reference to the manuscript.

Besides this brief mention of herself as a 'good woman', the writer does not identify her gender in any way throughout the text, which leads me to suspect that it was not considered relevant or important for her writing of the text. Perhaps this was because she knew her audience very well, and as the text was not designed for broad circulation (or for that matter for any circulation beyond what the single manuscript might find) she did not feel she needed to defend or excuse her act of writing as a woman. It could also be that her writing of this text was a form of devotional exercise that was acceptable for women. One indication that the Holkham writer may be thinking in this way is found at the end of the meditation on Mary Magdalene, which concludes with the appeal to Christ that 'whatever I write, thinke or speke of yowe and for yow, be it youre werk and not myn'.[19] The act of writing (which is not denied to the reader here) is lumped together with her other activities (that is, thinking and speaking) and then turned into Christ's work – performed for his benefit and for the profit of others. The text therefore outlines the ways in which the writer and the reader are meant to turn their conduct towards proper Christian ends, but whereas the extent of the activities suitable for religious-minded women were traditionally limited to thinking and speaking about Christ (and I would add reading), here they are able to expand their efforts to do God's work by writing appropriately pious texts that would benefit those who read them by teaching them about suitable devotional practices. In this way, the act of writing is open to these women, but at the same time, the kinds of texts they can produce are limited. Female religious could teach through their own example but not preach.

We can perhaps perceive a bias towards feminine material in this text, for a great number of the meditations deal with female figures from Christ's life on earth: Alexandra Barratt has provided several selections in her anthology (e.g., the woman of Samaria and Mary Magdalene). As analogues to this use of female figures, I would point to the widespread use of the Hours of the Virgin in this period, and could compare these meditations to the fifteenth-century *Myroure of Oure Ladye*.[20] Female perspectives on Christ's life and passion were very popular in late medieval England, and reflect upon the growing calls for affective responses to Christ's life and passion, which were made accessible through female intermediary figures such as the Virgin Mary or Mary Magdalene. Many of the female mystics known in late medieval England, such as those excerpted in Cosin V.iii.16, illustrate in their Middle English incarnations a preoccupation with the lives of Christ and the Virgin Mary – especially Christ's birth and death, both of which also witness his mother's intense involvement. These topics held great interest for late medieval Christians:

---

19 'A Collection of Prayers', ed. Barratt, p. 210.80–1.
20 *The Myroure of oure Ladye*, ed. J. H. Blunt, EETS ES 19 (London, 1873; rpt. Millwood NY, 1981).

This quest for a share in the sufferings of Christ, through identification with Mary, dominated the piety of Christian Europe in the fourteenth and fifteenth centuries. It gave rise to literally thousands of treatises, hymns, poems, sermons, and devotional images. [...] Mary was a natural focus for the attempt to realize for oneself the sufferings of Jesus, for she had stood by the cross, supported by John the beloved disciple, when the rest of the Apostles had fled. [21]

Vernacular gospel commentaries, such as Nicholas Love's immensely popular, early fifteenth century *Mirror of the Blessed Life of Jesus Christ*, played a significant role in later medieval English devotional culture, compensating for the lack of accessibility of the gospels in English: they often summarized the gospel narrative, guiding the reader very specifically in how to read and understand these materials.[22] Many female visionary accounts retell parts of gospel narratives as well (especially Christ's birth and passion), supplementing authoritative versions, and providing compilers and readers alike with additional materials on orthodox topics that were of great interest to the growing literate pious population.[23]

It is conceivable that the emphasis on female figures found in the *Feitis* relates to the circumstances of its production (and the gender of its writer). Yet we cannot underestimate the importance of the audience as a major determinant. As the meditations are written in the first person, the writer herself stands in as an original reader who has been asked to put these meditations down for her religious sister's use. It is likely that for both the original reader-writer and her religious sister (the reader of this version), the use of particularly female models for these meditations on Christ's life and passion was fitting, for women were often exhorted to follow the examples of female saints. The use of female figures from the New Testament likely played the same exemplary role, and in fact offers the reader something that female saints do not: they provide examples of Christ's mercy to women who did not always act in a saintly manner, who committed adultery and were engaged in prostitution, for example. These stories of women sinners offered the reader the opportunity to contemplate her own sinful state, and to seek Christ's mercy. Again, the text is responsive to the needs of the reader.

---

[21] E. Duffy, *The Stripping of the Altars: Traditional Religion in England c. 1400–c. 1580* (London, 1992), p. 260. See also T. H. Bestul, *Texts of the Passion: Latin Devotional Literature and Medieval Society* (Philadelphia, 1996).

[22] See Love, *Mirror* (2005).

[23] See C. L. Sahlin, *Birgitta of Sweden and the Voice of Prophecy*. Studies in Medieval Mysticism III (Woodbridge, 2001), p. 39 on Bridget's supplementing biblical accounts of the lives of Mary and Christ. Barratt has examined the influence of passion meditations on medieval English women writers—including Margery Kempe and Julian of Norwich: A. Barratt, '*Stabant matres dolorosae*: Women as Readers and Writers of Passion Prayers, Meditations and Visions', in *The Broken Body: Passion Devotion in Late-Medieval Culture*, ed. A. A. MacDonald et al. (Groningen, 1998), pp. 55–71.

In the manuscripts we have studied here, female models teach, while female readers, devotional practitioners, and scribes share their devotions with others. In the concluding section I consider briefly an example of a female practitioner who did not toil anonymously in a cell. Lady Margaret Beaufort provides an example of a pious laywoman whose translations of French devotional treatises were a form of spiritual practice.[24] Lady Margaret, mother to Henry VII, actively courted a pious public reputation. She translated the fourth book of the *De Imitatione Christi*, which was printed along with William Atkinson's translation of the first three books (undertaken at Beaufort's bidding) by Richard Pynson in 1504. This translation of Thomas à Kempis's treatise is the first text of the *devotio moderna* movement to be printed for an English audience. Her translation of a French version of the *Speculum Aureum*, commonly attributed to Denis the Carthusian but more likely the work of James of Guytroede, also a Carthusian, and entitled in English *The Mirroure of Gold for the Synful Soulle* (1506), was not as groundbreaking as her involvement in the *Folowynge of Christ* (as they entitled Thomas à Kempis's treatise), for as Alexandra Barratt has summarized, the *Mirroure of Gold* is a 'tissue of commonplaces'. Yet, she also notes that it was a popular printed text in the fifteenth and sixteenth centuries, going through many editions.[25]

In Bishop Fisher's memorial sermon for her, Beaufort's literary activities as a translator of devotional works are seen as part of her other devotional activities, performed 'for her exercyse & for the prouffyte of other'.[26] In his sermon, Fisher emphasizes Beaufort's study and reading, so that they appear to be a key part of her self-presentation as Fisher understands her. This parallels neatly with the description of holy women in the letter discussed earlier, where writing was included in the devotional busy work of religious women from the past. Beaufort's translations are designed to benefit both herself and others: in the first place, the translation act itself is a spiritual exercise, while in the second place, the printing of the translations is offered to the audience as appropriate devotional readings, just as we saw in the Golden Litany with Mawdlene's devotions.

Thus, devotional translations by well-to-do women with the right combination of aptitudes for study, languages and piety gained a foothold in late medieval England. These women do not preach, they do not write down original visionary experiences or biblical commentary, and they do not instruct others in how to live a devout life. Nevertheless, within late medieval England's conservative milieu their contribution is substantial. It was an expression of female lay piety that extended the devotional practices of reading, studying, praying and meditating into writing. By using writing as

---

24 Another useful example is Dame Eleanor Hull. See Hull, *Seven Psalms*.
25 A. Barratt, *Women's Writing in Middle English* (London, 1992), pp. 302, 301.
26 *The English Works of John Fisher*, ed. J. E. B. Mayer, EETS ES 27 (London, 1876; rpt. Millwood NY, 1987), p. 292.

an extension of their devotional practices they were able to blur the gendered binary of female reader and male scribe in the same way that female religious were starting to do.

By the fifteenth century in England pious women with literary interests or aspirations were able to find ways to treat the act of writing as a form or extension of their other devotions (e.g. praying, reading and meditating) rather than as something that was summarily denied them because of their gender and/or religious status. It appears that, alongside the development of a female visionary tradition of women writers, there arose a devotional tradition of meditational and instructional treatises that allowed women to consider writing as part of their devotional activities; that is, as a means of taking the convention of leading an exemplary life as a model for others to follow and putting this life – or their life practices – into a text, again for the profit of others who would benefit from their example and devotions. The texts of the Lambeth and Holkham writers made an effective meditational exercise accessible to one or more religious sisters. Margaret Beaufort's translations were an efficient and still conservative means of supporting her family's official position and standing, by offering the fruits of her devotional labours for the profit of other pious vernacular readers. I would like to believe that these women thought of themselves as part of a female devotional tradition made up of writers, readers and patrons that did not exclude but relied upon the participation of men, as writers, spiritual advisors and readers. It was not an exclusively female devotional tradition – their participation required a John the Evangelist or John Cressener to assist them – but it was one in which women found ways to contribute. Indeed, the Lambeth and Holkham manuscripts suggest that women writers of devotional texts were coming to be accepted, since they brought to their writings a gendered identification and a previous career as a reader of devotional treatises that qualified them to speak both to and on behalf of their audience. We must work towards an understanding of the various ways these pious women responded to the idea that writing devotional texts, like their other devotional activities, was not necessarily denied them, but could be viewed as a logical development of their devotions. Denied the avenue of preaching to convert or change the behaviour of those around them, these women writers pushed the envelope, transforming the ultimate goal of pious women – that is, to lead a good Christian life as an example for others to follow – into permission to put this embodied exemplarity into written form in a devotional text.

The texts considered in this essay show a commitment by female religious to putting text into practice: collecting devotions, reading and performing meditations and prayers and writing them down or having them written down. Their interests in current devotional trends spurred their efforts, as did their desires to see familiar subjects from new angles. By the fifteenth century, alongside the dedication to passion meditations and Marian devotions, there develops a rise in interest in the female devotional voice. This interest is fed by the influx of female visionary works from continental Europe, and also leads to the all-too-rare English female holy women writing down their experiences (or having them written down). Moreover, it allowed a very few women to write down their devotional practices as part of an effort to participate in pastoral instruction through texts by teaching from their own example and sharing their own experiences.

13

'Take a Book and Read':
Advice for Religious Women

Alexandra Barratt

Reading, prayer and meditation constituted a major part of the job-description for medieval religious. As the three activities were not so much a triad as a continuum, the boundaries between them constantly shifting, it is hard to know what exactly devout women, and their spiritual advisers, understood by the terms in the 300 years leading up to the dissolution of the monasteries. Prayer and meditation were particularly problematic. In contrast, reading seems less so, but it too was not always an activity distinct from the others, while the promotion of 'reading' *per se* led on to a more awkward question: what should one read? For reading is both transitive and intransitive: it is one thing to recommend reading, quite another to prescribe what is to be read. The reading of religious women is a large subject that has attracted much recent scholarly attention.[1] This paper will address a single aspect, that is, how far women religious had certain types of reading, even particular texts, prescribed (and others implicitly denied or forbidden).

At least three lines of enquiry are open to those interested in the reading practices of religious women in later medieval England. We can examine the relatively few texts composed by such women (at present virtually restricted to Julian of Norwich and Margery Kempe), for evidence of what they must have read (or had read to them); or we can analyse surviving manuscripts of religious texts for which there is internal or external evidence of ownership

---

[1] See, e.g., A. C. Bartlett, *Male Authors, Female Readers: Representation and Subjectivity in Middle English Devotional Literature* (Ithaca NY, 1995); Bell, *What Nuns Read*; M. Erler, 'Devotional Literature', in *The Cambridge History of the Book in Britain III: 1400–1557* (Cambridge, 1999), pp. 495–525; C. M. Neale and J. Boffey, 'Gentlewomen's Reading', *Cambridge History of the Book*, pp. 526–40; C. de Hamel, *Syon Abbey: The Library of the Bridgettine Nuns and their Peregrinations after the Reformation*, Roxburghe Club (1991); A. M. Hutchison, 'Devotional Reading in the Monastery and the Late Medieval Household', in De Cella in Seculum: *Religious and Secular Life and Devotion in Late Medieval England*, ed. M. G. Sargent (Cambridge, 1989), pp. 215–27, and 'What the Nuns Read: Literary Evidence from the English Bridgettine House, Syon Abbey', *Mediaeval Studies* 57 (1995), 204–22; R. Krug, *Reading Families: Women's Literate Practice in Late Medieval England* (Ithaca NY, 2002).

by such women, as individuals or in communities. Thirdly, we can study texts composed for and read by women (though not necessarily confined to a female audience), to see what they have to say about reading, and what reading matter (if any) they recommend. This last is the approach adopted here.

Treatises of advice written by men in both Latin and the vernaculars for religious women have a long tradition in the West, which there is no need to rehearse. More specifically, many such Middle English treatises survive, of which the thirteenth-century *Ancrene Wisse* is pre-eminent. Of the forty-eight less memorable texts listed in Jolliffe's *Check-List of Middle English Writings of Spiritual Guidance*, category O, 'For Those living under Rule', nearly half are written explicitly for a female audience. Of these some have a very narrow focus, consisting of guidance on a single virtue (typically chastity, obedience or humility) or on a particular topic (such as resistance to temptation), or they have a specific function, such as providing a form of confession adapted for women religious, or treating of the various spiritual and practical problems thrown up by the religious life. Most were implicitly written to supplement, not replace, such normative and legislative texts as the Benedictine Rule.

This may be why so many have nothing at all to say on the subject of reading, even though the very existence of such texts implies that religious women did indeed read, or listened to reading. Some of the texts also indicate that their readers could write: several claim to be composed in response to written requests from their future audience. For instance, the 'aberrant'[2] translation of William Flete's *De remediis temptationum*[3] in London, British Library, MS Royal 18 A x (Jolliffe O.8), addressed to a woman, begins:

> Dere sister, I haue in partie vnderstonde *by thyn writyng* of diuerse temptaciouns and taryinges that thu hast suffered ... a-geynes the wilken temptaciouns *I write the* here some remedies the wheche I have fownde in the writynges of holy doctours. (fol. 10v; emphases mine)

In another text (Jolliffe O.35),[4] composed in the early sixteenth century and addressed to the author's 'dear susterys Mary and Anne, wyth all the other devoȝth dyscyples of the scole of Cryste in youre monastery of Amysbury' (fol. 1), the writer acknowledges their request for instruction on the ceremony of monastic profession – a request that must have been conveyed in writing,

---

2   See B. Hackett, OSA., E. Colledge and N. Chadwick, 'William Flete's "De Remediis contra Temptaciones" in its Latin and English Recensions: The Growth of a Text', *Medieval Studies* 26 (1964), 210–30 (p. 223).

3   According to Hackett et al., the Latin text was composed before 1359 (ibid., p. 210).

4   Oxford, Bodleian Library, MS Additional A 42. This text has been usefully discussed and partially transcribed by Y. Parrey, '"Devoted Disciples of Christ": Early Sixteenth-Century Religious Life in the Nunnery at Amesbury', *Bulletin of the Institute of Historical Research* 67:164 (1994), 240–8.

given his own response. He agrees partly for practical reasons, partly because he assumes that written communication is more lasting than oral: 'wheras I can nott cum to doo hit personally, *to doo hyt with my pen*, wych may better a-byde with you þen thowe y had spoken it wyth my mowȝthe' (fol. 2, emphasis mine). Later, though, he allows for the possibility that some of his audience may not even be able to sign their own names, as he describes how when they take their vows they should

> vnder the wordes of your professyon when ȝe haue red hit, with your owne hond … write your name, or yf ȝe can nott, yn stede ther-of ȝe make a crosse + yn syne that hit is your owne dede. (fol. 28)

Reading and writing are therefore as much a part of the mental world of the consumers as of the producers of these texts. If so many have nothing to say on reading, it may be that their authors would argue that religious women already had their lives governed by monastic rules that dealt adequately with the subject. This position is rarely articulated, although the author of a treatise in Cambridge, Trinity College, MS O.7.47 (Jolliffe O.38), addressed 'vnto a mayden þat shuld leve vnde[r] þe rewle of holy religyone', does make it explicit when he urges his reader to seek in her 'rules and institutions' for amplification of any topic with which he deals inadequately:

> But þou, sister … halde þe streit weye … opon þe whilke religione is grounded, as þe rewles and þe instituciones of it proues … And þat shal be þi lesson and þi sermone, I mene þi rewle þat is þe cause of my writynge: þat yt wantes here [i.e. in this treatise], loke it þere. (fol. 81r–v)

Indeed, Chapter 48 of the Benedictine Rule, 'De Opera Manuum Cotidiana' ('Of Daily Manual Work'), pays considerable attention to reading, about which it has more to say than about manual labour as we would understand the term. For *lectio divina*, the reading of scripture, was of course fundamental to monastic praxis. The classic exposition is found in the *Scala Claustralium* attributed to the Carthusian Guigo II and written *c*.1150;[5] the Middle English translation, 'A Ladder of Four Rungs', which survives in three manuscripts,[6] defines monastic reading as 'a besy lokyng vpon Holy Wrytte with intencion of the wylle and in the wytte'.[7] The author describes how, having heard or read a verse of scripture, a person 'begynnyth to chewe it & breke it with skylle or

5   Latin text and French translation in *Guigues II Le Chartreux: Lettre sur la vie contemplative (L'échelle des moines)*, ed. E. Colledge OSA and J. Walsh SJ, Sources Chrétiennes 163 (Paris, 1970).
6   In *Deonise Hid Diuinite*, ed. P. Hodgson, EETS OS 231 (London, 1955, corr. edn 1958), pp. 101–17; extracts in *English Mystics of the Middle Ages*, ed. B. Windeatt (Cambridge, 1994), pp. 248–52.
7   *Deonise Hid Diuinite*, ed. Hodgson, p. 101.

reson', hence leading to meditation.[8] For *lectio* is not really the equivalent of 'reading': it represented a far more serious, engaged and considered activity than the sometimes cursory or even recreational occupation suggested by the English word today. As such, it was vulnerable to worldly interference. *The Myrour of Recluses*, a translation of the *Speculum Inclusorum* probably made for anchoresses, points out the potential dangers to a religious distracted 'in redynge or herynge of holy scriptures', whose 'mynde is al afeer fro the wordes and þenkeþ nat on hem'. This state of mind deprives such a person of the will, as well as of the ability, to study the word of God.[9]

The monastic concept of *lectio divina* created an uncomfortable dilemma, usually repressed or occluded, for religious women and their advisers in later medieval England. *Lectio* was first and foremost the prayerful reading and rumination of the Vulgate, and most women of the period are thought to have been ignorant of Latin. The depth and extent of this ignorance have surely been somewhat exaggerated,[10] (the fifteenth-century translator Dame Eleanor Hull – a laywoman – bequeathed a copy of the Vulgate in her will of 1460),[11] but certainly few women would have been capable of extensive unaided reading in the Latin text of scripture. Yet the 1407 Constitutions of Oxford, promulgated in final form in 1409, forbad the translation into English of scripture – not just of the complete text but also of short passages – and effectively made the reading and even possession of such translations *prima facie* evidence of heresy, unless a licence had been granted by the 'ordinary' or local bishop.[12] So from then onwards it was difficult, if not impossible, for male spiritual advisers to recommend unequivocally the reading of scripture, without risking charges of unorthodoxy and imperilling their spiritual daughters.

Some might argue that religious women were already living in a state of inhibition, their spiritual options severely restricted by their gender, when Arundel promulgated his *Constitutions*. For apart from the Wycliffite translation, only two extended English translations of biblical texts had been made for women before 1409. (In contrast, there are numerous Anglo-Norman texts that translate or paraphrase scripture.[13]) Richard Rolle, who died in 1349,

---

8   Ibid., p. 107.
9   *Myrour of Recluses*, ed. Harley, p. 16.
10   See A. Barratt, 'Small Latin? The Post-Conquest Learning of English Religious Women', in *Anglo-Latin and Its Heritage: Essays in Honour of A. G. Rigg on his 64th Birthday*, ed. Siân Echard and Gernot R. Wieland, Publications of the Journal of Medieval Latin (Brepols, 2001), pp. 51–65.
11   Hull, *Seven Psalms*, p. 204.
12   N. Watson, 'Censorship and Cultural Change in Late-medieval England: Vernacular Theology, the Oxford Translation Debate, and Arundel's *Constitutions* of 1409', *Speculum* 70 (1995), 822–64 (pp. 828–9).
13   A twelfth-century prose version of the Gallican Psalter is extant in twelve manuscripts, plus five manuscripts of later versions, and a fourteenth-century prose

translated the psalter for the recluse Margaret Kirkeby,[14] of which eighteen copies survive. He alternates Latin and English and seems to have deliberately made a literal translation, using accessible English vocabulary, to encourage his readers to learn some Latin:

> In þis werke .i. seke na straunge ynglis, bot lightest [easiest] and commonest. And swilk þat is mast lyke til þe latyn. swa þat thei þat knawes noght latyn. by þe ynglis may com til mony latyn wordis. In þe translacioun .i. follow þe lettere als mykell as .i. may. And þare .i. fynd no propire [appropriate] ynglis. i. follow þe wit [sense] of þe worde. Swa þat þai þat sall red it þaim þar noght dred errynge [so that those who shall read it need not fear making a mistake].[15]

Half a century later, a version of parts of the New Testament – St Matthew's Gospel, the Acts of the Apostles, the Pauline and Catholic Epistles – was, according to its twentieth-century editor:

> undertaken at the urgent request of the inmates of some religious house, more especially, to judge from the repeated references to the 'Suster' at the beginning and end of the various Epistles, of a woman vowed to religion.[16]

One reaction to the dilemma posed by the lack of access to scripture was to blur the boundaries between the elements that made up the monastic triad, conflating *lectio* with *oratio* or *meditatio*. A second strategy was to follow the example of the Rule of St Benedict and assimilate reading to work. Many treatises for women that have little to say about reading have plenty to say about work – not work that leads to economic self-sufficiency, but work that staves off the idleness that opens the door for sin. For instance, 'On maidenhood' (Jolliffe O.31), found in London, British Library MS Arundel 286, says that the second 'ward' of virginity is 'that maydens be noȝt ydel but euer ocupied traueylynge honest werkis: for ydelnes makeþ lecherous stirynges' (fol. 144v). Reading can be just one of many such 'honest works'. The text quoted earlier, found in Trinity College Cambridge MS O.7.47 (Jolliffe O.38), mentions reading only as one of several means to eschew idleness:

> Loke þou be not ydelle but outher þou be preyende, synggende, or redende or herande Godes wordes, or wirkande profitabil werke with þine handes, þat þe enemye fynde þe not ydelle. (fols. 80v–81)

---

translation of the whole of the Vulgate (Dean and Boulton, *Anglo-Norman Literature*, Items 445 and 469). See further S. Berger, *La Bible française* (Paris, 1884), and Dean and Boulton, *Anglo-Norman Literature*, pp. 238–63.

[14] *The Psalter or Psalms of David and Certain Canticles: with a Translation and Exposition in English by Richard Rolle of Hampole*, ed. H. R. Bramley (Oxford, 1884).

[15] Ibid., pp. 4–5.

[16] *A Fourteenth Century English Biblical Version*, ed. A. C. Paues (Cambridge, 1904), p. xxiv.

The virgin's 'lesson' or reading should be her rule, supplemented only by this present text: 'sette all þi stody & þi besynesse to knowe Godes wille & to fulfille it in werke' (fol. 81v). A fifteenth-century translation of Aelred of Rievaulx's twelfth-century Latin letter of advice to his anchoress sister recycles the familiar *sententia* from the Rule of St Benedict, 'ydelnesse is a deedly enenmy to mannys soule'. It goes on:

> I wolde thou were not vnoccupyed … thow shalt occupie the with som honest labour of thyn hondes and than shalt thow renne to som pryuat prayer. … And whan thow begynnest to waxe heuy of hem or wery, than take a boke and rede or do som labour with thyn hondes.[17]

Ancrene Wisse echoes and expands Aelred's sentiments when it lists reading among a range of desirable activities in Part One:

> Verseilunge of Sawter, redunge of Englisc oðer of Frensch, halie meditatiuns, ower cneolunges, hwen-se ȝe eauer mahen iȝemen, ear mete ant efter – eauer se ȝe mare doð, se Godd ow eche forðre his deorewurðe grace. Ah lokið swa, Ich bidde owe, þet ȝe beon neauer idel, ah wurchen oðer reden, oþer beon i bonen, ant swa don eauer sumhwet þet god mahe of awakenin.[18]

> [Reciting the Psalter, reading English or French, holy meditations, your kneelings, whenever you can attend to them, before or after meals – ever the more you do the more does God advance each of you in his precious grace. But see to it, I beg you, that you are never idle, but work or read or be at your prayers, and so always be doing something from which good may spring.]

Although writing hundreds of years before Arundel's *Constitutions*, the author here clearly distinguishes the reading of vernacular texts from the recitation of the Latin Psalter, in private or liturgical prayer.

Late in our period, in the early sixteenth century, the Syon brother Thomas Prestins made a translation of David of Augsburg's *Profectus Religiosorum*, almost certainly for the Bridgettine nuns. This expands the monastic triad to such an extent that reading becomes only one of seven possible spiritual activities, one of which is 'attending to good works':

> The .vi.th spiritual exercise is to haue oure mynde euer suspendyd & lyfftyd vp to god in prayers or meditacions, in remembryng the benefyttys of god, in thynkyng good thoughtys, in redyng holy bokys, in attending to good workys, & in the contemplacion of god.[19]

---

17 *Aelred of Rievaulx's* De Institutione Inclusarum: *Two English Versions*, ed. J. Ayto and A. Barratt, EETS OS 287 (Oxford, 1984), p. 6.
18 *Ancrene Wisse*, ed. Millett, I, 1.393–9, p. 18.
19 S. E. Hayes, 'David of Augsburg's *Profectus Religiosorum* in the Middle English

Reading is also listed among five things that the novice should use as seeds of meditation: 'holy redyng, holy communicacion or spekyng, good thoughtys, thankyngys to god, & praysyngys of god'.[20] Another text of a similar date, an anonymous treatise on preparation for communion found in Anne Bulkeley's Book (BL MS Harley 494), also mixes reading in with many other pious activities. The writer explains that worthy reception of communion demands

> þese and actuall rest of mynde, the which can not be had nor kept but of suche persons as gif themself moch to sylence, solitarynes, redyng, prayer, meditacyon, and contemplacion. And þerfor it is expedient to þat person þat will ofte tymes be commonede ... to stand solitary in prayer and vertuous study. (fol. 25)

The monastic triad is here embedded in a list of six, which is clearly progressive and cumulative, and reading is implicitly just one aspect of 'vertuous study'.

If some writers assimilate reading to work, others conflate, or even replace, it with meditation or prayer. The author of *Ancrene Wisse*, in the section devoted to Temptations, foregrounds the distinction (or lack of it) between reading and prayer. He designates reading, along with varied activity and spiritual comfort, as a cure or treatment ('salue') for sloth or accidie.[21] It can often be more profitable than vocal prayer (ironic, given the detailed attention devoted to such prayers in Part One). Indeed, reading *is* prayer, and he gives a detailed account of its spiritual dynamics and its link to meditation, quoting the famous passage from St Jerome's letter to Eustochium:[22]

> Redunge is god bone. Redunge teacheð hu ant hwet me bidde, and beode biȝet hit efter. Amidde þe redunge, hwen þe heorte likeð, kimeð up a deuo-tiun þet is wurð monie benen. For-þi seið Sein Ierome: *Ieronimus: Semper in manu tua sacra sit lectio; tenenti tibi librum sompnus subripiat, et cadentem faciem pagina sancta suscipiat.* 'Hali redunge beo eauer i þine honden; slep ga upo þe as þu lokest þron, and te hali pagne ikepe þi fallinde neb.'[23]

> [Reading is good prayer. Reading teaches us how and what one should pray, and prayer obtains it afterwards. During your reading, when it pleases the heart, there arises a devotion that is worth many prayers. For that reason Saint Jerome said, 'Let holy reading be ever in your hands; let sleep come upon you as you look on it, and the holy page catch your face as it falls.']

Translation for the Nuns of Syon Abbey: An Edition' (unpublished PhD dissertation, University of Nebraska, 1997), p. 70.

[20] Ibid., p. 163.
[21] *Ancrene Wisse*, ed. Millett, I, 4.1404, p. 105.
[22] Jerome, *Ep.* 22 (*PL* 22, 411).
[23] *Ancrene Wisse*, ed. Millett, I, 4.1554–61, p. 109.

He goes on to advise them to pray less, so they can read more, but also cautions them against excess. Walter Hilton, in Book One Chapter 15 of *The Scale of Perfection*, written for a religious woman, puts the situation very clearly if not bleakly. He acknowledges that religious in general have a range of strategies by which they can achieve virtue – reading, meditation and prayer, in fact – but that she is in a different situation: 'Redynge of Holy Writ mai thu not wel use.'[24] This does not mean women were not allowed to read scripture (after all, Hilton was probably writing before Arundel issued his *Constitutions*),[25] but rather that they were not able to do so,[26] though we may feel the distinction in practice somewhat academic. But what does Hilton suggest as a substitute? Not the reading of other vernacular texts but further 'gostly meditacione': 'therfore thee behoveth more occupye thee in prayer and in meditacioun', specifically on the topics of 'thi wrechednesse, thi synnes, and thi wikkidnessis'.[27]

Rolle, writing his *Emendatio vitae* in Latin the first half of the fourteenth century, did not have to solve this particular problem for religious women as vernacular readers. He was free to promote monastic *lectio* because he was writing for someone literate in Latin (possibly a secular priest). But of the seven separate Middle English translations of the *Emendatio*,[28] many were made for women religious, who we know owned some of the copies (e.g., the version found in Oxford, Bodleian Library, MS Douce 322 and London, British Library, MS Harley 1706).[29] Another version, in London, British Library, MS Harley 2406, faithfully translates the Latin of Rolle's chapter nine, on reading, as follows:

> Iff þou couetest for-to come to þe loue off Gode … be notht slowe and necligent for-to thinke gode thouchtes no for-to rede holy scripture. … Leue harde maters off holy writte to wise men þat hath studiede longe tyme þere-in; holy redynge helpeth vs muchel for-to profite in godenes … swiche redynge is gode to vs and a delicate feste, if we do it for-to know how we schal plese Gode and loue hym and notht for-to couet worship and fauoure of men. (fol. 49)

The only anxiety provoked by the reading of scripture here is that it could become a source of pride: reading must not become a scholarly activity that

---

24 Walter Hilton, *Scale of Perfection*, ed. T. H. Bestul (Kalamazoo, 2000), p. 45.

25 Watson accepts a dating of c. 1380–96 ('Censorship and Cultural Change', p. 861) for *The Scale*.

26 See *Scale of Perfection*, ed. Bestul, p. 45, note to line 334.

27 Ibid., p. 45.

28 See M. Amassian, 'The Rolle Material in Bradfer-Lawrence MS 10 and its Relationship to Other Rolle Manuscripts', *Manuscripta* 23 (1979), 67–78.

29 See H. Kempster, 'Richard Rolle: *Emendatio Vitae: Amendinge of Lyf*, a Middle English Translation, edited from Dublin, Trinity College, MS 432' (unpublished PhD dissertation, University of Waikato, 2007), pp. cix–cx.

might attract praise but should be practised purely for edification and devotion.

But other texts translated from the Latin after 1409 by less conscientious (or possibly more alert) translators have a particular problem if their originals enthusiastically recommended the reading of scripture. The translator may cut the Gordian knot by simply omitting the original reference to *lectio* altogether, as does the adaptor of the Middle English version of Bonaventure's *De Triplici Via* found in Cambridge University Library, MS Additional 3042 (Jolliffe O.47), a manuscript that belonged to a nun.[30] Quite the opposite technique is adopted by a Middle English translation (Jolliffe O.11) of the Epistle of 'Jerome' to Demetriade. This text tropes 'holy writt' as 'the worthi letters' of a great king – 'And þerfor we owen for to receyuen his letters and redden hem with greet reuerence' – and expands the Latin original's simple injunction, 'Ita Scripturas sacras lege',[31] so that this is only one of a range of options: 'gife þe to redenge or to herengge of holy writt or of holy doctours sawes or of holy wymmennes liifs'.[32] At least scriptural reading is still listed, although concealed among other possible choices.

The two translations of Aelred's *De Institutione Inclusarum* are instructive in their contrasting versions of a passage where the Cistercian eloquently discoursed to his Latinate sister on the joys and benefits of reading scripture. In the more literal Middle English version, found only in the late fourteenth century Vernon Manuscript (Oxford, Bodleian Library, MS Eng. Poet. a.1) and therefore made before Arundel's *Constitutions*, the passage reads:

> as a dredful douue, haunte ryueres of cler water. ... Ðyse ryueres beþ holy scriptures .... For þer is noþyng þat so put awey wyckede and vnclene þouȝtes as dooþ good ocupacioun in holy scripture.[33]

The much freer fifteenth-century translation still urges the recluse to 'beholde in the ryuers of holy wryt hou besy thyn enemy is to ouercome the and fle hym'. But the rest of the sentence is modified: 'ther is no thinge that ouercometh so sone the fende as doth redynge of deuoute thinge and prayer and meditacyon of Cristys passion.'[34] These three terms variously paraphrase rather than translate the Latin phrase *meditatio uerbi Dei*, 'an unequivocal reference to the reading of Holy Scripture'. The editors point out that 'the rather vague ME translation is no doubt quite deliberate and is an inter-

---

[30] See A. Barratt, 'Books for Nuns: Cambridge University Library MS Additional 3042', *Notes and Queries*, n.s. 44 (September 1997), 310–19 (p. 312).

[31] *PL* 30, 37C.

[32] London, British Library MS Royal 18.A. x, fol. 77v.

[33] *Aelred of Rievaulx's* De Institutione Inclusarum, ed. Ayto and Barratt, pp. 30–1.

[34] Ibid., p. 12.

esting example of the late medieval ambivalence towards recommending the reading of the Bible in a vernacular treatise'.[35]

A Middle English translation of the *Liber de modo bene vivendi*,[36] *The Maner of Good Living*, is extant in a single manuscript, Oxford, Bodleian Library, MS Laud. misc. 517 (Jolliffe H.23 and O.36) and is unusual in the amount of attention it devotes to reading. Its fiftieth 'exhortation' or chapter is on the theme, 'how necessary ys redyng to vs, or the heryng of redyng' (fol. 120). It emphasizes both the connection and the contrast between reading and prayer: 'when we praye, we speke to God. When we rede, God spekyth to vs' – an aphorism so often repeated elsewhere, for instance in the Bridgettine *Mirrour of Our Ladye*, as to become something of a commonplace.[37] It urges, 'if ye couette to be all-wey with God, euere praye and euere rede', though the writer goes on to privilege prayer over reading, saying unequivocally, 'it ys better to praye than to rede'. (*Ancrene Wisse*, as we have already seen, took the opposite view.) Reading, however, does have its own virtues:

> For by redyng we lern what we ouȝt to doo. ... By redyng, knowlege and vndurstandyng be increced. Redyng techyth vs to praye and to werke. Redyng informeth to þe actyue and contemplatyue lyves.

The Latin original concludes: 'in lege Dei esto assidua, habeto studium in divinis legibus, usus legendi sit tibi frequens'[38] – literally, 'be constant in the law of God (i.e. the scriptures), study the divine laws, let the practice of reading be frequent to you.' But the Middle English can only say, 'gyve þou ofte to prayer, perseuere in meditacion of holy scripture. Vse þou [accustome yourself] to rede' (fol. 120v).

This passage is verbally close to one in the translation of the *Counsels of St Isidore* (Jolliffe I. 22(c)).[39] The *Counsels* was written for men but the copy in Cambridge, Trinity College, MS O. 1. 74 is bound up with other texts for, or used by, women. It says:

35 Ibid., p. 82.
36 It was believed in the Middle Ages that Bernard of Clairvaux composed the *Liber de modo bene vivendi* (*PL* 184, 1199–1306) for his sister. More recently it has been attributed, though probably still wrongly, to Thomas of Beverley. See A. Mc Govern-Mouron, '"Listen to me, daughter, listen to a faithful counsel": The *Liber de modo bene vivendi ad sororem*', in *Writing Religious Women*, pp. 81–106 (pp. 83–4).
37 Versions of this aphorism also occur in Alcuin's *De Virtutibus et Vitiis* and the early Middle English prose text *Vices and Virtues*: I owe these references to Cate Gunn. See also N Watson, *Richard Rolle and the Invention of Authority* (Cambridge, 1991), p. 327.
38 *PL* 184, 1272–3.
39 There are several Middle English versions of this text: this was the most widespread, being extant in at least fourteen manuscripts.

Myche ȝeue þou þee to reding; take heede in meditacioun of scripture; bisie þee myche in þe lawe of God; haue a customable vce in [make a habit of reading] dyuyne bokis, reding þer-ynne treuli what þou schalt schone [shun]. Reding schewiþ what þou owist to drede; reding telliþ whider þou goost; in reding witt & vndirstonding encresiþ. Þou schalt myche profite in reding, if þou do as þou redist. (fol. 4)

Another version of the *Counsels*, found only in British Library, MS Harley 2388 (Jolliffe I. 22(a), O. 27) varies this, urging 'a custumabyll vse in þin seruice-bukis redyng' (fol. 60v). This adapts, or possibly misunderstands, the phrase translated in the other version as 'diuyne bokis', and the change is revealing as liturgical texts were, of course, in Latin.

Advocacy of spiritual reading is therefore widespread in these texts. But so, as we have already seen in passing, is a certain vagueness about specific reading matter. Some treatises self-reflexively recommend the reading of themselves. *Ancrene Wisse* is unequivocal on this. Once a week the anchoresses must read aloud the relevant portion of the Guide to their illiterate servants, while the author ends by advocating, with a degree of self-deprecating humour, that they should read some of his book to themselves every day – or else all his hard work has gone for nothing:

Of þis boc redeð hwen ȝe beoð eise euche dei leasse oðer mare. Ich hoopie þet hit schal beon ow, ȝef ȝe hit redeð ofte, swiðe biheue, þurh Godes muchele grace; elles Ich hefde uuele bitohe mi muchele hwile. Me were leouere, Godd hit wite, do me toward Rome þen forte biginnen hit efte forte donne.[40]

[Read from this book every day, when you have leisure, less or more. I hope that it will be very profitable to you, if you read it frequently, through God's great grace. Otherwise I have been wasting my time! God knows, I would rather set out for Rome than begin to do it again.]

The Maner of Good Living, which takes itself more seriously, demands a degree of attention close to that *ruminatio* otherwise devoted to scripture. Making use of the familiar metaphor of the text as mirror or *speculum*, it exhorts the reader:

take this boke and leye it euery hour bifore you. Ther-in looke ye as in a glasse … rede ouere this boke and rede it thorogh a-gayn and agayn, and ye shall know in it howe ye shall loue God and your neyghbour.[41]

More modestly, the adaptation of the *Diurnal of Devout Life* found in Anne Bulkeley's Book (London, British Library, MS Harley 494, fols. 6–19v) recom-

---

[40] *Ancrene Wisse*, ed. Millett, I, 8.336–40, p. 164.
[41] Oxford Bodl. MS Laud Misc. 515, fols. 1v–2.

mends its own reading as a practical remedy for human forgetfulness and as a way of supplementing oral communication. The recipient should

> often tymes to rede or here those thynges, þe whiche wolde alwey be had on mynde. Wherfor I haue, accordynge to your devout desyre and request, brevely in this lytell paper notyde thre exercyses þe which I haue many tymes counseylede yow to vse. (fols. 6v–7)

Another text to advocate its own reading is *The Doctrine of the Heart* (Jolliffe O. 3). The Latin original was written for nuns and indeed one manuscript of the English translation, Cambridge, Trinity College, MS B. 14. 15, contains a note on fol. 78 that it belonged to a London minoress, Dame Christine Saint Nicholas, who bequeathed it to her convent on her death in 1455. The passage relevant to our concerns does not appear in the Latin so is presumably a translator's addition of sentiments that it would have been presumptuous for the author himself to voice. It exhorts the nuns to read the text, 'not only with þe lippes of þe mouth but also and namly with þe lippis of þe soule'. The translator goes on:

> Clene and chast soules euer desiren so forto rede þat þei myght feele it sauourly with-in forth. Hertly redyng is a gracyous mene to gostly feling. In þis wyse þerfor schuld þis tretyce be rad and herd and þan wil Oure Lord worche be his grace, namly þer þe hertis be clene that redith it or heriþ hit. (fol. 1v)

The Doctrine of the Heart also praises the reading of saints' lives, just as *The Maner of Good Living* advocates reading 'the lyfe of seyntis or holy fadres'. It is perhaps surprising that more treatises do not explicitly recommend these stories. Certainly a number of women's religious houses owned copies of such lives in English, French and even Latin.[42] *The Doctrine of the Heart* regards such 'holy ensamples of seyntes lyues' as playing a very practical role as part of the nuns' spiritual armour:

> in þe begynnyng of ȝour chapitres [chapter meetings] þer is redde a lesson of the marteloge, þat is of seyntes lyues, wher-in þou maist hire how somme were scorgyd and somme y-brennyd and somme y-tormentyd … in token þat þou scholdest soffre mekely and paciently all reproues and blames of hem þat ben þi presidentis in chapitre. (fol. 40)

(The idea that attending the medieval equivalent of a department meeting approximates the suffering of the martyrs might strike a chord with many an academic!) This, however, clearly refers to public reading and collective

---

42 See N. R. Ker, *Medieval Libraries of Great Britain: A List of Surviving Books* (London, 2nd edn, 1964), *s. v.* Barking, Camsey, Shoreditch, Romsey, Tarrant Keynston and Wilton.

listening, similar to the edifying reading practised during monastic meals. But the later fifteenth-century 'abstracte owte of a boke þat is called formula nouiciorum', a condensation of Part One of David of Augsburg's *De Exterioris et Interioris Hominis Compositione* that was probably adapted for women,[43] does recommend the private reading of saints' lives:

> Rede þe liuis of sentis and þer doctrine þat bi þe exampulis of þer holy levyng þou may be alwey þe meker and informyd and inflamyd with þe more deuocion and provokyd to study þat þou may be illumyned in þi vndrestandynge.[44]

The Latin original of this chapter 'suggests that novices read the lives of saints so that they may then be able to appreciate Holy Scripture better',[45] but the Middle English version simply offers the lives as moral examples, and goes on to caution the novice against the dangers of the wrong kinds of reading:

> Rede not to þat intente þat þou be holde gretely lernyd bycause of curiosite, nor rede not suche thyngis as edifi not, for vayne redynge ingendereþe vayne þouhttis and quencheþe þe deuocion of þe soule.[46]

What other books, then, escape condemnation as 'vain reading' and are recommended to religious women? Unfortunately, only two treatises are helpful in this respect, and one is very late in the period. It is not surprising, given the conflation that we have seen of *lectio* and *meditatio*, that both recommend affective, meditative reading. One of these has already been mentioned: it is the version of the *Diurnal of Devout Life* found in BL Harley 494. The *Diurnal* is a very late text, published in the 1530s,[47] written for laypeople of both genders. But the manuscript version was adapted for and owned by a widow and later by her daughter, a nun: it is common to find texts originally written for one class of readership in the possession of quite another.[48] The *Diurnal* recommends reading in general, as the author believes that God communicates with us 'not only by secret inspiracions but also outward techynge and examples þat ofte tymes we here redde and see' (fol. 6). Specifically, he lays down a weekly scheme for passages to be read every day before the main meal. Its aim, he tells us, is 'to induce compunccyon' (fol. 14): it is therefore

---

[43] S. Marshall, 'An abstracte owte of a boke þat is called *Formula Nouiciorum* edited from London BL MS Arundel 197', *Mystics Quarterly* 29 (2003), 71–139 (p. 85).

[44] Ibid., p. 100.

[45] Ibid., p. 130.

[46] Ibid., p. 100.

[47] *STC* 6928 (1532?), *STC* 6928.5 (1532?) and *STC* 6928a (1542?, possibly 1534).

[48] A number of these treatises of advice to religious women survive alongside treatises aimed at other groups, such as laymen, male religious or married people, in manuscripts such as Cambridge University Library MSS Ii. 6. 55 and Ii. 6.39, both of which seem to have belonged to priests.

affective and not in any way intellectual. The prescribed readings, which are described metaphorically as food ('refeccion'), are taken from the 'Vita Jhesu secundum Bonauenturam', that is, the *Meditationes Vitae Christi* attributed to Bonaventure. This popular and widely disseminated text was written in Italy in the early fourteenth century by the Franciscan Johannes de Caulibus. At least ten Middle English versions survive (as do versions in numerous European languages), but there is only one complete translation: the Carthusian Nicholas Love's *Mirror of the Blessed Life of Jesus Christ*.[49]

The author of the *Diurnal* assigns specifically numbered chapters to each day of the week. If he had in mind Nicholas Love's translation, which seems likely as it had been printed several times by 1530, the scheme works out as follows:

Monday: Chapter 17 (Marriage at Cana)
Tuesday: Chapter 22 (Conversion of Mary Magdalene)
Wednesday: Chapter 23 (Samaritan Woman)
Thursday: Chapter 25 (Feeding of the Five Thousand)
Friday: Chapter 39 (Last Supper)
Saturday: Chapter 33 (Active and Contemplative Lives)
Sunday: Chapter 52: (Ascension).

He also gives detailed instructions on how to read. The woman does not, for instance, have to read the complete chapter, but 'oþer in part or hole, as may be sufficient to stere your hartes to compunccion'. After prefatory prayer, she should 'begyn to rede eueruthing reuerently, depely markyng every word that ye rede often tymes, asking grace to profyt' (fol. 14v). After she has finished reading she should turn to prayer, offering thanksgiving and penitence, and saying an *Ave* in honour of St Bonaventura. In other words, the *Mirror* is to be accorded the same kind of *ruminatio* as scripture and has indeed become a substitute for it, just as Archbishop Arundel had hoped it would when, *c.* 1410, he licensed it 'to be published universally for the edification of the faithful and the confutation of heretics and lollards'.[50] In this treatise reading has become highly formalized and also restricted in its content, as the same cycle is worked through every week, regardless of the liturgical season. In addition, the subject matter is limited as all the passages relate to meals.

The other treatise that recommends a particular text is *The Tree* (Jolliffe O.13),[51] which, together with its twin, *Twelve Fruits of the Holy Ghost* (39), survives in three late fifteenth century manuscripts and a printed edition

---

49 See *Nicholas Love: The Mirror of the Blessed Life of Jesus Christ*, ed. M. G. Sargent (Exeter, 2004), pp. xi–xiii.
50 Ibid., pp. xv and 7.
51 *A deuout treatyse called the tree & xii. frutes of the holy goost*, ed. J. J. Vaissier (Groningen, 1960).

of 1534/5 (*STC* 13608). Both purport to be letters addressed to a 'religious sister'. In *The Tree* the author exhorts her to be studious, in order to promote the interests of her order, 'as oþer of þin sistren don'.[52] Simultaneously, he adopts the common attitude that reading is one activity among many:

> If þou be wery in redyng. refressh þi soule bi prayer or be meditacioun or in sum maner oþer good charitable werk. now rede. now praye. now laboure bisely. and so shal þin houre be short. And þi laboure light.[53]

He also regards books as one of the necessities of life, analogous to food, drink and clothing, writing engagingly, 'if þou haue mete. drinke. and cloþing and a boke to loke vpon, it is I now [enough] to þe'.[54] In particular, he recommends:

> I wold þou were occupied. namly on haly dayes with redyng of deuoute bokes. as is. Stimulus amoris, or such oþer. In þe wich specialy I recomende to þi meditacioun. þe holy passioun of oure lord ihesu. And namly after complyn. and after matynes.[55]

The *Stimulus Amoris*, attributed in the Middle Ages to Bonaventura, is now thought to be the work of James of Milan. There is a Middle English translation, *The Pricking of Love*, extant in at least sixteen complete and partial manuscripts.[56] Two of these (British Library MS Harley 2254 and Downside Abbey MS Dartford) belonged to the Dominican nuns of Dartford.[57] The translation opens with extended meditations on Christ's Passion, to which the recommendation here must refer. Once again, reading is assimilated to meditation, as it is in the associated text, *xii frutes*, where the author praises those who are 'euer occupied in vertu, ouþer in deuoute wepyng and weylyng. or in holy redyngis. or herying of vertu, or ellis in holy meditaciouns of oure lordis passioun'.[58]

Of the many advice treatises directed at religious women, then, few have much to say on reading. What they do say is highly conventionalized and the specific texts they occasionally recommend are limited in range. There seems to have been no consensus about what books religious women should read, other than that – like male religious – they should ideally read the Vulgate. If they cannot do this, they must substitute edifying devotional reading rather than vernacular translations of the Bible. Other kinds of evidence, however, suggest that in reality women were not completely dependent on such advice.

---

52 Ibid., p. 15.
53 Ibid., p. 16.
54 Ibid., p. 18.
55 Ibid., p. 32.
56 See *The Prickynge of Love*, ed. H. Kane, 2 vols. (Salzburg, 1983).
57 Ker, *Medieval Libraries*, p. 57.
58 *A deuout treatyse*, p. 115.

The sheer number and variety of these texts of spiritual guidance written for women that we have considered (however modest the claims these 'poor relations' of *Ancrene Wisse* make for themselves) provide one indication of the range of women's reading. Another clue is provided by the manuscripts that we know belonged to women's religious houses or to individual nuns: these do indeed include copies of saints' lives, the *Pricking of Love* and Nicholas Love's *Mirror*, but religious women also owned other challenging and demanding texts. For instance, Sibilla de Felton, abbess of Barking, owned copies of the mystical texts *The Cleansing of Man's Soul* and *The Chastising of God's Children*. And while Margery Kempe did read (or rather had read to her) the *Stimulus Amoris*, her own book shows the influence of many other texts she records by name, such as the revelations of St Bridget of Sweden and of Elizabeth of Hungary, and the life of the thirteenth-century beguine Mary of Oignies. So even an 'illiterate' married woman ranged beyond the confines suggested by anonymous advisers. As for Julian of Norwich, the sources of her theology remain controversial but her mature thought was clearly nourished by texts rather different from the *Stimulus* or Nicholas Love, even though her originating desire for 'mind' of Christ's Passion fits comfortably within the parameters of the affective devotion promoted by both. There is therefore an interesting mismatch between what women were advised to read and what apparently they did read, as far as we can assess the evidence. If nothing else, this is a tribute to their enterprise, ingenuity and spirit of intellectual adventure.

INDEX

TABULA GRATULATORIA

Alexandra Barratt
Devorah Baum
Dr Stephen Bending
Johan Bergström-Allen
Mishtooni Bose
Jeanice Brooks & Mark Everist
Elizabeth J. Bryan
Tom Burton
A. E. Christa Canitz
Marc B. Cels
Susannah Mary Chewning
Helen Cooper
Susan Crane
Anne Curry
Roger Dahood
Richard Dance
Denise L. Despres
Jackie F. G. Duff
Elisabeth Dutton
Ruth Evans
Susanna Fein
Lynn Forest-Hill
David Freemantle
Vincent Gillespie
Joe Goering
Brian Golding
C. Annette Grisé
Cate Gunn
Ralph Hanna
Clare Hanson
Professor Dr Sieglinde Hartmann
Bob Hasenfratz
Leonie Hicks
Amanda Holton
Anne Hudson
Alice Hunt

Ann M. Hutchison
Catherine Innes-Parker
Chiyoko Inosaki
Eddie Jones
Josephine A. Koster
Juris G. Lidaka
Professor Alasdair A. MacDonald
Liz Herbert McAvoy
Gail McDonald
John J. McGavin
Professor Colin Morris
Charlotte C. Morse
Stephen Morton
Marianne O'Doherty
John Peacock
Derek Pearsall
Helen Phillips
Oliver Pickering
Ad Putter
Sherry Reames
Denis Renevey
Felicity Riddy
Elizabeth Robertson
Miri Rubin
David Russell
Sarah Salih
Sujala Singh
Myra Stokes
Elaine Treharne
Yoko Wada
Greg Walker
Nicholas Watson
Teresa Webber
Jocelyn Wogan-Browne
Naoë Kukita Yoshikawa

YORK MEDIEVAL PRESS: PUBLICATIONS

God's Words, Women's Voices: The Discernment of Spirits in the Writing of Late-Medieval Women Visionaries, Rosalyn Voaden (1999)

Pilgrimage Explored, ed. J. Stopford (1999)

Piety, Fraternity and Power: Religious Gilds in Late Medieval Yorkshire 1389–1547, David J. F. Crouch (2000)

Courts and Regions in Medieval Europe, ed. Sarah Rees Jones, Richard Marks and A. J. Minnis (2000)

Treasure in the Medieval West, ed. Elizabeth M. Tyler (2000)

Nunneries, Learning and Spirituality in Late Medieval English Society: The Dominican Priory of Dartford, Paul Lee (2000)

Prophecy and Public Affairs in Later Medieval England, Lesley A. Coote (2000)

The Problem of Labour in Fourteenth-Century England, ed. James Bothwell, P. J. P. Goldberg and W. M. Ormrod (2000)

New Directions in Later Medieval Manuscript Studies: Essays from the 1998 Harvard Conference, ed. Derek Pearsall (2000)

Cistercians, Heresy and Crusadse in Occitania, 1145–1229: Preaching in the Lord's Vineyard, Beverly Mayne Kienzle (2001)

Guilds and the Parish Community in Late Medieval East Anglia, c. 1470–1550, Ken Farnhill (2001)

The Age of Edward III, ed. J. S. Bothwell (2001)

Time in the Medieval World, ed. Chris Humphrey and W. M. Ormrod (2001)

The Cross Goes North: Processes of Conversion in Northern Europe, AD 300–1300, ed. Martin Carver (2002)

Henry IV: The Establishment of the Regime, 1399–1406, ed. Gwilym Dodd and Douglas Biggs (2003)

Youth in the Middle Ages, ed. P. J. P Goldberg and Felicity Riddy (2004)

The Idea of the Castle in Medieval England, Abigail Wheatley (2004)

Rites of Passage: Cultures of Transition in the Fourteenth Century, ed. Nicola F. McDonald and W. M. Ormrod (2004)

Creating the Monastic Past in Medieval Flanders, Karine Ugé (2005)

St William of York, Christopher Norton (2006)

Medieval Obscenities, ed. Nicola F. McDonald (2006)

The Reign of Edward II: New Perspectives, ed. Gwilym Dodd and Anthony Musson (2006)

Old English Poetics: The Aesthetics of the Familiar in Anglo-Saxon England, Elizabeth M. Tyler (2006)

The Late Medieval Interlude: The Drama of Youth and Aristocratic Masculinity, Fiona S. Dunlop (2007)

The Late Medieval English College and its Context, ed. Clive Burgess and Martin Heale (2008)

The Reign of Henry IV: Rebellion and Survival, 1403–1413, ed. Gwilym Dodd and Douglas Biggs (2008)

Medieval Petitions: Grace and Grievance, ed. W. Mark Ormrod, Gwilym Dodd and Anthony Musson (2009)

St Edmund, King and Martyr: Changing Images of a Medieval Saint, ed. Anthony Bale (2009)

Language and Culture in Medieval Britain: The French of England c. 1100–c. 1500, ed. Jocelyn Wogan-Browne et al. (2009)

York Studies in Medieval Theology

I   *Medieval Theology and the Natural Body*, ed. Peter Biller and A. J. Minnis (1997)

II   *Handling Sin: Confession in the Middle Ages*, ed. Peter Biller and A. J. Minnis (1998)

III *Religion and Medicine in the Middle Ages*, ed. Peter Biller and Joseph Ziegler (2001)

IV   *Texts and the Repression of Medieval Heresy*, ed. Caterina Bruschi and Peter Biller (2002)

York Manuscripts Conference

Manuscripts and Readers in Fifteenth-Century England: The Literary Implications of Manuscript Study, ed. Derek Pearsall (1983) [Proceedings of the 1981 York Manuscripts Conference]

Manuscripts and Texts: Editorial Problems in Later Middle English Literature, ed. Derek Pearsall (1987) [Proceedings of the 1985 York Manuscripts Conference]

Latin and Vernacular: Studies in Late-Medieval Texts and Manuscripts, ed. A. J. Minnis (1989) [Proceedings of the 1987 York Manuscripts Conference]

Regionalism in Late-Medieval Manuscripts and Texts: Essays celebrating the publication of 'A Linguistic Atlas of Late Mediaeval English', ed. Felicity Riddy (1991) [Proceedings of the 1989 York Manuscripts Conference]

Late-Medieval Religious Texts and their Transmission: Essays in Honour of A. I. Doyle, ed. A. J. Minnis (1994) [Proceedings of the 1991 York Manuscripts Conference]

Prestige, Authority and Power in Late Medieval Manuscripts and Texts, ed. Felicity Riddy (2000) [Proceedings of the 1994 York Manuscripts Conference]

Middle English Poetry: Texts and Traditions. Essays in Honour of Derek Pearsall, ed. A. J. Minnis (2001) [Proceedings of the 1996 York Manuscripts Conference]

Manuscript Culture in the British Isles

Design and Distribution of Late Medieval Manuscripts in England, ed. Margaret Connolly and Linne R. Mooney (2008)